ENVOYS EXTRAORDINARY

STRATFORD CANNING
From an engraving after a drawing by George Richmond

ENVOYS EXTRAORDINARY

The Romantic Careers of Some Remarkable British Representatives Abroad

BY

EDMUND B. D'AUVERGNE

AUTHOR OF
"THE DEAR EMMA" "NAPOLEON THE THIRD" "THE COBURGS"
ETC.

GEORGE G. HARRAP & CO. LTD.
LONDON　　BOMBAY　　SYDNEY

PREFACE

Britain's relations with foreign states appear at the present day to engross more than ever the attention of the public. Yet, though much has been written about the statesmen who have answered in the past for our foreign policy in Parliament, and even more about the fighters who have achieved by the sword what the pen could not effect, strangely little has been written about the men who have fought Britain's battles by word of mouth and artfully drafted notes in the courts of the stranger. Their greatest victory has been peace. Their triumphs would seem to be writ in water, and the triumphs of the war-makers endure in brass.

There is therefore some excuse for compiling the present volume, by which it is hoped to revive the memory of five British diplomatists, belonging to the last hundred and fifty years, who served their country, and humanity, well. James Harris, Earl of Malmesbury, Hugh Elliot, William Bentinck, Stratford Canning, Henry Bulwer—they belonged, indeed, not only to bygone generations, but were of a type and school of thought generally unpopular to-day. An Englishman, thought Harris, who could not perceive the superiority of his own nation over the rest of the world had no real mind. The same conviction, if not so cruelly expressed, abided in the minds of the other ambassadors of whom we treat, and probably in the minds of their fellow-representatives of Great Britain. We find such insularity a little absurd; but here from the absurd to the sublime there is not more than a stride. This unshakable belief in the supereminence of their country nerved his Britannic Majesty's envoys to interfere, as the foreigner often complained, not seldom in the cause of right. Far from suspecting it, they were animated with the crusader's zeal. The Kings of Denmark and Sweden fly at each other's throats—Mr Hugh Elliot, British minister at Copenhagen, rushes in to drag them apart. His Sicilian Majesty, in the undoubted exercise of his sovereignty, dissolves Parliament, exiles persons without trial, and so forth. These detestable proceedings, says Lord William Bentinck, are repugnant to the feelings of a decent Englishman, and must therefore cease. It was all most high-handed and improper, and his lordship was most rude to the Queen—but these things ceased. (Years after the same proconsul discovered that the practice of burning widows on their dead husbands' funeral pyres was abhorrent to his feelings—and that also ceased.) Stratford Canning at Istanbul heard that the Turks had put a man to death for recanting his profession of Islam. He decided that this was an abomination, and must never occur again. "But it is the law of the Prophet, the law of our land!" screamed the Turks. "Please do as I tell you," said the irritable old gentleman; and no more men were put to death in Turkey for reverting to the Christian faith. Such intervention in the domestic affairs of other states was haughty, oppressive, insolent; it was not always on the right side, as when Harris, more or less in love with the Princess of Orange, conspired to restore her feeble husband's sway; it was sometimes hotly resented, as by the Spaniards who dismissed her Majesty's minister from Madrid; but in Harris, Elliot, and the rest of the present company one is obliged to recognize the lofty arrogance of the British captains who swept the slave-ships from the seas, not caring much whether they flew a foreign flag or not. Unblushingly, our ambassadors intrigued to create a British party at every court to which they were accredited; but we need not often blush for them, for the British party was nearly always the party of liberty and progress.

I do not suppose these gentlemen were over-popular in foreign capitals, or that they made the English liked. But they believed that Britain was a great Power (as she may become again), and they believed in themselves as Britons. For his personal safety Henry Bulwer relied, he told the Spanish Government, on "the power of my country which resides in me, alone in the midst of evilly excited men, as well as in those mighty armaments which a word from the sovereign of Great Britain can call forth." To elderly Englishmen, and perhaps to a few young ones, the words may ring as clear and encouraging as the peal of the trumpet. Bulwer and his like believed in England's civilizing mission, and in their duty to exercise it.

But if they were thorns in the side of the foreigner, they were not less such in the sides of their long-suffering chiefs at Whitehall. In those spacious pre-telegraph days it was indeed easy for the representative of his Britannic Majesty to forget that the sovereignty of Britain resided anywhere but in him. Harris in an oft-quoted dispatch declared he had never received any instructions from home worth following. Lord Stratford's fine inattention to the orders of the Foreign Secretary earned him many a rebuke, and, most unfairly, the blame of causing the Crimean War. But the men on the spot were generally justified by the event. Bentinck was possessed of a wider vision than Castlereagh (faint praise enough!); had he been left a free hand the unification of Italy might have been anticipated by half a century, and at the cost of much less blood.

We shall not look upon their like again. They belong to an England that has passed away. The merits which I claim for them are in many quarters no longer regarded as merits. Their story may at least correct one theory very popular just now, of the mainspring of statecraft and of British policy in particular. Their Excellencies appear to have been almost unconscious of the economic motive which is now supposed to direct mankind. Their country's prestige, sometimes petty dynastic considerations, sometimes a policeman's habit of putting things in order and suffering no nonsense—these aims seem to the present writer mainly to have moved them. There are strangely few references to the famous economic motive in the letters of our ambassadors during the period covered.

These letters, contained in our State Papers and Foreign Office letter-books at the Public Record Office, have been very extensively consulted by the author in the preparation of this work. Wherever the course appeared in the least advisable, the narratives contained in memoirs and other published authorities have been checked and verified, and often corrected, by reference to the original official documents. The present book is addressed to those who may care to know more about the men who served us so loyally abroad, and about the processes, not seldom daring and romantic, by which the ends of our policy were pursued; but it is hoped that here and there some fresh light has been thrown on facts, not altogether unworthy of the notice of the serious historian.

EDMUND B. D'AUVERGNE

CONTENTS

	PAGE
JAMES HARRIS, EARL OF MALMESBURY	13
HUGH ELLIOT AND THE NORTHERN COURTS	89
THE FIGHT FOR SICILY	116
STRATFORD CANNING, VISCOUNT STRATFORD DE REDCLIFFE	182
SIR HENRY LYTTON BULWER	271
INDEX	311

ILLUSTRATIONS

	PAGE
STRATFORD CANNING	*Frontispiece*
CATHERINE II, EMPRESS OF RUSSIA	32
WILHELMINA, PRINCESS OF ORANGE	40
JAMES HARRIS, FIRST EARL OF MALMESBURY	54
WILLIAM V, PRINCE OF ORANGE	60
JAMES HARRIS, FIRST EARL OF MALMESBURY (AGED SEVENTY)	76
HUGH ELLIOT	90
GUSTAVUS III, KING OF SWEDEN	106
MARIA CAROLINA, QUEEN OF THE TWO SICILIES	128
LORD WILLIAM CAVENDISH BENTINCK	148
JOACHIM MURAT	176
STRATFORD CANNING (AGED TWENTY-NINE)	192
PRINCE METTERNICH	216
HENRY BULWER, AFTERWARDS LORD DALLING	272
ISABEL II, QUEEN OF SPAIN, AS A GIRL	286
GENERAL NARVAEZ	304

JAMES HARRIS, EARL OF MALMESBURY
(1746–1820)

ONE day, in the first years of King George III's reign, Mrs Harris, a lady living in a pleasant old house in the Close of Salisbury Cathedral, was astonished to observe some foolhardy person climbing the spire—the tallest in England. She called for her field-glasses; then, after a searching glance at the moving figure, exclaimed, "Good heavens, it is James!" It is not recorded that she fainted, as a lady might have done a hundred years later, on perceiving that it was her eldest son who was risking his neck. Already, probably, she was aware that James was very well capable of taking care of himself and that his courage was equal to any task he undertook.

This seems a suitable introduction to the diplomatist who vowed in later years never to leave a rung in the ladder of his profession unclimbed. The worthy Wiltshire family from which he sprang had not been thus tormented by ambition. Heard of as far back as 1565, they came in frequently from their country place to the house in the Close. The third Earl of Malmesbury, to whose piety we are indebted for an account of his grandfather's career and for an invaluable collection of his letters, writing in the forties of last century, laments the days when the "Provincial gentry filled and enlivened during a portion of the year our now deserted and mournful cathedral cities." It was to his father, and not, as it is now the fashion to do, to his mother, that the subject of our sketch attributed his "more than common success in life." It was the elder Harris's reputation and character, he says, "that introduced me with peculiar advantage into the world; it was as his son that I first obtained friends and patrons."

ENVOYS EXTRAORDINARY

James Harris, senior, is remembered as the author of a system of universal grammar entitled *Hermes*. The Sage of Fleet Street called him "a prig, and a bad prig." When he took his seat in Parliament for the borough of Christchurch John Townshend asked who he was, and was informed that his chief interests were harmony and grammar. "Why then does he come here," exclaimed the politician, "where he will hear neither?" He found friends, however, and was made a Lord of the Treasury in George Grenville's administration in 1763.

James the Less, meanwhile, after a hard time at a Salisbury school, found things very comfortable at Winchester. He says:

> There I did nearly what I liked, and as boys always wish to be men, I thought myself a man too soon. My father, at that time in office and living in London, kept me with him for six months before sending me to Oxford. I cannot even now decide whether this was a wrong or right step. I believe that seeing many of the leading men in Administration, hearing them converse on public business, contributed to form my mind to think on public affairs, and to give me an interest in them which, otherwise, probably, I might never have acquired; but the mixing at that age [seventeen] and raw from school, in all the gaiety and dissipation of London, filled my mind at the same time with false objects of admiration, false notices of excellence, and gave me, in my own conceit, a knowledge of the world so much greater than I supposed my fellow collegians could possibly possess, that I apprehend I carried to the University a considerable share of self-sufficiency and no great propensity to attend lectures and conform to college rules; and in fact the two years of my life I look back to as most unprofitably spent were those I passed at Merton. The discipline of the University happened at this time to be so lax that a Gentleman Commoner was under no restraint, and never called upon to attend lectures, or chapel, or hall. My tutor, an excellent and worthy man, according to the practice of all tutors at that moment, gave himself no concern about his pupils. I never saw him but once a fortnight, when I took it into my head to be taught trigonometry. [He attended anatomical lectures, as well, to the disgust of his mother.] The set of men with whom I lived were very pleasant but very idle

fellows. Our life was an imitation of High Life in London; luckily, drinking was not the fashion, but what we did drink was claret, and we had our regular round of evening card parties to the great annoyance of our finances. It has often been a matter of surprise to me how so many of us made our way so well in the world, and so creditably. Charles Fox, Lord Romney, North, Bishop of Winchester, Sir J. Stepney, Lord Robert Spencer, William Eden (now Lord Auckland), and my good and ever esteemed friend, the last Lord Northington, were amongst the number.

Though Fox surpassed him in fame, none of these succeeded so well in life as James Harris. He surpassed them all in the not unimportant particular of good looks. A strikingly handsome undergraduate of nineteen would not, I suppose, have sought his pleasure only in claret and card parties. Was he ever seen, one wonders, with

> Maidens who from distant hamlets come
> To dance around the Fyfield elm in May?

He got love, I suspect, when and from whom he wanted it; and, prizing it lightly, was able in his ripe years, cold-bloodedly, to advise a young aspirant to diplomatic honours

> to avoid what is termed abroad an *attachement*. If the other party happens to be sincere, it absorbs too much time, occupies too much your thoughts; if insincere, it leaves you at the mercy of a profligate and probably interested character.

This counsel, one may be sure, was the result of observation, not of personal experience.

In the autumn of 1765, his father being now out of office, James proceeded to the University of Leyden. Holland, the most opulent and populous of the United Provinces, still bulked large in the estimation of Europe generally. The ambitious English student thought it worth while to frequent the society and public amusements of Amsterdam and The Hague, "gaining a knowledge of the people and making friendships," we are told, which were very useful to him a score of years after.

The temptations to idleness, one presumes, were not so powerful under the leaden skies of Holland as at Oxford. Conscious that he had much leeway to make up, Harris read hard, studying history and law and mastering the Dutch language. He started a diary, which he kept up all his life. He was now thoroughly determined to make his mark in the world. With letters of introduction from Yorke, our minister at The Hague, he visited Berlin and was presented to the great Frederick. The monarch made on the young Englishman a disagreeable impression which time and better acquaintance by no means lessened. Harris has many anecdotes illustrating the King's stinginess and rapacity; more edifying are two other stories which should appeal to our sense of humour, as they did to his. Frederick congratulates our ambassador on the taking of Quebec. "Yes," replies his Excellency, "we have taken it, with the help of God." "Hah!" says the King, "God then is among your allies?" "Yes, sire," replies the Englishman, "and He is the only one of them to whom we don't pay a subsidy in cash." One of his Majesty's servants, the Grand Marshal of his court, was remarkable for what the Americans call 'dumbness.' He told everybody he had been present at a siege, but couldn't for the life of him remember whether he had been among the besieged or the besiegers. Our ambassador, the poet Sir Charles Hanbury Williams, when recommending the Earl of Essex to this functionary, thought it, therefore, not out of place to add, "You may be sure this is not the Earl of Essex whose head was chopped off by Queen Elizabeth." The Grand Marshal made a note of this, and, having presented the Earl to the Queen of Prussia, immediately added, "I am assured, your Majesty, that this is not the Earl of Essex who was decapitated by order of Queen Elizabeth."

From Berlin, Harris travelled on into Poland, then approaching its dissolution. As Yorke's friend, he was made much of by the titular king, Stanislas Poniatowski.

"Never seek high office" was the unhappy sovereign's warning to the ambitious stranger. But, observing that where the King was weak the Russian ambassador was all-powerful, Harris did not hesitate to accept the post of Secretary of Legation at Madrid under Sir James Gray, which was procured him in 1768, by the influence of Lord Shelburne.

It was a service done to his father's son. If Harris had given thus early exceptional proofs of sagacity or address he has not recorded them. His qualifications for the diplomatic career were a handsome presence, fearlessness, rather more learning than most of his contemporaries could boast, and an arrogant and unquestioning belief in the superiority of his own nation over all others.

> An Englishman who, after a long absence from England, returns to it with feelings and sentiments partial to other countries, and adverse to his own, *has no real mind*, is without the powers of discernment and plain easy comparison, and has no title to enjoy the superior moral, political and local advantages to which he is born.

So Harris wrote as an old man, but the very extravagance of the assertion proves it to be the expression, not of his considered judgment, but of inborn bias.

At the age of twenty-four James Harris, we may be sure, was far from sharing the growing opinion that England was in decline. Very quickly, too, he perceived the hollowness of Spain's pretensions to rank still as a first-class Power. The veteran Marqués de Grimaldi, then in charge of the Spanish Foreign Office, he judged to be a man of only ordinary ability and completely under the thumb of France. In the absence of his chief, the young *chargé d'affaires* found his opportunity. In 1764 the Spaniards had possessed themselves of the easternmost island of the Falkland group. In the following year the English made a settlement named Port Egmont on the western island. Four years later a claim to the whole group was made by Bucarelli, Spain's governor at Buenos Ayres. This claim was resisted by Hunt, the English naval officer on the spot, and it was agreed that the question should be referred to the two respective Governments. Hunt sailed for home. The matter was still under discussion when on August 23, 1770, Harris notified our Secretary of State that, according to his advices, a Spanish squadron was being equipped in the Plate river to dislodge the British settlers and to take possession of the whole archipelago.

In London considerable party capital was made out of the dispute. Whether or not Lord Chatham and his supporters were justified in accusing Lord North of weakness in dealing with the foreigner, young Mr Harris carried out the instructions he received with no want of vigour. He told Grimaldi that the only means of preventing the most fatal consequences to Spain was for his Catholic Majesty to disavow the proceedings of the governor of Buenos Ayres and to reinstate the settlers of Port Egmont. It is plain from our representative's dispatches that the Marqués was very much flustered by his manner of speaking. The matter, he said, would be adjusted in London between Lord Weymouth, our Foreign Secretary, and Prince Masserano, the Spanish ambassador to the court of St James's. It would be tedious, says Harris, to repeat the strange, inconsistent sallies that passion induced Grimaldi to make. Our *chargé d'affaires* can hardly be blamed if he hoped by bullying the court of Madrid to cut the ground from beneath Masserano's feet and win for himself the credit of a diplomatic victory. He saw no reason to temporize.

> There is not the least reason to doubt [he wrote] their sincere desire here of the continuance of peace, as well from their inabilities of supporting a war as from the dread they have of its consequences. . . . Their infantry is very incomplete, and notwithstanding the active efforts of General O'Reilly, still very ill-disciplined. . . . Their navy, since the arrival of the French-

man Gaultier, is considerably augmented and repaired; they have, however, very few seamen. . . . Their revenues have never been in a worse condition.

His Catholic Majesty Charles III did not indeed want a war; but the British demands, particularly the one that he should repudiate his lieutenant in America, were, he thought, inconsistent with the honour of his crown. The Family Compact which existed between the Bourbon princes justified his holding out. Choiseul, Louis XV's minister, was prepared to risk war with England. Meantime Lord Weymouth had been succeeded at the Foreign Office by Lord Rochford, who promptly displayed the energy expected of new brooms.

On January 4, 1771, the King's messenger, Otto, drove into Madrid and handed Harris several packets. That addressed to him contained his letters of recall. The negotiations with Prince Masserano had been broken off. There were other letters containing instructions for the Lieutenant-Governor of Gibraltar, his Britannic Majesty's consul at Cadiz, and the naval commandant in Spanish waters. These Harris sent on by Otto, directing him when he had delivered them to return to England by sea. In a like "safe and private manner" our *chargé d'affaires* sent off warnings to the other British consuls and the leading British business men in Spain. Having allowed these a start of eight days, he informed the Spanish minister of his recall. Grimaldi expressed his regret, and was the more sincere, no doubt, since he had learned that Choiseul was dismissed and that Spain in the event of war could no longer reckon on the help of France. The people at Whitehall had acted too hastily.

On February 7 Harris took formal leave of King Charles and started on his journey homeward. At Algoa, an inconsiderable village twenty leagues from the capital, he halted for the night. In the light of a lantern, it may be supposed, he caught sight of a passing traveller. He recognized Salter, one of the messengers.

Disclosing himself, he was handed a fresh dispatch from London. The Spanish ambassador had conceded all our demands, in consequence of the French king's dismissal of Choiseul. The night was pitch-dark and the roads worse than was the wont in Spain. Notwithstanding, Harris turned about and rode straight back to Madrid. At ten o'clock in the forenoon he presented himself to Grimaldi, no doubt with the intention of exchanging congratulations on the settlement of the dispute. But the Marqués seized this opportunity of signifying his indignation at the high-handed procedure of the English court and of snubbing the young man who had plagued him. Mr Harris had presented his letters of recall; therefore he had lost his diplomatic character. His Catholic Majesty had the right to expect, not a *chargé d'affaires*, but at least a minister plenipotentiary till such time as an envoy of higher character should be accredited to him. In the interval Mr Harris, for whom the Marqués had the highest regard, could only be considered a private English gentleman. So much bemused by want of sleep and the fatigue of his ride that he had difficulty in penning a concise account of the incident to his superiors, Mr Harris went down the stairs of El Pardo. He had not long to wait for his revenge. On March 7 he was apprised by one of the Marqués' own messengers that the Spanish court had been notified by Lord Rochford of his elevation to the rank and office of minister plenipotentiary, pending the arrival of Lord Grantham as ambassador. Accordingly Mr Harris once more made his bow to the King of Spain, and Grimaldi said he was very pleased.

So Harris had cause to be. The age abounded in opportunities for young men,[1] but it was unusual for one to be appointed minister before he had completed

---

[1] Harris's night ride back to Madrid could only have been performed by a young man. Nowadays, by means of motor-car or aeroplane, an octogenarian can travel all over Europe with less trouble. Science is making the world easier for the aged and therefore limiting the opportunities of youth.

his twenty-fifth year. The reward was generous, for the satisfactory result of the transaction about the Falkland Islands was due not so much to his efforts as to the change of ministry in France. However, on the papers being laid before Parliament, it was agreed that "the young gentleman at Madrid had done his duty very well." He was transferred as minister plenipotentiary to Berlin. Every one would not have taken this to be promotion. His emoluments amounted to less than the £800 a year he had received in Spain, and Berlin was not then looked on as a very important station. Britain was mainly interested in the attitude of the two great western Powers. Prussia, in close concert with Russia and the Emperor, was busy about the dismemberment of Poland. At Whitehall this was described as "a curious transaction," but as one which was not likely to prejudice England so long as the equilibrium of the bandit Powers was maintained. Harris, while frequently deploring the subservience of the court of Petersburg to the court of Berlin, conceived no possibility of Europe's being seriously disturbed till such time as the three allies disagreed among themselves, or by their still stricter union were able to carry their ambition beyond the utmost limits of moderation.[1]

"That Berlin was a disagreeable post for an English minister, and that there was little respect shown them, and that from the temper of the two courts there was at that instant no probability of any material business occurring between them," was pointed out to the young diplomatist by his sometime friend and sometime rival, William Eden (afterwards Lord Auckland). Harris did not deny this; but when Eden went on to say that the King would be glad if he would go to Copenhagen, to sustain and comfort his unfortunate sister, the Queen of Denmark, he refused the transfer on the ground that there was that in the character of King Frederick which might one day transform Berlin into the liveliest centre

[1] May 8, 1773. S.P. 90/93. Public Record Office.

of politics in Europe. The *rôle* of Perseus did not appeal to this young man. On learning that his master had conferred the riband of the Bath on Murray Keith for his chivalrous and courageous intervention at the Danish capital on behalf of the Queen, Harris may for a moment have regretted his cautiousness. To his friend Batt he admitted that he was growing fat and lazy. He disliked the Prussian capital.

> No place can be worse for the comforts of social life. Berlin is a town where if *fortis* can be construed honest, there is neither *vir fortis nec fœmina casta*. A total corruption of morals reigns throughout both sexes in every class of life, joined to penuriousness. The men are constantly occupied how to make straightened [*sic*] means support the extravagances of their life. The women are harpies debauched through want of modesty rather than from want of anything else. They prostitute their persons to the best payer, and all delicacy of manners or sentiment of affection are unknown to them.

Mr Harris will have his sedate friend Mr Batt believe that his manner of life was as sober as his. It is, however, significant that the notorious profligate the Duc de Lauzun, afterwards better known as the Duc de Biron, speaks of the British minister as his most intimate friend in Berlin and says he took him about everywhere. Mr Harris is described by Dr John Moore as living in a style which did honour to his country and himself, a style which, like the abused Berliners, he found it impossible to maintain on his straitened means. On July 3, 1773, we find him writing to Lord Suffolk[1] to implore an augmentation of his salary (which was five quarters in arrear) or a special gratuity from the King—any further encroachments on his private income must fall heavily on his family. Lord Suffolk's reply has not been preserved to us, but Harris acknowledged it with gratitude.

Thiébault, a French writer of memoirs, has it that little notice was taken of the British ambassador at Berlin.

---

[1] S.P. 90/94. Public Record Office.

JAMES HARRIS, EARL OF MALMESBURY

The Englishman, however, says that he was always received by his Prussian Majesty with particular marks of favour; and this is borne out by the terms of Frederick's letter to him when he was appointed to another court. Harris could not have reproached himself with having left anything undone to humour the old man. Aware of his dislike for his nephew and heir and his disapproval of his comparatively prodigal way of life, Harris refused to lend the Prince money, though one thinks it might have been worth incurring the aged monarch's displeasure in order to gain the goodwill of his successor. Tact also forbade him to support the Polish ambassador or to put in a word on behalf of Poland with his own Government, as his friend King Stanislas had invited him to do. Recognizing the necessities of his position, Stanislas bore him no grudge on this score and continued to speak of him as his friend.

But, in spite of all, when the British minister presented his letters of recall in September 1776, and set his face homeward, he must have realized that he left Old Fritz no better disposed towards Britain than when he was accredited to him. It was Harris's first failure.

II

For over two years the world had been watching the struggle between Old England and her undutiful sons across the Atlantic. The tenacity of the Americans, rather than their actual achievements in the field, led our enemies to forecast the result. The insurgents found defenders in the House of Commons, to the amused astonishment of the non-parliamentary nations. "You might as well try to explain snow to an African chief," groaned Harris, "as our party system to foreigners." There were those who expected the lopping off of its greatest branch to bring down the old tree of British monarchy. Britain's navy was neglected. Disgracefully, we hired German troops to fight our rebellious colonists.

ENVOYS EXTRAORDINARY

Old Frederick prophesied our downfall. The attitude of France and Spain made it sure that upon any signal success of the Americans they would come into the war against us. George III and his ministers looked around and saw that England had no friends. The three eastern Powers were not, indeed, enemies. Their interests nowhere clashed directly with Britain's. But Vienna followed the lead of Berlin, and the King of Prussia could not forgive England for having, as he held, abandoned him in 1763. There remained Russia, that strange great newcomer into the European concert, whose armies had penetrated to Berlin, shattered the febrile strength of Sweden, and threatened to drive the Turk beyond the Danube and the Black Sea.

The Empress Catherine was not known to bear any ill-will to Great Britain. Our ministers somewhat ingenuously thought she might become an ally. Young Mr Harris had complained that her minister Panin was the mere instrument of Frederick. Harris had not done much at Berlin, but his knowledge of the forces which drove the machine of Russian diplomacy might be usefully applied to countering them. True, he was not by temperament exactly the man one would select for the *rôle* of suppliant. On the other hand, his comely person ensured him a cordial welcome by the most amorous of female sovereigns. Early in 1777, somewhere about the completion of his thirty-first year, he was informed that his Majesty had been pleased to appoint him his ambassador to the court of Petersburg.

Before leaving England he looked round for a wife. On July 28, 1777, he married a sixteen-year-old girl, Harriet Mary, younger daughter of Sir George Amyand, a deceased baronet. Her elder sister was the wife of Gilbert Elliot, afterwards known as Lord Minto, and Gilbert's sister had married William Eden. Harriet was a slim little thing, so frail in appearance that her husband had some joke about her being the portrait of Nobody. Later on she filled out. Elliot, who fetched her back from Petersburg in 1781, wrote, "She is really extremely pretty, and a little rouge, which she puts on very well, is a great advantage to her." She was very fond of her sister, and wrote her innumerable letters in a fine, legible hand. A bright little worldling, arch, merry, and adventurous, she is at her best describing the fashions and court functions and retailing the gossip of her circle. Her views or prejudices were those natural to the wife of his Britannic Majesty's representative. She cried out in horror at the execution of people of her own class in France, apparently oblivious that every week in England hundreds of people of both sexes, many of them children of fourteen, were hanged for trivial offences. If, following the example of the blacks of Haiti, the slaves in our colonies were to mutiny, she thought the planters would be justified in demanding the execution of Wilberforce. She recognized her own, the eighteenth, century as the age of unbelief, and surmised that it might be succeeded by an age of superstition. She was no puritan. She saw no reason for setting her face against Lady Hamilton, whom she met and dined with at Naples. Her liking for the famous Emma was not shared by her sister or her son. In Italy she was detained at Venice, not out of any curiosity about its art treasures, but because the laundress took so long to wash her linen. Her letters contain few allusions to the beauties of art or nature. She and her husband looked on the world with the eyes of Peter Bell.

But to the tinsel splendours of the Muscovite court they opened in wide admiration. The chest containing the wardrobe of Harriet and of Harris's sister Gertrude, who accompanied them, was lost at sea, and both ladies had to make their bow to her Imperial Majesty in clothes kindly lent by the Russian ladies. The Empress was then (January 1778) approaching her half-century. Her capabilities as a ruler were as notorious as what people termed her gallantries. At a first glance the new envoy was struck by her "incredible vanity." No doubt Catherine liked to be flattered, but, like a purring cat beneath its fur, she remained very much on guard. Harris erred, too, in asserting that the leading men at her court were too rich to be bribed, too headstrong to be persuaded, and too ignorant to listen to plain truth and conviction. His own strength and weakness lay in his conviction that the welfare of England was to be preferred above all things by all men, even by Russians.

He lost no time in acquainting Count Panin, Catherine's chief minister, with his Government's desire for an alliance with Russia. The Count, he saw, was surprised; but he promised to submit the proposal to his mistress, premising that she would never entertain the idea of an offensive alliance. On the Sunday following he took the Englishman into the Grand Duke's apartment and informed him that the Empress was touched by the attitude of our court, but in view of the diversity of their interests would like to have an exposition of a general system and of our idea of a defensive alliance. This was not encouraging. In the conversation that ensued Panin denied with an oath that Russia was under the influence of any other Power. "What!" he exclaimed. "Did you suppose we would suffer ourselves to be *led?*"

Harris persisted in that opinion and peevishly denounced the plausible and insidious wiles of the house of Bourbon. In March France entered into an alliance with the Americans and declared war on Britain. The ambassador could hardly have expected any better answer from the Empress than that which he got in May. She would ally herself with England against France only on the condition that we joined her in the war against the Turks. After all, it could have made little difference to the eastern empire how the balance of power inclined on the Atlantic shores. But Harris, although a suppliant, was not the man to take such a reply meekly. Knowing that the condition would be rejected by his court, he pointed out stiffly that we had already rendered material service to the Russian fleet in the Mediterranean in its operations against the infidels. He blamed Panin for not having declined the proffered alliance out of hand, observing that the rejection coming at the end of four months suggested calculation and was bound to make a bad impression in London.

That possibility troubled her Majesty so little that she directed her ambassador in England to protest against our rough handling of neutral shipping. She wished, she explained, to spare Harris so disagreeable a commission. He was not grateful. If the remonstrance had been transmitted through him, he observed, it would have occasioned less noise. This was ungracious of our ambassador, for the Empress noticed him more than any other members of the diplomatic corps, and, indeed, more than any strangers. She invited him to all her card parties. She took him, with only two other courtiers, to her country seat, La Grenouillère, and talked to him about painting, of which he knew little, and about gardening, of which he knew less. The wits of woman and man were evenly matched. Harris pricked up his ears when his hostess continued to discourse on the genius of the ancient Greeks and on the possibility of their descendants becoming the first people in the world, if properly assisted to succeed. If King George really wanted help from the Empress, wrote the ambassador (June 4, 1779), the best means to obtain it would be to encourage this romantic idea.

> She is now so warmly bent on it that such a conduct, dexterously managed, would give us the firmest hold of this court; and as its execution would instantly appear impracticable we need not be apprehensive of having engaged ourselves too far in an unpleasant transaction.

At that date the project appears to have been in itself by no means impracticable; and it is not at all certain that the dismemberment of the Ottoman Empire in Europe and the erection of an Hellenic state might not have been carried out by Britain, Russia, Austria, and France, with hardly more difficulty than the partition of Poland occasioned.

The Empress smiled but to deceive, in our ambassador's opinion. He was Sir James Harris now, having been knighted by her Majesty and invested with the insignia of the Order of the Bath in January 1779, at the request of his own sovereign. He and his wife were among the few strangers privileged to attend performances at the imperial theatre at Peterhof. There in June Catherine spoke to him between the acts and asked him if he had it officially confirmed that Spain, following the lead of France, had declared war against Britain. He seems to have seen the news only in the *Hamburg Gazette*. Taking advantage of the Empress's sympathetic tone, he said that there appeared to be a kind of crusade forming against us, and if we were to be abandoned by the only great Power in Europe capable of withstanding so formidable a league, he scarcely knew whether our exertions, great as they certainly would be, could enable us to stand against it. This sounds odd language in the mouth of a British ambassador. Catherine endeavoured to reassure him. "I always was and always shall be the firm friend of Britain," she said, and then reminded him, as she should not have had occasion to do, that our resources and national spirit were great. "Be assured," she concluded, "that nothing can be sincerer than my friendship for England." At that point the curtain rose, and Sir James was unable to get this assurance put into the shape of a pledge of assistance.

He was, he complains, without instructions. But the times called for special enterprise, and he was prepared to risk disavowal. Presently the Autocrat's indignation was roused by the Spaniards' searching and making prizes of two Russian trading ships. For some time past Sir James had been systematically courting the favour of Patiomkin, who was not only the Empress's favourite but the inveterate enemy of Nikita Panin. Through him

JAMES HARRIS, EARL OF MALMESBURY

the Englishman procured the singular privilege of a private audience with the sovereign. He writes:

On Monday, the 22nd July, at the masquerade given at the Grand-duchess's birthday, some time after Her Imperial Majesty's card-party, at which I had assisted, was finished, Mons. Korsakoff came up to me, and desiring me to follow him, conducted me a back way into the Empress's private dressing-room, and on introducing me, immediately retired. The Empress, after making me sit down, began by saying that after her own affairs, ours were those which she had most at heart . . . and [she] should be happy if I could obviate the obstacles which ever presented themselves to her mind in every plan she had formed to be useful to us.

The action of the Spanish privateers inspired Sir James to suggest she should make a strong and spirited declaration to the courts of Versailles and Madrid and support it by a considerable naval armament, thus restoring equality to the war and setting free the various European Powers to take each the part their interests and sympathies assigned to them. What he hoped for, I suppose, was that the doubtful neutrality of a Russian armada would compel our enemies to keep a large fraction of their fleets in observation. Catherine made a non-committal reply, and said she had no doubt our navy was a match for both French and Spaniards. She hinted that the best way of procuring peace would be for us to renounce our American colonies. Harris asked her if in the like circumstances she would purchase peace on such terms. She replied with great vehemence, "J'aimerais mieux perdre la tête." To her objection that she had no right to intervene in a quarrel so remote Harris insisted that her intervention would cover her with glory and set her above Peter the Great. "She seemed much pleased with the idea," but said some very powerful objections remained. She knew, of course, that the ambassador was trying to drag her into the war on the side of his own country. "Our conversation," concludes Sir James, "having lasted upwards of an hour, she dismissed me, and it being quite dark, it was with some difficulty I found my way through the intricate passages back to the ball-room."

As he had been requested, the ambassador recapitulated his arguments in writing. Two days later, finding herself in his company at supper, the Empress turned to him and assured him she was thinking over what he had said. "You must not be surprised," she told the others present, "if I have secrets with Sir James Harris. We were neighbours in the country (near Peterhof), and neighbours always have secrets."

This was all very well. Harris had had his opportunity of speaking directly to the Autocrat behind the backs of her ministers, but now Patiomkin warned him that she had referred his proposal to Panin and told him to let her have his written opinion upon it. "By employing various means, unnecessary to repeat," as Sir James tells us, he obtained an abstract of this opinion before it was submitted to the Empress. Panin described Prussia as the sentinel of Russia, and concluded that there was no ground for supporting England. The answers, as he conceived them, to these contentions the Englishman embodied in a draft which Patiomkin promised to place in his mistress's own hands. Again he reminded Catherine of the help given by the British fleet to hers. She may have remembered that it was with the help of the British consul at Leghorn that the unfortunate young adventuress who claimed to be the daughter of her predecessor Elizabeth had been kidnapped and sent to die in a Russian prison. But empresses are no more grateful than the rest of their sex. Presently Harris heard that she had gone off into the country. She appeared to forget such weighty issues by the sickbed of her favourite Lanskoi. Vainly England waived the right of searching Russian ships; vainly, at his ambassador's suggestion, George III wrote to Catherine, suggesting she might make a naval demonstration on his behalf. On January 9, 1780, Panin, confined by sickness to his room, handed Harris his sovereign's coldly worded rejection of our proposals.

JAMES HARRIS, EARL OF MALMESBURY

The previous August the townsmen of Drake had beheld the fleets of France and Spain sailing unmolested up the Channel. An alliance with England was not like to be profitable. But Catherine had a lurking doubt. "I would do everything to serve you," she told Harris one evening at supper, "short of involving myself in the war." The handsome Englishman renewed his arguments. She stopped him. "Si j'étois plus jeune," she said, "je serois peut-être moins sage," a remark which may have had only a political sense. She would give money to the poor, she said, if Rodney beat the fleet of Spain. Rodney did beat it, and relieved Gibraltar. "I am better than my word," whispered her Majesty to Sir James on entering the ball-room. "I will not only give a thousand rubles to the poor, but I give you this ball and entertainment on account of Rodney's victory."

But, either because England was too successful at sea or not successful enough, the Russian ruler continued to protest against our interference with neutral shipping. What had her Majesty to fear? inquired Lord Hillsborough, new at the Foreign Office. "Her mercantile marine is the best guarded in the world, for she has one man-of-war to every merchantman." This sneer irritated the Empress. She became more definite in her demands, and in March sent out to the other courts a list of her five points to be guaranteed by the armed neutrals. These were:

(1) Neutral vessels may freely navigate along the coasts of the belligerent countries, from port to port.
(2) Belligerents' property, other than contraband, shall pass freely in neutral bottoms.
(3) The definition of contraband to be that given in Articles 10, 11, of the Russo-British treaty of commerce.
(4) Blockade to be recognized only if effective.
(5) These points to be observed as principles of law in all prize-court proceedings.

Harris, writing at a later date, gave it as his opinion that, if England could have done without Russia, she should at once have rejected these new-fangled doctrines, but if her need of assistance was great she should have recognized them as far as Russia was concerned and so secured a powerful friend. Instead, as he puts it, a merely trimming answer was returned from London. He was instructed secretly to oppose, openly to acquiesce. The convention between the Northern Powers, known in history as the Armed Neutrality, was approved by the Empress in June. Harris, in disgust and despair, asked to be recalled. Lord Stormont, now at Whitehall, told him to remain where he was.

He was likely to do as well there as any of his countrymen, for he was still *persona gratissima* at the Russian court. At a masquerade the Empress chose him for her escort. "It was I who dubbed you knight," she said, "and it is your duty to protect me against bores." Encouraged by her kindness, the ambassador again tried his powers of persuasion at a private interview. "What harm has my Armed Neutrality, or rather Armed Nullity, done you?" she asked good-humouredly. "All the harm in the world," was the answer. "It establishes new rules which cover our enemies, supplies them with materials for building ships of war, and confounds our friends with our foes." "Listen," said Catherine; "make peace! The time has come for it." Harris replied that nothing less than the Peace of Paris would afford a basis for negotiation. Her Majesty hotly repudiated the charge of being anti-English. Harris appealed to her generosity to save England. She said she was weary of showing generosity which was never requited. Having warned her against misinterpretation by her ministers, the Englishman withdrew.

This interview took place at the end of 1780. Gibraltar resisted all the assaults of France and Spain. Harris took heart again. "England when united in itself is a match for all Europe," he wrote. One regrets he did not take

CATHERINE II, EMPRESS OF RUSSIA
From an engraving after a painting by Rosselin

up that attitude at Petersburg. Instead, he resorted to chicanery and bribery, and in the end gained nothing. He apologized to Lord Stormont for having been perhaps too profuse in his expenditure of secret service money. Having passed three years in Spain and five at Berlin without having had recourse to a practice repugnant to his character, he had hoped to have no need for it in Russia. But he soon discovered his error. He was surrounded by spies and had none. No servant of his was too insignificant to escape the solicitations of his rivals. When he left his secretary writing he was obliged to lock him in, not because he mistrusted him, but lest he might inadvertently leave the door open. For information that was reliable and worth having, he had to pay handsomely —and on one occasion at least he was forced to pay for what he knew already. He had already sunk £20,000 of his own in the public service, but was willing to stand the loss if the authorities at home deemed his expenditure in this way excessive. It does not appear that he procured any very valuable intelligence, except about the affairs of individuals. "If you know as much about the affairs of State as you do about mine," said one of Patiomkin's associates, whose necessities he had been informed of and which he was willing to relieve at a price, "I can be of no use to you." "And," retorted the ambassador, "till you make me as well acquainted with the one as I am with the other, I shall be of no use to you."

As it turned out, Patiomkin did little for us, beyond perhaps inducing his mistress not to extend the protection of her Armed Neutrality to our latest enemies, the Dutch. Even the bait of Minorca was refused, Catherine suspecting it was designed to engulf her in the war. She offered mediation in concert with the court of Vienna, but the British Cabinet would not tolerate any intervention between the King and his rebellious subjects, and rejected the idea of an armistice as necessarily fatal at the time to the success of our arms in America.

Yet Gilbert Elliot, coming in August 1781 to take

his wife's sister home, observed nothing of the coolness on the part of the Empress of which Harris complained. He saw Harriet and Sir James playing cards with her Majesty. She motioned them to sit next to her in her barge. He saw Harriet dining at Patiomkin's table—"a distinction," he was informed, "which never befell a modest woman before." Her Majesty's whole behaviour on the occasion of Harriet's *congé* was infinitely gracious. Elliot and his sister-in-law travelled home through Poland. Approaching the King's country seat, they discovered his Majesty seated on a bench by the roadside. Harriet alighted and was presented. A very pleasant conversation went on for half an hour in French and English, Lady Harris being seated next to King Stanislas. The travellers had supper with the King, and the lively Harriet danced a polonaise in the garden with him or with Gilbert—the letter is not clear on this point.[1]

Sir James remained at Petersburg, disgusted with the Empress. He admits that she had offered to impose peace on Holland if we would subscribe to the principles of the Armed Neutrality. He declares himself to have been completely isolated. He had lost faith in Patiomkin. He had no one who could be trusted to convey anything direct to the Empress. He was vilely and absurdly slandered. He accuses Panin of spreading a report that he had tried to burn the Russian fleet and poison the Grand Duke and his family by means of certain plants new to the Russians, the hot-scented geraniums! Fox's first brief tenure of office in the spring of 1782 brought back the smiles to the face of Imperial Majesty. The new Government, she hoped, would be more reasonable and by recognizing American independence bring about a general peace. Görz, the Prussian minister, began to make himself agreeable to Harris, and talked of an alliance between Britain, Russia, and Prussia. England was saved by her seamen. "Vive la Grande-Bretagne!

[1] *Life and Letters of Sir Gilbert Elliot*, vol. i, p. 66.

Vive Rodney!" wrote Patiomkin on hearing of the defeat of de Grasse off Dominica on April 12.

Harris took heart again. He easily persuaded himself that these Muscovites were longing to help our country. On June 26, 1782, he had "a very important secret" to communicate to his Government. The Empress was preparing a powerful armament to compel the acceptance by the Dutch of our peace terms. "This intention," goes on the letter, "is so profound a mystery that I am almost afraid of mentioning it, even in cipher. . . . Not a soul knows it, except those very few who enjoy her Imperial Majesty's complete confidence." Alas for Sir James Harris! Six weeks later he gloomily admitted that there was no longer any hope of her taking vigorous measures against our formidable adversary. He was happy to observe that the Secretary of State (Lord Grantham) had not placed too much reliance on his expectations. This time, we hope, our ambassador had not paid too highly for his exclusive and tremendously secret information.

Although the naval power of France was broken, the American provinces were lost to Britain. Peace was in sight. "A new face, new manners, new flatteries are necessary here," wrote Harris.[1] He was sure both his intellect and his health would break up if he spent another winter so near the Pole. In three months he had aged twenty years. He had nothing to do. He despised Görz's proposal.

> We should keep aloof, form no connexions with any Power whatsoever, be civil to all, particular to none, and wait for the moment when our alliance is sought for with eagerness, when we may enter into it in the only manner becoming such a Power as Great Britain.

Hearing of his illness, his wife and sister hastened from Lyons, in the depth of winter, half across Europe to his bedside. His prayer for recall was at last granted

[1] Add. MSS. 38774, f. 208.

by his old friend Fox, who was again at Whitehall. In August 1783 he took leave of the Empress, confident, as he wrote, that he left a smooth and pleasant road for his successor, Alleyne Fitzherbert, to walk in.

III

A treaty with Holland having been signed in the summer of 1784, Britain was officially at peace with all the world. But peace between Britain and France was regarded by most men, certainly by Harris, as merely a breather. While the soldiers and sailors took a rest, the diplomatists manœuvred for positions and continued the fight on the political chessboard. Three years prior to the great Revolution Sir James spoke of the French monarchy as too deeply rooted ever to be shaken, and Frederick and the Emperor looked on England as a decaying Power. In a forecast of the future entitled *England under George VI*, published about 1760, it was pointed out how impossible it was that the American colonies could ever unite or free themselves from the mother country. We need not, therefore, be surprised that to so unprescient a generation the little Dutch republic still appeared a Power well worth courting. The Hollanders did not love us any the better because we had defeated them and taken away their factory of Negapatam, on the Coromandel coast. On the other hand, the Prince of Orange, who held the anomalous office of Stadholder or hereditary Captain-General and chief magistrate of the republic, was known to have inherited strong British sympathies from his mother, a daughter of George II. Harris was acquainted with his Highness, and on this account presumably Fox offered him the legation at The Hague. Sir James had already refused Madrid, "on the score," as he obscurely puts it, "of my wife and children." The Hague, on the other hand, as a mere legation, he deemed unworthy of his reputation. Harris was the friend and follower of Fox, but Pitt thought so highly of him that, on forming his administration, he granted him the salary of an ambassador and promised to raise him to that rank when the opportunity occurred, if he would go to Holland with the credentials of a minister plenipotentiary. On November 22 we find Pitt writing to his Foreign Secretary, Lord Carmarthen, "I do not suppose it can be right to take any step except hurrying Sir James Harris, whose presence at The Hague becomes very essential."

France, it appeared to the new Prime Minister, was about to clutch the United Provinces once more in her embrace. The Emperor Joseph, the ruler of the territory we now call Belgium, had repudiated the unnatural convention which, in the commercial interests of the Dutch, forbade the navigation of the lower Scheldt and blocked access to the port of Antwerp. In addition the enlightened despot laid claim to a segment of Dutch territory near Maastricht. Since Antwerp was in those days supposed to be the rival of London, it might have been expected that England would eagerly associate herself with any power to combat the Emperor's project. The Marquess of Carmarthen hoped, indeed, that Frederick would intervene, if only because the Stadholder was the husband of his niece; but the old man was too wily to play our game. In the meanwhile the Dutch invoked the good offices of France, their ally in the late war. Vergennes, the French minister, listened sympathetically to their complaint, and in November sent a strongly worded protest on their behalf to the court of Vienna. By this Pitt seems to have been more alarmed than by the original threat to the prosperity of the Port of London. He foresaw an enormous increase of French prestige in the country which he considered still worth securing as an ally. Hence the haste with which Harris was sent over, to represent England as the honest broker and the true friend of the United Provinces.

He arrived in the first week of January 1785. Amid

the scenes of his early manhood, in the sedate red-brick houses reflected in the placid canals under a dull sky, he ought to have found himself at home. But familiarity, and perhaps the cold splendours of Petersburg, had engendered contempt. Having first asked whether his post was to be looked on as a permanency, he perceived the necessity of taking a house and entertaining generously. "If I mean to do anything here," he writes (January 28, 1785), "I must wield the spit as well as the pen. Dutch hearts lie to the leeward of their stomachs; and if I now at this moment make any impression on them, it is from the beef and pudding they see in the background." Later he announces that he has signed the lease of a house for five years.

> I am making up my mind to dullness and gravity; my eyes to black teeth and white lips; my nose to the stench of tobacco and unwashed toes; and my stomach to cheese, butter, and herrings. The experiment will cost me a few moral as well as physical indigestions; but in five or six months, I hope to become as square and solid, mentally and corporeally, as the most massive burgomaster in the republic.

The country we now call Holland, after its most important province, then constituted the federal republic of the United Provinces. These provinces were Holland, Zeeland, Utrecht, Gelderland, Overyssel, Friesland, and Groningen. Each province had its own legislature or States, and the whole union was directed by the States-General seated at The Hague. As in most federal republics, there was a party which favoured the central Government and another more tenacious of the privileges of the individual states. At the time of Harris's arrival the former styled itself the Patriots, a name which stank in English nostrils.[1] It was they who, by their sympathy with the revolted colonists and their eagerness to snap

---

[1] According to Horace Walpole, the most popular declaration a Parliamentary candidate could make was that he never had been and never would be a 'patriot.'

up the American market, had supplied England with grounds for attacking the republic. They were strongest in the province of Holland. Naturally, they inclined towards France, and, because they were the inheritors of the republican tradition, were in opposition to the Prince of Orange, the hereditary president or Stadholder.

His Highness William V, though credited by his enemies with formidable powers of dissimulation, had been at any rate unable to conceal his fondness for the country of his mother. When the indecisive engagement off the Dogger Bank in August 1781 was acclaimed as a victory for the Dutch fleet, the Captain-General of the republic's army and navy was heard to exclaim, "I hope the English did not lose much." It is not to be wondered at that the Patriots accused him of neglecting his duties. By posterity this unworthy descendant of William the Silent is most gratefully remembered as the founder of the fine collection of pictures at The Hague. In one of these he is shown as a dull-looking man, short of stature like his grandfather, with a fleshy face, protuberant lips, and an upturned nose. Next to him is the portrait of his consort, Wilhelmina, sister of that Frederick William whom Harris had refused to assist in his financial embarrassments at Berlin. Like most princesses of her epoch, she is portrayed as stout, deep-bosomed, full-faced, and over-upholstered. Another portrait shows her on horseback, a long-nosed, wholly unattractive female. But royalty could not have been so ill-favoured as it is generally represented by the painters of the eighteenth century. Perhaps it was a convention of art to make them ugly, as kings were to be shown in Roman costume. Harris's dispatches breathe something like a tenderness for the Princess of Orange, a tenderness which her firmness and masculine qualities could not have inspired unless backed by some kind of sex-appeal. Mirabeau says she made an enemy of the Duc de la Vauguyon by rebuffing his passionate advances.[1]

[1] Mirabeau, *Histoire secrète de la cour de Berlin*, vol. ii, p. 225.

> The Princess of Orange is accomplished to a degree [writes the ambassador], with a strong mind and quick penetration, but she is depressed by misfortunes of every kind. Her domestic life is deprived of happiness. Naturally high-minded she can ill brook the bad breeding of the wives of the factious Patriots.

Of this lady's husband Sir James had as poor an opinion as M. de Vérac, the French ambassador. "Such a man can never win any game; and unless a sleeping potion is administered to him, total ruin must result." The particular game which Harris wanted the Prince to play was not a very pretty one. Throughout the year 1785, while Vergennes was striving to maintain the treaty rights of the Dutch against the Emperor, the British envoy was busily trying to poison the people's minds against the mediating Power. He asserted that France would take Luxemburg and Namur as the price of her intervention. Finding that the Patriots were not to be hoodwinked, he busied himself stirring up disaffection against the States-General and in forming an Orange party.

> If it were possible [he writes] by any means whatsoever to gain over the Princess of Orange, to open her eyes to the interests of her children, and to induce her to prevail on the Prince's party to consent to the Emperor's views on the Scheldt (provided the Emperor on his part would consent to reinstate the Prince in the full privileges of his high office), this country might still be restored to its ancient system. If this should not happen, we might then look forward to the reduction of this country to a state of perfect insignificancy, as the best event which can befall England, it being evident that the Republic had better be annihilated than remain as it is.

In other words, the Stadholder was to be persuaded to sacrifice the commercial interests of his country, and incidentally those of the Port of London, in order to preserve his own dignities; and Sir James preferred the total ruin of a friendly state to seeing it pass under the influence of France.

WILHELMINA, PRINCESS OF ORANGE
From an engraving after a painting by John Hoppner

JAMES HARRIS, EARL OF MALMESBURY

By incessantly snubbing their Stadholder and threatening to curtail his authority the Patriots certainly played into the Englishman's hand. On August 19 the Princess admitted him to a private interview. She told him that she looked up to his royal master as the only real support the house of Orange had left.

> She spoke with much good sense and great sensibility on her own position, and without losing her dignity, endeavoured to interest me deeply in her situation [says Harris]. I on my side spared no pains to gain her confidence and to persuade her that I mean nothing but good to her and her House.

A few words passed between them at a ball, watched on all sides though they were. On September 2 the Princess and the ambassador met secretly in the gardens of the House in the Wood. His Excellency predicted that so soon as the agreement with Austria had been reached a treaty of alliance between France and the United Provinces would be signed, and this would be followed by the abolition of the Stadholder's office, and not improbably by the impeachment of the Stadholder himself. Her position, he insinuated, watching her face as he spoke, was desperate. It called for vigorous action. He was ready to obey her orders, but England by acting singly would only aggravate the evil. In the end she besought him to ask his colleague at Berlin to appeal for help to her uncle, the King of Prussia. Harris's dispatch concludes:

> I clearly perceived that she was by no means on a footing of confidence with the Prince, and that although she never mentioned his name but with an appearance of respect, she neither trusted him herself nor was trusted by him. I fear this division extends still further than public subjects; that they are as little agreed on domestic ones, and this circumstance makes it a very difficult task to obtain the confidence of the one without losing that of the other. . . . He is so jealous, not of her virtue, but of her sense and power, that he would not even go to Paradise by her influence; and she has in general that kind of contempt a

high-spirited woman feels for an inferior male being. . . . Hitherto, I have carried my cup even; and indeed it is not so much myself I fear, as the eyes of officious spies and informers, from whose eyes and tongues no one is safe.

In the first months of his arrival at The Hague he had noticed that a strange link-boy dogged his footsteps, although he was accompanied by two torch-bearers of his own. There were gossips, no doubt, who attached other than a political significance to the Princess's meetings with the handsome Englishman. For this reason, he told her, he declined the honour of dining with her.' One way of engaging a woman's interest is to hint that her name has already been coupled with one's own.

Like all public personages prior to the Revolution, her Highness thought it compatible with her dignity to adopt on occasions the most despondent tone. She and her children were going to the friendly province of Friesland. "I leave The Hague," she said to Harris, "possibly never to return to it. A few days will wrest from the Prince every remnant of authority, and I trust he is too high-minded to remain *un stadhouder en peinture*." She hoped her children would be happier in a less splendid situation. She had been often advised to separate her interests from those of the Prince. To that she would never subscribe. At times she had wished the Prince possessed many qualities he had not and could be divested of several that he had; but these were feelings which she conceived in her own heart. "I am bound to share his fate," she concluded, "let it be what it may."

Something, decided Harris, had evidently happened since he had sat next her at supper the previous evening. He proceeded to drag this out of her. She explained that a French officer, M. de Maillebois, who had been specially recommended to the Prince by the King of Prussia, had offered to put into her hands an authority equivalent to her husband's if she would contribute to his securing the command of the army. Moreover, her alliance had been solicited by Peter Paulus, one of the Patriot leaders. What did Sir James think about these proposals?

He denounced them as false and dangerous. He did not pause to consider that they might be to the Princess's advantage. He saw only that the scheme would throw her into the arms of the French party. The proposal, he said, could only be sincerely made by men who were infinitely weak or infinitely honourable, which certainly was not the character of the Patriots. "I dwelt the more on this," he says, "as I was fearful despair might make her clutch at this slight twig." He dwelt on the significance of the two proposals coming on the same day.

To Joseph Ewart, our *chargé d'affaires* at Berlin, he wrote in support of the Princess's appeal for help. In the Prussian King's attitude may be traced the inspiration of the proposals made to his niece. France, Spain, Austria, and Russia, he pointed out to Ewart, were now in alliance, and Holland would shortly be in the power of France. England and Prussia were isolated, and were not a match for such a coalition. His Prussian Majesty expressed a polite concern for his niece, and thought that the Prince of Orange had better come to terms with Amsterdam. He made it clear that he had no intention of pulling the chestnuts out of the fire. Harris was left to play a lone hand.

It looked as though he had lost the game. On September 20, 1785, the preliminaries of an understanding with the Emperor were signed. His Imperial Majesty renounced his project of opening the Scheldt in consideration of an indemnity of ten million florins paid by the United Provinces. On November 9, as Harris had anticipated, this was followed by a treaty of alliance between France and Holland. The allies were to assist each other in case of attack, with troops, ships, and cash, and undertook to guarantee each other's territory. From Lord Carmarthen the ambassador received urgent but unnecessary instructions to oppose the ratification of the treaty at The Hague. Under the pretence of showing his wife the sights of Amsterdam, his Excellency visited the city in order to foment the opposition. He failed. The treaty was approved by a majority of the States-General on December 1.

"French gold!" shouted Harris. But France then, and for a long time after, had not a louis to spare. It was not for him to reproach his adversary with questionable methods of promoting their interests. His Britannic Majesty's representative was deep in a conspiracy against the integrity of the state to which he was accredited. By showing himself freely in society he hoped to carry on his operations undetected. He went too far, however, in inviting Peter Paulus to dine with him. The shrewd Hollander guessed what he was about. "I must expect," wrote the conspirator, "to have the whole force of their opposition to encounter. The foundation, however, is laid." Trinquetti, the Sardinian Consul-General, was in his pay, and through Count Mirabel, the Sardinian minister, he sounded the deputies from Zeeland and succeeded beyond his hopes in influencing their reports to their constituents. He sent his agent, Baron Kinckel, into the insular province to foment the jealousy with which the inhabitants always regarded their richer neighbours. Van der Spiegel, the Pensionary or Governor, was a strong Orange partisan. On December 16, 1785, we find Harris writing to the Foreign Secretary:

> I have received this morning the strongest assurances that the Province of Zeeland will go any lengths to which I choose to push it, and *is ready to separate from the Union and put itself under the immediate protection of England.*[1] I replied with expressions of great applause to the laudable spirit they manifest, and encouraged it by every vague assurance I could make. I avoided, however, touching on their offer of throwing themselves into the hands of England till I know in what manner your lordship orders me to receive it.

This was as well. Carmarthen's reply is dated a week later.

[1] The italics are the present writer's.

Sir:
The idea of the province of Zeeland separating from the Union and receiving the protection of England, can by no means be encouraged. That so respectable a part of the Republic should endeavour to resist the despotic system of the present ruling faction is most desirable; but when the bare supposition of the serious consequences which might result to this country even from the Seven United Provinces engaging in a war, demands no trifling degree of consideration, the defection of a single province cannot by any means justify on our part, a risk of such a nature.

Meanwhile the Patriots continued their agitation against the Stadholder. But neither Vergennes in Paris nor de Vérac, his man at The Hague, threw himself as passionately into the quarrel as did Sir James Harris. De Vérac assured his chief that the Patriots contemplated nothing unconstitutional. They proposed merely to limit the Stadholder's military powers. Harris told a different story to his Highness. The villains intended to strip him of all his dignities, force him to abdicate, and indict him for high treason. The Princess was to be declared *gouvernante* during the minority of her children with a council of regency to assist her. A princely adventurer, the Rhinegrave of Salm, precisely one of those impoverished princelings for whom the English country gentleman had a bottomless contempt, was to take command of the federal forces, and already disposed of a considerable body of volunteers or free corps. The French, it was alleged, had spent £50,000 in bribes. As a matter of fact, it was not till well on in March 1786 that Vergennes went so far as to authorize his minister at The Hague to spend money, and only if absolutely necessary to strengthen the good cause.[1]

In fairness to Sir James it must be said that in backing the Prince of Orange—solely, of course, in the interests of his own Government—he had the support of a considerable volume of public opinion in the republic itself.

[1] Pierre De Witt, *Une Invasion prussienne en Hollande*, p. 67.

ENVOYS EXTRAORDINARY

Among the provinces Zeeland (as has been seen), Gelderland, and Friesland stood by the Stadholder, out of jealousy of Holland. Even in Amsterdam, and perhaps generally throughout the country, the unrepresented masses persisted in regarding the descendant of William the Silent as their defender against the capitalists and merchant aristocracy who controlled the States-General. It need not be said that William V was incapable of imagining, much less of fulfilling, the mission which the common people assigned him. The prince who puts himself at the head of the poor folk and vindicates their rights against the rich and noble is yet awaited in other countries besides Holland.

Orange favours were as common in the Dutch streets as now in Belfast. Harris says a poor woman was hanged at Rotterdam merely for wearing the Stadholder's colours. In defiance of popular sentiment the States-General decreed that a gate leading out of the Parliament House at The Hague, which had been hitherto used exclusively by the Stadholders, should now be affected to the use of the deputies. On March 17, 1786, Mynheer van Gyslaer, the deputy for Dordrecht and one of the most conspicuous leaders of the Patriots, attempted to assert this new privilege. An angry crowd collected on the drawbridge and refused to let him pass. When the courageous deputy insisted the people threatened to throw him and his carriage into the water. He might have fared no better than the brothers De Witt, who not much more than a century before were torn to pieces by an Orange mob, close to this very spot, had he not been rescued by a squad of horse-guards. A man who appeared to be the ringleader of the rioters was seized and found to be the barber of one of the Prince's chamberlains. He was condemned to death for high treason against the republic. At the instance of Gyslaer he was, however, reprieved at the place of execution as the noose was being slipped over his neck. Harris expresses himself as disgusted at the failure of a plot so ill combined and so ill executed. The result gave renewed confidence and energy to what he called the Faction.

> The friends of the old cause, disheartened by ill success, gradually leave The Hague and retire to distant provinces. The more timid even dare not see or speak to me [says the ambassador], and many whom I found well disposed on my arrival here have gone over to the opposite party. . . . The Hague itself is more like a besieged town than an open village. . . . The police has, I am told, 1200 spies in its pay.

Unmoved by a memorial in favour of the Prince addressed by Sir James to the States-General and a mild remonstrance by Thulemeyer, his Prussian colleague, the Provincial States of Holland at the end of July relieved his Highness of the command of The Hague garrison. This annoyed the Stadholder. He threw his hat on the floor and stamped upon it.

He could not, however, stamp on the obstinate Hollanders. "The pear is not yet ripe," sadly mused Harris, though he was thinking of an Orange. He reproached the Prince with having no guts, and was meditating a plan to suborn the city council of Amsterdam when news came of the death of old Frederick. Now that his wife's brother was King of Prussia, William V showed fight. He sent his troops to occupy two little towns in Gelderland which had flouted his authority. Harris clapped his hands. Holland retorted by ordering the troops of the province to take no commands from the Stadholder. As in America seventy-five years later, soldiers hesitated in their loyalty between their native state and the head of the federation. The Prince of Orange established his headquarters at Nymegen, and turned expectant eyes towards Berlin.

The high hopes formed by his Highness and by Harris were not immediately realized. But King Frederick William II showed himself not unmindful of his sister's uncomfortable position and sent a special envoy, Harris's old friend Görz, to see what might be done at The Hague. Having first called at the British legation, Görz paid a visit to M. de Vérac. Why should not France join with Prussia in restoring the Stadholder to his rightful position in the state? The Frenchman could only reply that the Most Christian King did not propose to interfere in the internal affairs of the republic, but considered himself the guardian of its liberty, its independence, and its constitution, as well as of its territorial integrity. The Prussian went away in a huff and reported the result of his overtures to Harris. He might have withheld his confidence had he seen a letter addressed by his friend to Lord Carmarthen. His aim, wrote Harris, was to commit France and Prussia to a military quarrel. "Next to recovering the republic for England," he said, "the rendering it a useless friend to France is, I presume, the principal object of my residence here."

Sir John Dalrymple had written from Berlin, inquiring whether an insurrection might not be raised in Holland itself. Harris assured his Government that he intended to act singly, independently of the Prussian and Orange interests. But a commercial treaty had just been concluded between France and England. Harris was requested to use arguments, and not assurances, in dealing with his Dutch friends.

His designs were penetrated by a man who had met him in England. The famous Mirabeau was hovering round Potsdam on a secret mission. He writes of "this bold and artful Harris, who, determined to advance his fortunes at any cost, seeks to embroil his nation, which is rather clever than wise."[1] This is harsh. Mirabeau, visiting the Elliots at Bath in 1783, had made furious love to Lady Harris, and, not succeeding in subduing her within a week, as he had expected,[2] entertained uncharitable memories of her and her husband.

---

[1] Mirabeau, *op. cit.*, vol. ii, p. 11.
[2] *Life and Letters of Sir Gilbert Elliot*, vol. i, p. 88. Sir Gilbert's "John Bull of a wife" would not allow Mirabeau to sleep under her roof at any price.

The months went by, and the tension between the legislature and the executive (to apply the terms of American constitutional law to Dutch institutions) did not relax. His Prussian Majesty, preoccupied with the pursuit of Fräulein Voss, a Prussian Pamela, was apt to forget his injured brother-in-law; and, to make matters worse, when the coy lady yielded she used what influence she had on the side of France. His Highness of Orange decided to strike a blow for himself. Profiting by a dispute between the city and the state of Utrecht, he attempted to gain possession of the town. On May 9, 1787, his troops were defeated by the Rhinegrave at the head of a body of volunteers. Seeing that the Prince could not save himself, Harris went home to try his powers of persuasion on his own Cabinet. He took with him a letter from the Princess to the King. At a dinner at the Lord Chancellor's he contended that, if war should ensue, France had no army or revenue or ministry to sustain it. Delays were dangerous. The diplomatist found Pitt and his colleagues more pliable than the Empress of Russia—more pliable than his own King, who could be persuaded only with the utmost difficulty to sanction an advance of £20,000 to be spent on raising troops for his cousin. Later on a further sum of £70,000 was wrung from him.

Back at The Hague, our minister continued to suborn deputies and to aid and abet the disturber of the Republic's peace. He set spies on the French ambassador. "For God's sake," cried the weary Carmarthen, "bring the well-disposed Dutch to some plan of active co-operation without delay!" Harris hardly needed the spur. To his delight, the Princess of Orange announced to her partisans her intention of appearing at the capital and putting herself at the head of her party. "If the Princess of Orange can by her presence give Their High Mightinesses [the States-General] what God has, I fear, refused them, and make them act like men," wrote Sir James on June 25, "I will adore her as an angel."

To lull suspicion, while the chiefs of the Stadholder's faction were awaiting her Highness's coming at the House in the Wood, the Englishman went to sup with his adversary de Vérac. Apparently he did not possess the self-control which was indeed rare in those days, but which might have been considered in all ages indispensable to a diplomatist. "His conversation was wandering," reports a French witness, "and though a first-class player, he appeared unable to sort out his cards and made the grossest blunders."[1] Returning to his house at midnight (June 28, 1787), he was met with the news that the Princess had been stopped by a band of volunteers on her way to The Hague upon crossing the border of the province of Holland. Very soon (for distances in the Netherlands are not considerable) the details of the incident filtered through. Orders had been given by General van Ryssel and a committee of defence sitting at Woerden to detain any important equipage till further instructions were received. The Princess waited. Woerden was not far away. Soon the messenger returned. General van Ryssel begged her Highness to proceed no farther. In the agitated state of public opinion her presence at The Hague might produce an undesirable explosion. Wilhelmina was astonished and indignant. Another messenger was dispatched with a written protest to the general. Night was coming on, and she was allowed to proceed under escort to pass the night at Schoonhoven.

Before dawn she penned a letter to the States-General, declaring that her sole reason for proceeding to the capital was to promote a reconciliation between the rival factions. She expected that the action of the officers at Woerden would be disavowed by the Provincial States, and that she would be allowed to continue on her journey without molestation. The news spread abroad. Harris apprehended a rising of the Orange party, which would have had no chance of success. At five in the afternoon

[1] Pierre De Witt, *op. cit.*, p. 225 *n*.

the Provincial States approved their committee's action and postponed a further reply to the Princess's letter.

Fearing that her Highness might be kidnapped by the bands under the orders of the Rhinegrave, Harris sent Kinckel to recommend a retreat. The emissary found her already back in Gelderland, on her way to Nymegen. There she was welcomed with cries of *Oranje boven!* and every manifestation of loyalty.

How much our minister had hoped for from the Princess's *coup d'état* may be measured by his dejection. "Check to the Queen," he announced, "and in a move or two, checkmate. . . . My bile runs through the pores of my fingers and mixes with the ink as I write." He hoped Lord Carmarthen and his colleagues would not measure his merits by his success; if they did he might end his days in the Tower. But his lordship rallied him. "Don't be so disheartened by a check to the Queen, let her be covered by the Knight and all is safe. . . . The event may still be productive of good. If the King, her brother, is not the dirtiest and shabbiest of kings, he must resent it, *coûte que coûte.*"

Frederick William would indeed have been the shabbiest of brothers if he had failed to resent the affront to his sister as it was represented to him by her friends. She was supposed to have been encircled by men with drawn swords, to have been placed under arrest; no respect at all had been shown her. . . . Thulemeyer, knowing the facts, however, contented himself with a protest, which in his English colleague's estimation was shameful to a degree. He even told his court that Mr Pitt would resign rather than actively engage in the quarrel. Harris implored Ewart to contradict this at Berlin. Unfortunately for Holland, the sagacious Vergennes was dead, and his portfolio had passed to Montmorin, a weaker man. Moreover, France's eyes were now turned inward. There was no inclination among the French to be involved in such a storm as Harris was blowing up in his teacup. Jockeyed by the headstrong envoy, Pitt sent for the Prussian representative in London and told him that the insult to the Princess was a matter for his master in which the French had no concern whatever. Should Prussia determine upon action in Holland, Britain would support her against interference by France.

"She wants to drag me into a war with France," Frederick William grumbled when he received his sister's complaints. But, egged on by England, he mobilized his forces and addressed what was in effect an ultimatum to the States-General. He would be satisfied with nothing less than a public disavowal by the authorities of Holland of their subordinates, the punishment of those concerned in the fancied outrage upon her Highness, and a formal invitation to the Prince and Princess to return to The Hague, with a positive assurance that there would be no further attacks upon the Stadholder's rights and privileges. There had been no outrage, no insult, persisted the stubborn Hollanders. They were sure of help from France. But Pitt took a strong line. He assembled a fleet and warned Montmorin that any concentration of troops in the direction of the Low Countries would be viewed by his Britannic Majesty's Government as an unfriendly act. To save his face the French Foreign Minister recalled de Vérac. In their hour of need the provinces were left without a French representative to counsel them. Notwithstanding, at the instance of Amsterdam, the States-General rejected the humiliating demands of Prussia.

With difficulty Harris (so he tells us) restrained the Orange partisans from attempting a rising in Holland. He was himself warned to leave The Hague *in time*. Having sent his family away, he stuck to his post. "If I am *De Witted*, don't let me be *outwitted*, but revenge me," he asked Carmarthen.

Fräulein Voss's sympathies with France were not perhaps so keen as was supposed. Or the King of Prussia may have deafened his ears to the voice of the siren. The word of command was uttered in Berlin, and on September 13, 1787, a Prussian army, 24,000 strong, under the orders of the Duke of Brunswick, invaded the United Provinces. The Princess of Orange, followed by her maids of honour, went out from Nymegen to meet her deliverers. In Gelderland generally they were received with acclamation. The States-General prepared to resist the invaders as they had resisted Louis XIV. The dykes were cut; but the Duke had consulted his almanac and timed his march by the tides. The waters sluggishly creeping over the meadows merely wetted the feet of the advancing host. The Dutch troops, not numbering altogether more than 10,000 men, under the command of the Rhinegrave, retired beyond Utrecht. Panic seized The Hague. The Grand Pensionary and the Patriot leaders took refuge in Amsterdam, but not before Harris had prevailed on them to leave a regular force to preserve order. The Provincial States of Holland hurriedly passed a resolution apologizing to the Princess and inviting her to present herself at the capital.

She came indeed, but she was preceded by the triumphant Stadholder, in a coach drawn through the streets by his enthusiastic adherents. "This [September 20, 1787] is the most glorious day I ever shall see," declared the jubilant ambassador. "Never were politics and sentiments so intimately connected." (For an instant the Foreign Secretary in London may have doubted whether they had not been too intimately connected.) Sir James was overwhelmed by the benedictions of the masses, by the compliments of the upper classes, and by the congratulations of the military. Although a stranger to sentiment, he confessed that his eyes were full of unshed tears when he met the Prince. In a long audience his Highness voiced his gratitude to England. The Princess of Orange on her arrival was not less kind. Their Highnesses ought to have known, but it seems to me that they owed their salvation to Prussia, not to Sir James.

ENVOYS EXTRAORDINARY

A new States-General and new States for Holland were quickly got together, purged, of course, of all anti-Orange elements. Van der Spiegel was made Grand Pensionary of the United Provinces which he had tried to disunite. King Louis was notified that all the disputes which had lately troubled the commonwealth were now happily composed—an assurance which must have given the harassed King much relief. But Amsterdam, behind its dykes and entrenchments, looked sullenly on, declining to recognize the Government set up by foreign bayonets. Harris entreated the Duke of Brunswick to complete his work by reducing the insolent city. There was no fear of a French attack, he pointed out; Britain was ready with her fleet and an army of 35,000 men to co-operate with him. Any better terms having been refused them at Harris's particular instance, the burghers on October 6 formally recognized the new state of things and capitulated. A deputation waited on the Princess to apologize for the insult offered her near Schoonhoven and to inquire what form of satisfaction she demanded. Harris was all for severity, and only upon specific instructions from Carmarthen forbore from recommending personal punishments. Having kept the deputies waiting two days, the magnanimous lady condescended to accept the apology and to remit any punishment due to the offenders, except that they should be dismissed from their public offices and declared for ever incapable of holding them again. She would not, however, pledge herself for their not being proceeded against in the course of law, if it were found that they had been guilty of offences against the State. The credit for this last proviso is taken by Harris, who thought it a good thing to hold a rod in pickle for the unfortunate Patriots. He was disgusted that Paulus and other leaders of the faction should escape by merely relinquishing their functions. Apparently the defeated party had no confidence in the lenity of the victors, for they emigrated to France in embarrassing numbers, to return in

JAMES HARRIS, FIRST EARL OF MALMESBURY
From an engraving after a painting by Sir Joshua Reynolds

1795 in the ranks of the victorious French Republican armies.

No one in 1787 anticipated that day. The Dutch were taught how wicked it was to stop a princess's carriage and make her pass the night in an inn. All decrees in any way offensive to his Highness were revoked by the submissive States. The Prince and Princess of Orange ruled as well as reigned over the United Provinces. Lynden, the Dutch minister to our court, pretended to be pleased at the event. "I am sure Harris will enjoy it," said George III. But the French had received a slap in the face which dimmed the honour of the ancient monarchy. Lafayette and Mirabeau alike protested against the abandonment of the Hollanders. Meanwhile the Duke of Brunswick was left under the impression that he was an invincible commander and that Prussian troops were irresistible.

IV

However much sentiment had been mixed with his policy, Sir James Harris had now to show the reinstated Stadholder that he had not been working entirely for the fine eyes of the Princess. By a treaty of alliance the republic was to be subordinated to Britain. But the Dutch, in the modern diplomatic jargon, were 'realists.' The Prince of Orange and the new Grand Pensionary beheld themselves seated firmly in the saddle. Their adversaries were ruined and exiled. Said his Highness to the Pensionary, or the Pensionary to his Highness,

> with a knowing wink,
> "Our business was done at the river's brink;
> We saw with our eyes the vermin sink,
> And what's dead can't come to life again, I think."

Or in some such form of words they reminded one another that what the kind English had done could not now be undone. A treaty of alliance with Britain? With all their hearts! But, lest they should be suspected of betraying the country (to which after all the Stadholder had his obligations), they proposed that England should restore their ravished factory of Negapatam and thus obliterate the painful memories of the war of '81.

It took our ambassador the best part of a year to carry the treaty through.

Give them back their Indian possession, he at first advised his Government, otherwise all our labour will have been in vain. His dispatches during this twelvemonth are full of alarming reports of the concentration of French troops at Givet and in French Flanders. The French were draining the man-power of the bishopric of Liége, a favourite recruiting ground for the mercenary troops on whom the Prince of Orange relied to uphold his authority. The Dutch commodore Melvil, homeward bound from the Mediterranean, where he had royally entertained Sir William Hamilton and his *chère amie*, the lovely Emma, was ordered upon Harris's instructions to anchor off Flushing in preparation for a hostile demonstration from the direction of Dunkirk. The French and Spanish and Austrian ambassadors were hand in glove to undermine British influence. The Dutch were being daily reminded that England had proved a very expensive friend. But Pitt thought he had done quite enough for the Stadholder, though it may seem to some that Prussia had done much more. He would only surrender Negapatam in exchange for Trincomalee, on the coast of Ceylon, and Riouw, in the East Indian Archipelago.

To that, replied Van der Spiegel, our people will never consent. The Grand Pensionary himself, and of course the Prince of Orange, assured Harris with tears in their eyes that they personally would do *anything* for England; but somehow they failed to bring the States round to their view. Drafts of the treaty were prepared and torn up. Lord Carmarthen bewailed the ingratitude of the Dutch. Had we not delivered them from the odious tyranny of the Patriots? Despairing of moving his own Government, Harris took a high hand with his friends at The Hague. When the Pensionary announced his inability to persuade the Amsterdam deputies, the Englishman taxed him with having *promised* to do so and said that in London he would be charged with having broken his word. A group of deputies were roundly told that if they did not pass the treaty British protection would be withdrawn, and they would certainly be exposed to the vengeance of the Patriots. Harris was careful to use this threat in presence of the burgomaster Reindorp and the deputy Dedel, whose houses had been destroyed by the hostile faction. He spoke with equal directness to the Stadholder. At the same time he wrote and circulated a pamphlet embodying similar warnings. From Carmarthen he wrung a guarded permission to assure the Dutch that his Britannic Majesty would not require in exchange for Negapatam anything really detrimental to their interests—but, added his lordship, the ambassador, if directly questioned, was not to say that we would take anything else than Trincomalee![1]

As finally drafted the treaty bound the contracting parties to help each other with troops and ships if either were attacked. The assistance of the Dutch in Europe might not seem very valuable to Britain, but the case was otherwise in the East Indies, where the governors and naval commanders of both Powers were instructed to co-operate. Neither state was to disarm or make peace without the other's assent. The Prince of Orange's approval of the treaty is explained by the clause which bound his Britannic Majesty to guarantee the office of Stadholder to him and his heirs and to maintain the existing form of government in the United Provinces against any assault or enterprise whatsoever. The dominant party in the republic, having thus admitted the right of a foreign Power to determine the form of government in their own country, were obliged to

[1] F.O. 37/22. Public Record Office.

swallow the much debated eleventh article, which ran as follows:

> His Britannic Majesty agrees to treat with the United Provinces for the restitution of Negapatam, and is disposed to concur in their desires as soon as an equivalent can be agreed upon, and will require nothing but what is favourable to the interests of both parties in the East Indies; the negotiations to this end shall begin at once upon the conclusion of the treaty of alliance and shall be concluded within six months of that event.

With this the obstinate Hollanders had to be content; and the treaty was agreed to by the States-General on April 15, 1788, to be formally ratified on May 8. "The Dutch skiff," in the words of Ward and Gooch, "appeared to be once more in tow behind the British ship of the line."[1] It remains to be said that Britain did not retrocede Negapatam and that she found pretexts for not opening the promised negotiations. And we ultimately got Trincomalee as well.

Nevertheless, when Sir James Harris was promoted to the "character" of ambassador by his grateful sovereign in March 1788, the populace vied with the Stadholder's court in doing him honour. One regrets that Harriet was not by him on this joyful occasion. His Excellency was spurred on to complete his work by forging a triple alliance between Britain, the United Provinces, and Prussia. The idea had again been mooted at Berlin. It was favoured by Count Herzberg, the new king's minister, only on the condition that the parties guaranteed one another's territorial integrity. But this did not suit Mr Pitt. He knew that Prussia proposed to swallow another large slice of Poland, and that by upholding her fresh acquisitions England might be dragged into difficulties with Austria and Russia. The negotiations languished. Presently Harris was informed that Frederick William was about to visit his sister at Loo, the Stadholder's country seat in Gelderland. Upon the conclusion of the Dutch treaty the nimble diplomatist hurried over

[1] *The Cambridge History of British Foreign Policy*, vol. ii, p. 177.

to London, and brought back with him a letter from George III to the Prince of Orange recommending the projected alliance. This letter was written in Harris's presence and probably at his dictation. The day of his return he had news from Ewart. The King of Prussia was disgusted by the slow progress of the negotiations; he was full of doubts and suspicions; he was being worked on by a powerful anti-English clique at his court. Pondering this intelligence, Harris continued his journey to Loo. There he met the Princess. She had returned from meeting her brother and was able to confirm what Ewart had said. The French had stationed agents at three separate points on the King's route to waylay him and to represent the impolicy of a British alliance, which would be sure to bring him into conflict with the three remaining Powers. Sir James was described to him as an artful and dangerous man. The King was afraid of him.

Harris was at this moment without definite instructions. He was so much the less embarrassed. Three years previously (March 15, 1785) he had written to Ewart, "I never yet received an instruction which was worth reading." He would seize the opportunity to nobble the Prussian King behind the backs of his advisers, hoping that his Majesty bore him no grudge for having refused to help him to raise a loan while he was heir presumptive. Within another twenty-four hours Frederick William II arrived at Loo. The Englishman scanned his entourage closely. He had no fear of the minister Alvensleben, but in Stein he recognized a probable opponent. With secret satisfaction he also recognized the King's valet, whom he had known in Berlin. It is alleged[1] that in the course of one of his missions our handsome representative procured certain secret papers from a foreign embassy by the simple expedient of making

[1] By Charles Ross, editor of the *Cornwallis Papers* (1859), who vouches for the anecdote as quite authentic but gives neither name nor place. He may have had it from Harris's secretary, whose name was Ross.

love to a lady closely related to the ambassador concerned. This story may or may not be true, but, by his own confession, Sir James resorted at least on this occasion of the Prussian King's visit to methods which were not over-nice. The royal valet had a hundred ducats slipped into his hand by a person in the service of the Stadholder, and, less ostensibly, of the British ambassador. It was whispered in his ear that he could earn as much again if upon any pretence that seemed good to him he kept Counsellor Stein from speech with his master till a late hour on the following day. The worthy fellow was not too proud to take a bribe. Twice next morning Herr von Stein presented himself at the King's door, and twice was denied admission. Meanwhile, behind the door, the artful and audacious Harris brought his strong mind to bear on the King of Prussia's weak one, and left him all but persuaded of the advantages of a British alliance. Still, Harris, I suppose, had his anxious moments until that night, during the progress of a *fête* in the park, his Majesty drew him behind a pavilion and told him that he was ready to conclude a preliminary treaty there and then. Harris lost not a minute in seeking out Counsellor Alvensleben, and they sat up the rest of the night together, he tells us, preparing the necessary documents. Next morning, the draft treaty having been approved by the King, it was copied out in fair and signed by Harris and Alvensleben on behalf of their respective countries, in presence of the Grand Pensionary Van der Spiegel, at two in the afternoon of June 13, 1788. Hearing what had been done, the Prince of Orange embraced Harris. "Je vous dois mon stadhoudérat et mon bonheur," exclaimed his Highness in the language he preferred to his own. The treaty was to bind Prussia also to uphold his dignity and office.

But it did not guarantee the prospective gains of Prussia, for which reason Count Herzberg was very wroth when he learned what had been done in Gelderland. However, as he was pleasantly reminded by Ewart,

WILLIAM V, PRINCE OF ORANGE
From an engraving after a painting by Ozias Humphry

nothing now remained but to complete the treaty. This was done four months later. The most important clause pledged the parties to support each other with a force of at least 20,000 men, or their value in cash. The Prussian troops were not to be employed outside Europe, and the contingents were not to be furnished unless the attacked party had already put a force of 44,000 men in the field.

Britain's isolation was ended. She thus stood, with Prussia and the Dutch, opposed to France and the two empires. In September Sir James Harris was raised to the peerage under the title of Baron Malmesbury; and in the same month, to the professed sorrow of the Dutch, he relinquished his mission to the little republic which he had bound, as he thought, securely about the feet of Britain. He had scored his only real success.

v

Writing in 1790, Lord Malmesbury prophesied that civil war would break out in France, and that there would be no need to reckon with that country as a friend or a foe. His lordship, surveying mankind from courts and club-houses, did not so much as suspect the existence of the forces about to crack the evil and artificial crust of eighteenth-century society. Almost as far back as the memory of man extended, government had been carried on by kings and aristocrats. They schemed to enrich themselves, they quarrelled with the Church, they disputed savagely the succession to the crown, and all the time they plotted and made war against each other. To the stupid masses they seldom gave a thought. The people had to pay taxes and do as they were told. In England it was not thought always advisable even to let them do the fighting. Parliament sometimes prayed the King to take foreign troops into his pay, to defend this country which could not defend itself. There were German princes and Swiss cantons always eager to hire out men to fight anybody's battles. Hence the significance of that clause, so frequent in treaties, which provided for a cash equivalent in lieu of troops.

Presently France declared war against the Emperor in his capacity of King of Hungary. England looked on, deeming this to be only a little different from the wars between states which had always been going on; nor, since her alliance with Prussia was purely defensive, did she feel called on to intervene when Frederick William declared war on France in support of his nominal overlord. The German invaders were driven back at Valmy. Even then Malmesbury and his like failed to realize what was happening. Lord Auckland spoke of "the strange success of the rebel rabble."[1] But the strange successes were repeated. Soon the rebel rabble was knocking at the gates of Antwerp. Though not disposed to make war on the French because they had adopted a republican form of government, Pitt and Grenville were true to the old policy of keeping Belgium out of the hands of a rival Power. The United Provinces were threatened. Frederick William was reminded by us of his promise to protect the Stadholder. But the three eastern Powers were too busy carving up Poland to heed what was going on in the extreme west of Europe. Desperately, upon France's declaration of war upon Britain, Grenville threw Poland to the wolves. At length, in the summer of '93, the two German Powers, in consideration of a subsidy from London, turned their glances once more towards the revolutionary flame which was ever burning more fiercely. The Prussian King marched with his troops to help the Duke of York in Flanders. His zeal for what Pitt now spoke of as "the common cause" quickly evaporated. His Majesty could not see why he should waste Prussian blood to recover these provinces for his Austrian rival. His reply to his allies' complaints was to quit his army, leaving it orders not to engage in any serious operation.

[1] *Hist. MSS. Commission Reports*; Dropmore Papers, vol. ii, p. 329.

Grenville expostulated and appealed to the treaty. As to that, answered Jacobi, the Prussian representative in London, we had not helped his master when he moved against the French in '92. King George turned in this extremity to the architect of the alliance. Lord Malmesbury had taken a long holiday in Switzerland and Italy (where he met the Hamiltons), and was now once more at home. He had dabbled in domestic politics and broken with Fox because of his revolutionary sympathies. He must go to Berlin and bring the King of Prussia round to a sense of his obligations. Lord Yarmouth, the ambassador on the spot, was not strong enough. "You must tell the King of Prussia," said George III, "that if he allows himself the same moral latitude in regard to treaties as he does in still more sacred ties [referring to his marriage vows] all good faith is at an end." His Britannic Majesty partly attributed his royal brother's backslidings to his association with a sect called the Illuminés (better known as the Illuminati). Suspected of Jacobinical ideas, these people were in reality Christian mystics, a species of eighteenth-century Buchmanites.

On November 22, 1793, Lord Malmesbury started on his special mission to Berlin. He spent a month on the journey. "Voilà Ulysse revenu à Ithaque!" exclaimed Van der Spiegel when he called at The Hague. At Brussels he encountered the Earl of Yarmouth, who was very angry at his going to Berlin.

> Quite overcome with passion [Malmesbury describes him], he would not listen, but went on begging his own questions—went on accusing me with breach of confidence, friendship, etc.—a perfect angry child, who vents his passion on the first object he meets. But his real anger was with the ministers, which he did not dare shew; he therefore vented it on me, who, he knew, would take more from him than any other person in the world. There was not an unpleasant thing he did not say, nor an unpleasant reference he did not make. He glanced more than once at a challenge, and if I had not known him so well, I must have lost my temper with him.

ENVOYS EXTRAORDINARY

The irate lord said that the special envoy would not be well received at Berlin because of his Treaty of Loo. This he "unsaid" in the morning, and the diplomats parted on tolerable terms, Malmesbury going on to Ath to meet the Duke of York. The French were pushing the allies across their frontier. His Royal Highness talked too much, and my lord told him so. At the table of his colleague, Lord Elgin, Malmesbury met a strange, sensible, learned, flighty and coquettish lady, afterwards better known as Lady Holland. At Frankfort he talked with his crony Kinckel. He was put on his guard against Lucchesini, an Italian who had gained the favour of Frederick the Great and was now at the Vienna Legation, doing his best to embitter Prussia against Britain and Austria. By the time Lord Malmesbury reached the Prussian capital he was pretty well posted as to the intrigues and influences against which he would have to contend. To court the King's mistresses would have been waste of energy. Plutus, not Venus, swayed the latest courts of the *ancien régime*.

At his first audience with King Frederick William Lord Malmesbury forgot King George's instructions to chide him for his immorality. On the contrary, he complimented him on his known good faith, exalted motives, and the like. In fact; he almost apologized for asking a question which seemed superfluous—was his Majesty going to stand by the treaty and assist Britain against the vile French republicans who had had the impudence to declare war against her? He was most anxious to do so, his Prussian Majesty answered, but he had not in his treasury enough to pay the expenses of a third campaign. Unless his allies came to his assistance, he would have to withdraw from the war. He was willing and ready, he said at a second interview, to raise an army of 100,000 if his allies would defray the cost. He proposed the territory to be conquered in France as security for a loan—a suggestion which sounded feasible to the envoy!

Malmesbury communicated with his Government and came again. What sum, he inquired, had the King in his mind? Frederick William consulted a paper folded in his pocket-book, and announced that the lowest sum on which he could raise the army was twenty million dollars, without reckoning the cost of bread and forage. The Englishman looked glum. What sum, asked the King, was Britain prepared to advance? Malmesbury hesitated. "Come," said his Majesty. "I am prepared to stake my resources, and England should do the same. Let us not be afraid of committing ourselves. Make your offer." Thus adjured, Malmesbury declared he was empowered to offer two millions sterling—England to furnish two-fifths, Austria, the United Provinces, and Prussia itself each a fifth, the money to be charged against France. There was a pause. Finally the King said he would accept the offer, provided the Empire would find the bread and forage and that he would be dispensed from his quota.

On this basis brisk bargaining went on between our ambassador and the ministers Haugwitz and Finck. There was much good humour and reiterated assurances given on the parties' *foi de gentilhomme*. Meanwhile Morton Eden at Vienna was trying to secure Austria's acquiescence in the scheme. He failed. The blame is thrown by Malmesbury on the Marquis Lucchesini, who undoubtedly was averse from Prussia's taking action in the west; but as our ambassador himself admitted, in a dispatch dated March 9, 1794, the court of Vienna feared the King of Prussia more than it feared the French, and the court of Berlin considered that of Vienna as a most dangerous and inveterate rival.[1] Thugut, the Imperial Chancellor, would not pay a kreuzer to put the successor of Frederick at the head of a powerful army. The central Powers were still snarling viciously at each other over the carcase of Poland. To make matters worse, the Emperor named the Archduke

[1] F.O. Prussia, 64/32. Public Record Office.

Albrecht of Saxe-Teschen to the supreme command of the allied army, a step which made it impossible for the King of Prussia to take the field.

Malmesbury spent the middle weeks of March in efforts to soothe the injured majesty of Prussia and to persuade the sovereign that no personal insult had been intended by his suzerain. Frederick William muttered something about the *dessous des cartes*, and Lehrbach, the Austrian minister, made himself disagreeable. Let us quit this unsympathetic atmosphere, suggested Haugwitz, with whom so far Harris had got on very well; let us go to The Hague and draw up another treaty. The King of Prussia, no doubt glad to be rid of the importunate visitor, signified his approval. The plans for the journey were already made when his lordship reluctantly communicated to the King a proposal from Grenville. Britain offered to hire 30,000 Prussian troops, to be under British orders, for a monthly subsidy of a million sterling. This offer was to be stated by Malmesbury as an ultimatum. Clearly his lordship did not so state it; for upon its rejection by Frederick William II, who refused to hire out his troops to anybody, he posted off to Holland with the affable and conciliatory Haugwitz.

By the treaty drawn up on Dutch soil Prussia engaged herself to furnish a force of 62,400 men, to act under a Prussian commander with the armies of Britain and the Provinces, "wherever it should be judged most suitable in the interests of the two Maritime Powers," all conquests to be at their disposal, in return for a subsidy of £50,000 a month, a payment of £300,000 at the beginning of the campaign, and another of £100,000 at the conclusion, cost of bread and forage in addition. Of these sums £400,000 was to be paid by the Dutch and the balance by England. It was Easter-time. Good Friday fell on April 18, but Malmesbury had such influence with the slow-going Hollanders that the treaty passed the States-General on the following day. It was not a very good treaty. As the *Quarterly Review*[1] was to point out half a century later, instead of getting 100,000 men for £800,000 per annum, we had eventually to pay near £1,200,000 for 62,400 for six months nominally. But already Malmesbury had received Grenville's sanction for this modification of the original project; and, with the treaty signed in his pocket, he hurried over to London to hasten the dispatch of the stipulated moneys.

> The ministers [he tells us] were so fully employed in their discoveries and examinations of seditious and treasonable practices, that I had very few and short conversations with them; and although I constantly pressed their sending me back, I neither could obtain any fresh instructions from Lord Grenville or put the subsidy in a way of being paid till the 23rd of May.

The anxieties of the home Government were by no means unfounded, but to a professional ambassador his country's relations with foreign Powers naturally appeared the most vital concern. While thus kept on tenterhooks he had a conference with his sovereign, who thought the war ought to last and that a premature peace would only conceal, not cure, the evil. King and diplomatist were now aware that they were fighting not merely France but a principle subversive of their own society.

His lordship got away at last, on May 24, 1794. His instructions were to hasten the movement of the Prussian forces towards Liége, and on no account to let them be employed on the east side of the Meuse. The troops were sorely needed. Eight days prior to the envoy's departure the Duke of York and his allies were signally defeated at Tourcoing. At Maestricht Malmesbury met Haugwitz. The promised English gold had not yet reached the Prussian pocket. "It is to no purpose," wrote Malmesbury to Grenville, "that I endeavour to convince M. de Haugwitz that the money due is at this moment as much the King of Prussia's as if it were in his treasury." Without the money the Prussians would

[1] *Quarterly Review*, vol. 75 (1845), p. 414.

not move. The Poles, moreover, were again up in arms, and Frederick William hurried east. Near Mainz the English agent met the Marquis Cornwallis. This distinguished soldier and administrator had lately returned from India. He was so acceptable to the Imperial court that he had been offered, but had refused, the command of the allied forces. He and Malmesbury together proceeded to the headquarters of Field-Marshal Möllendorf, the commander of the Prussian troops on that side. To the old soldier of Frederick the idea of the court at Berlin disposing of his army and putting him under the orders of a foreign diplomatist was naturally abhorrent. Cornwallis was quite silent, grumbles Malmesbury, and left all the military reasons advanced by the Marshal against marching without a word of reply. To such reasons the man of treaties and protocols was deaf. He called for the instant execution of the bond. There came an urgent appeal from the Austrians to the Prussians to occupy Trier. The corps under Kalckreuth, already detached for service with the Imperialists, could be sent, said the angry peer. Not a single one of the 62,400 men provided for by the treaty was to be diverted from the Holland front. The preservation of the Stadholder's realm was becoming almost as much a monomania with Malmesbury as the preservation of the Kingdom of the Two Sicilies was soon to become with Nelson. Möllendorf pointed out the dangers of a long march down the Rhine with his rear and left flank exposed to the enemy. His lordship persuaded himself that the veteran's mind had lost its energy, that he was overruled and led by the crowd of advisers about him, etc. He would not credit the reports of French victories, which, if the Prussian army were removed, would expose Central Germany to invasion. Malmesbury declared himself unable to do business with the old man. "Möllendorf was a dotard, his mind was gone, nothing remained but his vanity and malice." Courier after courier rode into Berlin, bearing imperious demands from Malmesbury for the exact fulfilment of the treaty. Haugwitz was invited to come to the camp, to exert the authority with which, his lordship sarcastically put it, he supposed him still to be invested. On June 26 the Austrians were severely defeated by Jourdan at Fleurus. They retreated towards the Meuse. It was hard on the haughty ambassador when Grenville wrote that, in view of the melancholy posture of affairs, the actual distribution of the allied forces left nothing to be wished for (August 16). Six weeks earlier Pitt had said as much.[1] Haugwitz notwithstanding was to be told very firmly that the King of England did not by any means renounce the right of directing the further movements of the Prussian troops, according to the express terms of the treaty.

Malmesbury professed to come round to the views of his principals. The autumn he passed very pleasantly, in the country behind Frankfort, riding, dining, and drinking "old Hock at a guinea the pint," not sorry that there was a Prussian army between him and the republicans. The money sent by England to be spent in the defence of Holland was being used by Frederick William on the banks of the Vistula. Under secret orders from his court Möllendorf concluded what was in effect a truce with the French. As the winter drew near the inhabitants of the Rhine country grew clamorous for peace. Lord Malmesbury could not understand such wicked madness. On his lands in quiet Wiltshire foreign armies were not trampling down the crops, burning the farmsteads, and fighting pitched battles. Until the invention of the aeroplane Britons always had a difficulty in realizing the horrors of warfare. At sea we were doing very well, adding islands and territories to our empire. "I disapprove of every measure," passionately protested the patriotic lord, "which at this moment can put peace into people's heads." With horror he perceived in the Prussian officers a strong tinge of democracy and "a dislike for the cause for which they ought to be fighting."

[1] *Historical MSS. Commission Reports*; Dropmore Papers, vol. ii, p. 592.

England had now turned to Vienna, in an effort, fruitless as it proved, to induce Austria to subject her armies to British control on the usual cash terms. On October 19, at an end of his patience, Pitt stopped the Prussian subsidy, and on November 24 Malmesbury was informed that the Prussian army had orders to withdraw from the Rhine. His lordship washed his hands of the business, declaring he would speak his mind very plainly in a letter to Haugwitz.

There was still work for Malmesbury to do in Germany. Most reluctantly the Prince of Wales had agreed to marry the daughter of the redoubtable Duke of Brunswick, in whose powers of leadership the reactionary states continued to repose great confidence. Malmesbury was directed to bring the Prince's betrothed to England and to profit by the occasion to invite her father to assume the command of a new allied army to be mustered behind the Waal. The Duke declined the flattering invitation; he subordinated his policy to that of the power which completely encircled his limited dominions. The rest of his time at Brunswick the diplomatist devoted to schooling the Princess Caroline in her duties as future queen of England. In March 1795 he took her to London and handed her over to the tender mercies of Prince George. His Royal Highness never forgave Malmesbury for his share in effecting his wretched marriage, merely official though it was. Caroline had no reason to thank him either, though Lady Malmesbury at any rate proved herself one of her most zealous partisans in her hour of trial.[1]

VI

In England Lord Malmesbury met his friends of Orange. They had fled from their country, which under the name of the Batavian Republic was now the ally of

[1] Although this chapter in Lord Malmesbury's career hardly belongs to diplomatic history, its human interest would have tempted the present writer to include it here had not the subject been brilliantly and exhaustively dealt with by Judge Parry in his book *Queen Caroline*.

France. This country was no loser by the change of government. We seized the Cape, Demerara, and the other Dutch colonies. Spain had also joined forces with the great republic, but her dominions overseas were not so easily snatched at. Prussia made peace with France at Basel. But Austria was induced to continue the war by the promise of British and Russian money. Meantime the star of Bonaparte was rising higher and higher. At Montenotte, at Lodi, at Rivoli, the hapless whitecoats went down before him. All Northern Italy was his. Yet, with tireless persistence, the Austrians, led by octogenarian generals, returned again and again to the charge, invariably offering themselves to be beaten in detail according to Bonaparte's plan.

Vast sums of English gold went this way—to maintain a system of society which no longer suited the needs or served the interests of any but the few. The poor English people were starving, and positively begrudged the money spent on the preservation of privilege and property. They cried, "Bread, peace, and no Pitt!" If there were not peace there might soon be no Pitt. The reflection may have occurred to some, if not to the statesman himself. At this moment he certainly desired peace,[1] and Grenville, who desired it by no means so eagerly,[2] supported him loyally enough.[3] Learning through a French refugee in London that the Directory was prepared to consider terms, the English negotiated—"to gain time, to penetrate the intentions of the French Government, *and perhaps also to conclude a peace if it appeared acceptable*," says a modern French historian.[4]

Admitting Pitt's sincerity, we remain surprised at his choice of Lord Malmesbury as a negotiator. The

[1] I follow Holland Rose and Ballot (*Les Négociations de Lille*).
[2] E. D. Adams, *Influence of Grenville on Pitt's Foreign Policy*.
[3] See *The Cambridge History of British Foreign Policy*, vol. i, Appendix D.
[4] G. Pariset, *Histoire de la France contemporaine*, vol. ii, p. 322. The italics are the present writer's.

diplomatist had ever been distinguished by his hatred of the French, and his only success had been scored off them and their Dutch allies. He was unfamiliar with France. The new ideas prevailing in that country were as strange and abhorrent to him as to his master. Even so the Cabinet took care to limit his powers very strictly. He was to concede no point and sign nothing without previous reference to London. His instructions were to express to the Directory England's desire for a just and honourable peace, but this was not to be concluded without the concurrence of Austria, and that Power entirely disapproved of his mission! Withal, he was to insist on enjoying all the rights and privileges belonging to a public minister, according to the law and customs of nations received in Europe. These instructions are in very striking contrast to the suppliant attitude enjoined on him as ambassador to Berlin and Petersburg. He who was to grovel at the feet of a neutral despot was to stiffen his back when addressing a victorious republic. Grenville obeyed his chief, but it is plain that his hatred of the Revolution seriously tempered his will to peace.

Our envoy left London on October 15, 1796. He took with him his secretary, Ross, also George Ellis, the man of letters, Lord Morpeth, and Lord Leveson-Gower. Apparently to his surprise, he was treated by the officials on French soil with perfect courtesy and by the people with cordiality. He did not reach Paris until the 28th. ("No wonder he travelled so slowly, since he went on his knees," sneered Burke, who was, of course, bitterly opposed to any kind of negotiations with the Republic.) In Paris he could reckon on the friendship of a small group of anglophiles, ready to secure peace by the sacrifice of France's recent acquisitions. Among these were Talleyrand and the Swiss banker Perregaux, an associate of the Director Barras. The Jacobins were shocked,[1] we learn, by the splendour of his entry. However half-hearted his chief may have been, Malmesbury,

[1] F. V. Aulard, *Paris pendant la réaction Thermidorienne*, vol. iii, p. 542.

with so many failures behind him, was genuinely anxious to bring his mission to a successful conclusion. From the first he adopted a conciliatory manner, going so far as to don the tricoloured cockade—a step which Grenville could not bring himself to sanction or to condemn in writing.

The ambassador had his first interview with Delacroix de Contaut,[1] the Directory's Minister of Foreign Relations, on the morrow of his arrival. "I confess," he had written to Grenville, "I have the feeling of an unsteady head on the edge of a high precipice"; but he accustomed himself surprisingly well to this unfamiliar atmosphere. Delacroix must have been a novel experience after the Panins and Haugwitzs. The minister was a somewhat pedantic old *conventionnel*, who throughout his political career had certainly displayed an inflexible determination to keep his head on his shoulders, but who approached his duties with breadth of vision and a grasp of sound fundamental principles. Both he and the curious junta to which he was responsible eyed the British envoy's credentials askance. Evidently he had not the full powers of a plenipotentiary. His Government declared they would not make a separate peace, but he had no authority to speak for their allies. Britain proposed as a basis for the negotiations a reciprocal surrender of conquests *pari passu*. Delacroix found this vague. Was it proposed, he inquired, to return to the *status quo ante bellum* or to accept the *uti possidetis?* Malmesbury had to confess he did not know, but would send a messenger to London to find out. He could not answer any question without sending to London. Very soon in the *Rédacteur*, the Directory's official organ, Delacroix was represented as greeting the envoy with the polite inquiry, "How are you?" and Malmesbury as replying, "I thank you for your kind inquiry, but before I reply to it I must send a messenger to London for instructions."

Grenville in his memorandum had rather tactlessly

[1] Father of the famous painter.

spoken of the uninterrupted success of his Britannic Majesty's arms. This nettled the Directory, which in its reply, "without suggesting that the double purpose of his Britannic Majesty's Government was to set aside the partial propositions of other Powers by making general propositions of its own, and to throw upon the Republic the odium of prolonging the negotiations," declared itself willing to treat as soon as definite proposals were put before it and the British representative could produce his powers to act for Britain's allies. Grenville characterized the Directory's insinuations as offensive and injurious, and repeated his former proposition. Malmesbury was called on to be more specific. He could not be till the Directory accepted the general basis laid down by his principals.

A deadlock resulted. Malmesbury spent a very unhappy fortnight. "If we escape the guillotine here," he wrote to his young friend Canning, now Under-Secretary in Downing Street, "how shall we escape the Tower in England? . . . Send me a specific *projet* and broad instructions. If I am to go on again with notes and memorials, I had better be recalled. I have written freely to Pitt and clearly to Lord Grenville." He threatened to recall himself.

The Austrians' attempt to relieve Mantua was defeated by Bonaparte at Arcola on November 18. At last Grenville condescended to be more explicit. In a confidential memorandum to be submitted by Malmesbury he required that all territory taken from the Emperor should be restored, including, of course, the Belgian provinces, and the Milanese, of which Bonaparte was in sovereign possession. Rather than let Belgium remain annexed to France, Britain was prepared to hand back all the French settlements she had taken during the war. As regarded France's ally, the new Batavian Republic, if the Dutch returned to their old allegiance to the Stadholder, little would be asked of them; otherwise Britain would not relinquish certain of her prizes.

Malmesbury and Delacroix went through this memorandum point by point. The Belgic provinces had been formally annexed to the Republic; therefore their retrocession was contrary to the law and constitution. What Dutch possessions were the English minded to keep? Malmesbury could not deny that these were the Cape of Good Hope and Trincomalee. With a foresight beyond the Englishman's span, Delacroix predicted that the Cape might become the nucleus of one of the most fertile and productive colonies of the East (*sic*), of more importance to England than the Netherlands would be to France. Its possession would confer the mastery of the Orient. As to the West India islands, they would be conquered, said Delacroix, by the spirit of liberty —"alluding, of course," explained the peer, "to the abolition of slavery," which in his lordship's opinion would destroy the islands. At parting the minister inquired if the severance of Belgium from France was a *sine qua non*. Malmesbury replied that it certainly was, and one from which his Britannic Majesty would not depart.

Grenville was prepared not to insist on the restoration of the provinces to Austria so long as they went to a Power not controlled by France. Prussia was the Power he thought of. And from Vienna Morton Eden sent word that Austria would resist such a cession by force of arms. The death of the Empress Catherine shook the constancy of the Austrian Cabinet. On the last day of the year the Emperor announced that he would become a party to the negotiations if France would accept the British basis. He was too late.

The news from Russia had also reached Paris. Malmesbury admitted that "the Empress had been killed so often" that he was inclined to discredit the intelligence. It was also known in Paris that the new Tsar, Paul, was no friend of Austria or of Britain. On December 19 the ambassador was disappointed by receiving a curt note informing him that the Directory could not accept the confidential memorandum as the basis of a treaty. He was called on to submit an ultimatum. Malmesbury had none to give, and knew well that this was demanded in order to throw the responsibility for the breach upon his country. He made answer that he was ready to discuss any counter-proposal. He was told that the Directory could listen to no overtures contrary to the constitution of the Republic, which forbade the dismemberment of France; since, moreover, Lord Malmesbury announced at every stage in the negotiations that he must communicate with his court, it followed that his continuance in Paris was superfluous and improper. Therefore he was invited to take his departure within twice twenty-four hours.

On December 29 he was back in London.

VII

Half a century lay behind Lord Malmesbury. His eyes were not less brilliant, but they gleamed now from beneath a mane of snow-white hair. *Le lion blanc*, a French journalist had called him, and the young men growing up around him eagerly caught at the nickname. Among these disciples was George Canning, Under-Secretary at the Foreign Office. The world had changed since young James Harris rode back through the night to Madrid to recover his ambassadorship. More truly than when he despaired of his mission at Petersburg he might have now exclaimed that new faces and new manners were wanted. Yet when Pitt, seeing England abandoned by all her allies except Portugal, determined, in the spring of 1797, on another bid for peace, he could pitch on no better man than Malmesbury to resume the negotiations with France, despite the objection of the Directory that another nomination would have augured better for a prompt conclusion of peace.

Pitt had been openly attacked by his political opponents for continuing the war to keep Belgium out of

JAMES HARRIS, FIRST EARL OF MALMESBURY (AGED SEVENTY)
From an engraving after a painting by Sir Thomas Lawrence

the hands of the secular foe. That stumbling-block was now removed from the path to peace. In April Bonaparte, within a few marches of Vienna, dictated the preliminaries of Leoben to the discouraged Austrians. The terms of capitulation were kept secret by Thugut, the Emperor's Chancellor, but before they were actually signed Grenville knew that they would include the definitive cession to the Republic of those maritime provinces which were so much more important to us than to their Austrian suzerain. With a heavy heart Pitt resigned himself to the inevitable. All the more was it necessary to retain the Cape and Ceylon, "the possession of both which points," wrote Grenville, "is of the greatest importance to the defence of the East Indies under the new state of things which would arise in Europe from the possession of the Netherlands by France." In addition we wanted to keep Trinidad, a Spanish island, as a set-off against the continued occupation of the Spanish half of Hispaniola by our enemies, and Martinique or Tobago. With these not unimportant exceptions, his Britannic Majesty was prepared to restore all his conquests from the French and their allies, Spain and the Batavian Republic.

On July 5 the negotiations were opened in the Hotel de l'Intendance at Lille. This town had been selected for the purpose, ostensibly on account of its neighbourhood to England, actually in order to keep the keen-sighted English diplomatist as far away as was practicable from Paris. His lordship was accompanied by Ross, by Mr Wellesley as secretary of the mission, by his friend George Ellis, and by the young Lords Morpeth and Leveson-Gower. France was represented by Letourneur, who had given up his seat on the Directory to Barthélemy, a moderate and a reputed advocate of peace; by Pléville de Peley, an old admiral who had lost a leg in the wars; and by Hugues Bernard Maret, afterwards Duke of Bassano, a friend of the new Director, and inferentially, therefore, well disposed towards England. Letourneur's qualifications for diplomacy may be estimated by his objecting, when Malmesbury demanded the Cape, that the Dutch ought not to suffer since they had been dragged into the war by France; an observation which his lordship noted with a smile. But his proposals, said the ex-Director, would be listened to, provided they contained nothing contrary to the French constitution. The Low Countries having been lost, the British delegate saw no harm in admitting this at the outset. Although the concession was made conditionally upon the other side's agreeing similarly to propose nothing contrary to the laws, integrity, and treaty obligations of Britain, Malmesbury presently learned that he was blamed by Grenville for having given away so much. Without surprise we read at a later stage the envoy's complaint that he was placed in an embarrassing position by the difference of intentions and opinions between the minister under whose orders he was bound to act (Grenville) and the minister with whom he wished to act (Pitt).

The French delegates were hardly in a better case. They had been sent to conclude a peace, and among their masters, the Directors, only one, Barthélemy, sincerely desired it. Of his colleagues, Rewbell was definitely for carrying on the war. Barras and the other two inclined one way or the other as their own interests pointed. As to Delacroix, his last negotiations with Malmesbury had left him deeply distrustful of England. For two months at Lille the delegates, French and English, strove hard for peace, with little backing from their Governments. The French adopted the wise plan of showing their instructions to Malmesbury and discussing them with him before they proceeded to deliberate officially. Ordered to reject the British demand for Martinique and Trinidad, the republican envoys wrote to Paris to suggest a compromise. France might cede Senegal (which was not, under the Constitution, an integral part of her territory) to England in lieu of Trinidad, and Spain might indemnify her by handing over Louisiana. It would have been a poor bargain for England, even more so in the form favoured by Delacroix, who seriously discussed the idea of asking for Gibraltar or Jersey in exchange for the forlorn factory on the edge of the great desert. Meanwhile Malmesbury was officially informed that the King of England was required to abandon the title of King of France and to restore the ships "taken charge of" by Hood at Toulon. The ambassador thought the empty title of pretence inherited from the Plantagenets hardly worth disputing, but, aware of the unconciliatory temper of the man behind him, he fought hard to persuade the French that it was purely honorific like the titles of King of Jerusalem, Cyprus, etc., borne by certain Italian sovereigns, to which, he might have pointed out, the Grand Signior never objected. But the delegates of the Republic dared not give way. Their tenacity, which was imposed on them, appeared to the Englishman to be dictated by policy. "Pléville did not say a word; his eyes were shut all the time. Letourneur spoke very little to the purpose, Maret very well and very much like a gentleman."

His lordship's hopes were dashed on July 15 by the communication to him of a declaration on the part of the Directory that France was forbidden by secret treaties to consent to the alienation of any part of her allies' territory. Britain was asked as a preliminary to the negotiations to restore everything she had taken, and the French argued that they were forbidden by their constitution and engagements to cede anything in return. To send this note to London, Malmesbury saw at once, would mean the immediate rupture of the negotiations. Very sensibly he asked for an interview with the representatives of the Republic and warned them of the fateful consequences of the Directory's intimation. Letourneur, he said, as a late member of the governing body, ought to have known and to have apprised him of France's treaty obligations when he first outlined his proposals for compensation. Tactfully the English peer forbore, however, to press this point, and listened while the flustered ex-Director explained that the note was not to be taken as barring further discussion. England was invited to submit a counter-proposal, and if that failed the French would submit one themselves. With this very important assurance tacked on to it, the truculent dispatch from Paris was forwarded to Whitehall.

By this time Malmesbury had some reason to believe in the goodwill of one at least of the French delegates. He may have had in his pocket a letter handed on the previous day (July 14) to Mr Wellesley by Cunningham, an Englishman long resident at Lille. To facilitate the negotiations, ran the letter, it might be convenient for his lordship to get in touch with the one person on the delegation capable of managing the business; in which case it was possible to produce an intermediary in the entire confidence of that person and animated, like him, only by zeal for the public interest. Malmesbury sent the trusted George Ellis to interview the intermediary, who proved to be one Pein, a retired inspector of postal services. The person referred to was Maret. He was an intimate friend of Barthélemy, and his advice to his lordship was to mark time and to give him every opportunity of preparing his colleagues for any proposals he had to submit. Pein's *bona fides* was established by a sign fixed by Malmesbury. The delegate at their next meeting took his handkerchief out of one pocket, passed it over his face, and then placed it in the other pocket.

Thus satisfied, the British delegate kept in close touch with Maret by means of frequent conversations between Ellis and Pein. "What is going on now ex-officially," he told Grenville on August 6, "is much more important than what passes officially." By the French [1] this underhand intercourse is regarded as a ramification of the widespread conspiracy between England and the royalists which was directed by Wickham, our agent in Switzerland. Maret's overture was made possible so early in the day thanks to one of those inventions of which

[1] G. Pariset, *op. cit.*

Malmesbury and his like recked not at all. A telegraph of the semaphore type was now in operation between Lille and the capital. There can be no doubt, therefore, that the delegate already knew of the dismissal of the uncompromising Delacroix and the appointment of Talleyrand as his successor, although the official announcement was not made till the 15th. The new Minister for Foreign Affairs was in favour of peace, or, at any rate, so far as the prospects of peace favoured his operations on the Stock Exchange. Maret was perhaps his instrument; but it is at least probable that both men honestly adopted the same policy. Malmesbury does not appear from his correspondence to have known that Talleyrand was behind his friend on the delegation; or perhaps he concealed his knowledge from George Ellis, to whom Canning wrote on July 27 to inform him that Talleyrand was in communication with "Bobus," otherwise Robert, Smith of whom he was a great friend. ("Bobus," brother of the famous wit Sydney, was then a young barrister, an Etonian chum of the Under-Secretary.) "We have good reason to believe," added Canning, "that Maret has a commission (whether from the French or Dutch we do not know) separate from his colleagues to treat for the surrender of the Cape for a sum of money."

Malmesbury should have been mystified, therefore, when four days later Pein told Ellis that if we would give up the Cape we could have peace in a fortnight. The Spaniards and the Dutch when questioned by the Directory, at the instance of the delegates, would not hear of surrendering any of their ancient possessions. In vain Maret pointed out that they would not recover them and would lose much beside if the war was renewed. The go-between, when asked why France did not bring pressure to bear on her obstinate allies, haltingly explained that in such an event she would have to compensate them with money. It is to be noted that he did not suggest England should pay it. Malmesbury expressed his belief in the good faith of Maret and his agent. According to

Ellis, Pein positively refused the offer of a loan of £200, but the French will have it that Malmesbury paid him 7500 francs, and as much as 25,000 francs to another agent, Pierre Lagarde, who was now watching events at Lille on Talleyrand's behalf.[1]

Neither Maret nor the ex-Bishop of Autun, we may be sure, would have been insulted by the offer of a substantial *douceur*. Without it, however, they were capable of working for peace. Both were hoping for the triumph of the anti-war party in the approaching contest between the executive and the legislature. "Patience, patience!" counselled Maret as the weeks dragged on without the promised counter-proposal arriving from Paris; "if we do not advance with a giant's stride, at least I hope our progress is sure." By this time Malmesbury had completely grasped the situation. "The issue of the negotiations," he wrote, "depends less on what happens here than on what is going to happen in a very short time in Paris." That he tried to influence the course of events by the methods usually most successful with mankind is indisputable. It was afterwards alleged—and by Talleyrand, of all men—that the British delegate during the progress of this and his previous mission distributed upward of £36,000 among journalists and obscure conspirators. On September 9 his lordship wrote to Grenville, "I forgot to mention that 'Robert' is arrested, but he is not in possession of a single paper or proof of any kind. I fortunately stopped fifty louis I was going to remit him on Tuesday evening."

The rumour of his liberality brought a good many suspicious visitors to Malmesbury's door. A Mr Potter, who on October 24, 1796, had waited on him in Paris with *des projets insensés*, now reappeared, stating that he was authorized by Barras to demand half a million sterling as the price of peace. Our emissary suspected a trap, and dismissed him. The same intimation was made on August 19 by a Mr Melville, of Boston, "about

[1] Pariset, who does not cite his authority.

twenty-six years, reserved and vulgar." He claimed to know Perregaux, which it has been proved was true. Dismissed by Ellis, the Yankee returned to Paris and swore he had been bribed by the perfidious British. Pein was told of these overtures and asked what he thought of them. He said he would not be surprised if Barras and Rewbell took a bribe. The retired post-office inspector would presumably have reported these intrigues to his principal, and it may be suspected that it was by no mere coincidence that Maret, in the course of conversation with Malmesbury, found an opportunity of referring to his shattered fortunes. "Those will no doubt be repaired when you are appointed ambassador to London," cheerfully his lordship assured him.

The summer dragged on. It is comforting to reflect that men in those days could toil on in the heat of cities apparently without any yearning for a breath of the sea or the countryside or for a surcease from their labour. The political sky seemed to brighten when Malmesbury, resplendent with his star, was seen at the theatre in the French delegates' box. "Peace is in sight," whispered the Comte de Saint-Simon,

> qui des fondements jusqu'en faîte
> Refaisait la société.

If France makes peace at all, said Malmesbury less confidently, it will be at the expense of her allies; but while Cabarrus tried in vain his persuasive arts on the stubborn Hollanders, Godoy at Madrid, so far from yielding Trinidad, spoke of recovering Gibraltar and Nootka Sound. With their ears attuned to every murmur in Paris, Maret and Malmesbury kept the negotiations alive.

> I pledge myself [wrote the Englishman] to fight desperately every inch in the East and West; to cavil at the ninth part of a hair; to wrangle till I am hoarse for titles, dignity, treaties, ships and what-not; nay, to live on patiently at Lille for the sake of maintaining the smallest portion of these.

Canning was urged not to let Pitt be seduced by the pro-war faction.

> If I am to remain here in order to break off the negotiations creditably and not to terminate it successfully, I must instead of resigning my opinions resign my office.

Followed Fructidor! The Moderate party in Paris was overthrown, and with it vanished all hopes of peace. Malmesbury announced to his Government "the most unlucky event that could have happened." Talleyrand, of course, hastily accommodated his policy to that of the winning side. Maret looked anxious. On September 11 (a week after the triumph of the Directory over the Legislature) Lord Malmesbury was informed of the recall of the French delegates to Paris. They took leave of him in presence of their successors, Treilhard and Bonnier, very courageously, as he thought, assuring him of their esteem and expressing the hope that they had merited his.

On the same day Malmesbury wrote to Canning, "If you do not intend that I shall remain here alone and in my shirt (for I shall be compelled to pawn my clothes if you do not send me the means of going on) send me messengers and boxes." Wellesley had been taken off to India by his brother; Ellis and Leveson-Gower had gone home, tired out by the protracted deliberations. His lordship was not reduced to pawning his clothes. On September 14 Treilhard inquired if he was authorized to treat for the restitution of all the former possessions of France and her allies remaining in the hands of Britain. Malmesbury's reply was that he had answered that question as far back as July 15 and had waited ever since for a counter-proposal. Since, then, his lordship had not the powers asked for, said the new delegates, he was invited to return within twenty-four hours to London to procure them. He was assured that this invitation was given solely in order to speed up the negotiations. Had that assurance been sincere, they would certainly have dropped a hint as to the possibility of sending a messenger.

JAMES HARRIS, EARL OF MALMESBURY

Lord Malmesbury was used to failing, and accepted this dismissal, as far as can be gathered from his diaries, more cheerfully than he had given up his missions to Prussia and Russia. Of course, he was aware as he hurried back to London that not only Grenville but his sovereign would be better pleased by the breakdown of the peace negotiations than by their success. In fact, had he returned carrying with him the cession of the Netherlands and the Cape, he could not have been more cordially welcomed by minister and Majesty.

> Lord Grenville [Malmesbury tells us] seemed to doubt the necessity of any further note; I strongly for it; that if we said nothing, our enemies would have it to say, we had left them at Lille and refused to go on with a negotiation they never intended to break off. Lord Grenville admitted my reasoning, and said he would mention it to the Cabinet.

It was not necessary to convert Pitt to this step, for he by no means despaired of a peace. He was beset by secret agents. One of them, O'Drusse, styled by Malmesbury, perhaps in jest, vicar-general of the Bishop of Autun, reported that Talleyrand, provided he remained in office, would undertake to get us one of the Dutch settlements, Ceylon probably, for £200,000. Malmesbury's old acquaintance, Mr Melville, of Boston, was also in London, ready to 'square' Barras with a mere £450,000. The veteran diplomatist saw in these pretended negotiations merely dodges for rigging the stock market. In any case, he pointed out to the Prime Minister, the offers were not supposed to come from "the whole firm," but from Barras and his set. He trusted that Mr Pitt in responding had been very explicit as to the terms and the price— that no cure, no pay, should be stipulated; not a penny to be given till after the ratifications, and every article valued and paid for *ad valorem*.

> I see doubts and dangers in all this secret intelligence. I admit the desire of getting the money, but I question the power of delivering the thing purchased. Barras confessedly the only one

in the secret; he and his expect to persuade Rewbell, and to prevail on him to take his share of the bribe. *Thence* my apprehensions; and it clearly appears that O'Drusse and Pitt's informants act separately.

We go farther than Lord Malmesbury and suspect Mr Melville, of Boston, of being one of those speculative busybodies in whom his country is prolific. That he never produced any authority from Barras is certain. "If Pitt gives you half a million sterling, will you make peace on his terms and give me fifty thousand?" That is what the Yankee adventurer fancied himself saying to the Director and possibly what he did say. The reply of Barras is not recorded—it may have taken the shape of kicking Mr Melville downstairs. Had the Directors or Talleyrand had it in their power to sell a peace, it would have been done long before, when they could have counted on the support of Barthélemy and other moderates. As it was, the French delegates remained at Lille till October 17, and then departed, throwing upon his Britannic Majesty's Government the responsibility for continuing the war.

That is not the fair view. Nothing could be more preposterous than to propose that France should retain the major part of her acquisitions on land, while Britain should relinquish all the conquests made by her sailors. It may be that Bonaparte was opposed to the surrender of the Cape, but the rupture must be attributed mainly to the French Government's hopes of utterly ruining their island foe. They could not foresee, it has been well observed, the destruction of the Dutch fleet by Duncan and the not easily comprehensible failure of their expedition to Ireland—still less the rapid rise of the young Corsican general at the expense of the Director attorneys. In England all murmurs against the war were stilled in face of the implacable temper of the foe. Hitherto the French Republic had been waging war, at least in appearance, in self-defence. The rejection of our olive-branch at Lille meant that France had embarked on a war of conquest; the tradition of Louis XIV was soon to be continued by Napoleon Bonaparte.

No blame for the rupture can be attached to the British negotiator. At Lille, rather than at Madrid or Petersburg or The Hague, Malmesbury showed his talent as a diplomatist. Ready enough to give way on such trivialities as the obsolete title of his sovereign, he was unyielding in his determination that England should emerge a gainer from her long struggle. He who had passed his life in the courts of the Old Régime won the friendship and respect of the men of the Revolution. But though no word of disappointment is to be traced in his writings, it may fairly be concluded that this last failure decided him never again to accept a diplomatic mission. He pleaded his growing deafness when invited to do work again abroad. In 1800 he was created an Earl and Viscount FitzHarris. To the last a commanding and venerable figure in political society, he passed his time between his house in Spring Gardens and his country seat, Park Place, near Henley. He survived his friend, the Prince of Orange, who died in exile in 1806, and his much loved Princess, who died on her return to Holland in 1813 at Loo. Having lived, as he noted in his diary, longer than any of his forbears, the first Earl of Malmesbury died at his town house in Mayfair on November 20, 1820, aged seventy-four years.

Laid beneath the spire which, according to legend, he had climbed as a boy, he was spoken of as having reached the pinnacle of his profession. Talleyrand is quoted as saying of him, "I hold Lord Malmesbury to have been the ablest British minister of his time—it was impossible to surpass him, all one could do was to follow him as closely as possible." This is expert opinion; but it is higher praise than the facts of the diplomatist's career appear to warrant. The bitter reviewer [1] exaggerates in

[1] *Quarterly Review*, vol. 75 (1845), p. 414. By the courtesy of Mr Murray, the reviewer is revealed as the redoubtable John Wilson Croker. His review of *Endymion* is described in the *Dictionary of National*

saying that it was Lord Malmesbury's fortune all through his life to be baffled and bamboozled, as indeed he was by Catherine's ministers and by Haugwitz. But very few definite successes, as has been seen, can be placed to his credit. It was his mistake to resort in desperation to bribery and undignified tricks inconsistent with his character. Meeting rogues on their own ground and with their own weapons, he courted defeat. His suppleness was more to be admired at Lille in his negotiations with men whose ideas were profoundly antipathetic to him. His enormous prestige Malmesbury owed not to his triumphs, but to his experience, which was immense. We are glad that his countrymen forgot his failures and rewarded him as his devotion to his country deserved.

Biography as a "specimen of that worst style of criticism which starts with the assumption that because the reader does not like the work, it is bad, and proceeds to condemn whatever does not fall in with the critic's individual ideas."

HUGH ELLIOT AND THE NORTHERN COURTS

WHEN the Earl of Malmesbury warned a young aspirant to diplomatic honours to keep clear of *attachements* he probably had in mind an experience which might have checked the career of Mr Hugh Elliot, a fellow-ambassador of not less ability than his own. The two were kinsmen by marriage. Hugh, born in 1752, was a son of Sir Gilbert Elliot and a member of that powerful Border family nicknamed the "Scots Greys." He was younger brother of Gilbert, afterwards first Earl of Minto, and brother-in-law therefore of Malmesbury's wife. We suspect an early attachment between them. True, telling him of her marriage, Harriet wrote, "Never was wedding so merry as mine!"—but that is exactly what a bride would say to the man who had not asked her to marry him. The two had met in their childhood at Twickenham. To remind him that they had once slept in adjoining rooms the lady in her frequent letters called him Pyramus and signed herself Thisbe. Accepting his invitation to stand sponsor to his daughter, she wrote in 1782:

> I sometimes think over past times, and reflect that if anyone had told us when we sat upon my couch, you at my sick feet, by my fireside in George Street, that in four years I should be writing to you from Petersburg, to you, *a married man!* at Berlin, we should have looked upon them as worthy of a strait waistcoat. All I can say is I can never be more sincerely attached to you and wish you more sincerely well than I did then, and that this attachment will ever continue the same and as truly as if you were my own brother. . . . As to Mr Harris [she goes on in French], I leave him to speak for himself. If you devote yourself to politics as much as he, your wife will find out that she has married a mere gazette.

Lady Harris was wrong in her dates. Neither she nor

Hugh was in the neighbourhood of George Street in 1778. Her tender memories must have carried her back five years, to the time preceding Elliot's departure for Berlin. At that time he is described by Thiébault, a French memoir-writer, as *assez bel homme*, and, though never renowned like Malmesbury for good looks, he was afflicted with an adventurous Byronic temperament which would have given him the advantage with romantically inclined young ladies. He had wanted to be a soldier in days when few men felt any special call to die for their country. Failing to get a commission in the Guards, he ran away to Constantinople, fought with the Russian army, swam the Danube holding on to the tail of a Cossack's horse, and came home, flushed with glory, to beg his stern father's pardon. He was pointed to as a macaroni, a character which young men of his class affected in those days, as they now occasionally contrive to get sent down from Oxford, grow stubbly beards, and wallow in the morasses of Bloomsbury. His vagaries, his love affairs, his apparent irresponsibility, sorely distressed his family. The Duchess of Northumberland, her Grace of Queensberry, Lady Townshend, looked kindly on him. He never would marry, he often declared, unless his wife would agree to living as far away as the next street. When his father's influence procured him the appointment of British minister to Bavaria at a salary of £3 a day, a Russian officer of his acquaintance wrote:

> What! Elliot, the friendly, the sociable, the light-hearted, the careless, the gallant, the *petit maître*, is about to immure himself in the recesses of a cabinet? But this is to rob society! Since the lively Elliot takes on the sombre sedate air of the diplomatist, I do not despair of one day seeing the Pope in the uniform of a hussar.

At the mature age of twenty-two doubtless the new British envoy no longer recognized himself under the polished Muscovite's description. No such melancholy transformation was, however, imposed on him by his new character. There was little diplomatic business to

HUGH ELLIOT
From a painting at Minto House
By kind permission of the Earl of Minto

be transacted between the Governments of London and Munich, and that little could be safely handled by his secretary and late tutor, Mr Liston, who thus qualified himself for ambassadorial rank later on. The Elector's court was modelled on Versailles—rather, on the Trianon. The English newcomer's air of melancholy, his alternate fits of gaiety and gloom, enormously interested the Bavarian ladies. They pursued him along the alleys of Nymphenburg. Among those who overtook him, or whom he overtook, was the pretty Countess Daun. She signed her love-letters "Delta." Elliot escaped the fate of Hylas, but an old court coat of his was seized on by the maids of honour and cut up between them for love tokens. The young man scowled on such frivolity. Like most of his contemporaries, he was quite unable to live within his means. As his purse grew lighter his heart grew heavier. He withdrew from society, forswore the sex, and applied for leave to fight the insurgents in America. This was refused, but by way of a change he was accredited to the Imperial Diet at Ratisbon, in addition to Munich. For a time he lived, very economically, on an islet in the Danube. He corresponded with Mesmer, took up philosophy, advised Delta to do the same, and tried without success to convince her that friendship was better than love. From this austere view he was himself presently converted—some say by the charming wife of Count Neipperg. He not only loved again, but suffered another lover, a Bavarian prince, to correspond with a noble lady under the seal of his Britannic Majesty's legation. Liston, who acted as postmaster, was pestered at all hours of the day by ladies inquiring for letters from their lovers. We are not surprised to learn that Mr Elliot made no enemies in Munich, and must agree with Mr Pitt in thinking it unnecessary of him to pay a round of visits upon his departure to say how glad he was to go.

Such an indiscretion might have spoilt his chances of advancement had he been anyone else than the son of the powerful Sir Gilbert Elliot, the King's special confidant. At the age of twenty-five he was deemed by Lord Suffolk worthy of promotion and accredited to Berlin, in succession to Harris. That his appointment was opposed in certain quarters, probably by Lord Barrington among others, need not be imputed entirely to factious malice; but Berlin, as we know, was not then considered a mission of the first importance. Although Fox six years later declared that "Alliances with the Northern Powers ever have been and ever will be the system of every enlightened Englishman,"[1] Prussia wisely held aloof from western affairs and looked eastward and southward. Within six weeks of his taking up his duties, however (May 9, 1777), the young ambassador was directed by Lord Suffolk to keep his eye upon Lee and Sayre, two American gentlemen who were on their way to the Prussian capital to enlist King Frederick's interest in the rebel cause. It was beneath his Prussian Majesty's dignity to treat with insurgents, Mr Elliot was assured; but upon the arrival of the transatlantic visitors Herr Zegelin, one of Frederick's confidential ministers, came over from Potsdam and took rooms in their hotel on the same floor.[2] Elliot knew very well that the Americans were tempting the Prussians with offers of their trade and that they were placing orders for cloth and other commodities in Berlin. Of what followed there are various accounts. He set spies on the rebel agents. For a price, he was told, he could be put in possession of the strangers' papers and replace them without detection. The ambassador approved the design. He waited. Presently he was informed that the business was too risky and must be abandoned. Then, rash as the Angevin king, he exclaimed as he sat at table, "I would give a great deal to see those papers!" or, as he afterwards maintained, "an account of their doings before they came hither." The words were heard, as he possibly expected they would be heard, by his servants. That day the room

---

[1] Malmesbury, *Diaries and Correspondence*, vol. ii, p. 40.
[2] S.P. 90/101. Public Record Office.

of the delegates was entered—some say by the window, others by means of a pass-key—and their portfolio was carried off. Lee sent for the police. The hotel-keeper said the servant of the British ambassador had attempted to suborn him. Promptly Elliot came forward and assumed full responsibility for the deed. He confessed to using those rash words at table in the hearing of others, and, having restored the portfolio to its owners, he submitted himself absolutely to the discretion of his Prussian Majesty. His court, he declared, had no knowledge of or share in the business.

This is Lady Minto's version of the episode, based, she tells us, on her grandfather's letters and his dispatches to Lord Suffolk.[1] Carlyle imagines the theft to have been committed by the chief housebreaker or pickpocket of Berlin. Thiébault has it that Elliot wormed himself into the confidence of the Americans (which sounds unlikely) and never let them out of his sight.

> One evening shortly after they had gone to a party, their dispatch-box was abstracted. It was brought back next day with the money, jewels, and letters of credit which it had contained still in it, but without the credentials and instructions which it had also contained.

The King of Prussia told a correspondent that it was left behind, without being opened, on the stairs.

To everybody's surprise, old Frederick appeared to be satisfied with the Englishman's frank confession and did not demand his recall.

> If I were to act with vigour [he writes] it would be necessary for me to forbid this man the court, since he has been guilty of a public theft; but not to make a noise, I suppress the thing. I shall not fail, however, to write to England about it, and indicate there was another way of dealing with such a matter.

Lord Suffolk, of course, in his official dispatches

[1] No dispatches giving an account of the incident are to be found among the State Papers of the period.

severely rated the over-zealous envoy. The expressions he had uttered at table "were highly improper to be used by the representative of a court which disclaimed and will ever disclaim to trust the crooked paths of duplicity and treachery." Mr Elliot was enjoined to refrain from vivacities of language and to discourage so criminal an activity on the part of his dependants. But before many months had passed he was informed that the irregularity of the transaction would be forgiven in consideration of the zeal which prompted it, and that £1000 would be paid into his bank to indemnify him for his expenses. One is left in doubt whether these expenses included the thief's honorarium; also, whether the purloined casket or portfolio contained Count Schulenburg's note to Mr Lee inquiring what formalities were observed by the French and Spanish Governments in admitting American privateers to their ports.[1]

Foolishly Britain stood by the letter of the Navigation Act of Charles II's reign and refused to admit ships from the newly acquired Prussian province of East Friesland carrying the produce of other parts of the monarchy. Yet our court was astonished when Elliot reported his Prussian Majesty's refusal to allow auxiliaries, recruited by England in Hesse-Cassel and Anhalt for service in America, to pass through his dominions. It does not appear that our representative exerted himself to conciliate the old sovereign. "Who is this Hyder Ali?" maliciously inquired the King. "Sire," came the quick reply, "he is an aged despot who has robbed his neighbours and is now in his dotage." "It was a revenge that Satan might have envied," chuckled Elliot, telling the story. It was before this, we presume, that he complained of the King's coldness to his close friend, Prince Henry of Prussia. Fox, who took over the now united Foreign Departments in March 1782, and who was most anxious to engage Frederick's sympathies, could hardly be blamed, therefore, for deciding to recall the ambassador

[1] R. H. Lee, *Life of Arthur Lee* (1829), p. 97.

—at his Majesty's direct request, according to Sir Gilbert Elliot, though this was denied by Prince Henry. The notice was sent to Elliot unaccompanied by any promise of future employment. Before, however, it could be given effect to, the Rockingham Ministry was turned out. Lord Grantham, taking over the seals of office from Fox, persisted in the proposed change at Berlin, but hoped shortly to transmit to the retiring envoy some mark of the continuance of their master's favour. This took the form, on October 29, of Elliot's appointment to Denmark in relief of Morton Eden. Upon his taking leave Old Fritz sent him a snuff-box with his portrait set in diamonds—a gift, said Prince Henry, which was to be taken as a proof that his transfer was not due to any pressure from Berlin.

His quitting Prussia precipitated what appeared at the time to be a catastrophe in Elliot's domestic life. Over and over again he had expressed, like Harris, his contempt for Berlin men and Berlin women; but by the end of his second year in the city his name had been coupled with that of a young Prussian heiress, Charlotte Krauth.[1] She was a flaxen-haired, blue-eyed beauty, the daughter by a former husband of Mme de Werelst, wife of the Dutch ambassador. To judge by his letters, the Englishman appears to have been half-ashamed of his passion. He speaks of the girl in no very flattering terms, though, according to a Frenchman (Dampmartin) who knew her, she had brains as well as beauty. "Beware of Miss Cabbage,"[2] one friend warned him, "for she is artful and knows very well that you love her." James Harris, writing from the banks of the Neva, reminded his colleague that sprouts are hard to digest—and he ought to have known, for his own cold heart had thawed a little while he was in Berlin in the warmth of Charlotte's

[1] By the usually accurate Burke she is stated at this time to have been the widow of one Krauth, of whom I can find no mention in contemporary letters.
[2] A free translation of *Kraut*.

eyes. Deaf to these warnings, Elliot announced on July 9, 1779:

> I am married in private without her mother's consent to the Krauth; after the *éclat* of my attachment to her, I had the choice between folly and dishonesty—my affections pleaded for the first, my conscience forbade the latter. My project is to keep the matter secret till the King's death. The Prince of Prussia, Prince Henry, etc., are as much my friends as princes can be. I despise the world too much to fear its vicissitudes, and think her worth sacrificing life and fortune to.

A child, a girl, was born to the pair. In 1781 Lady Harris paid a visit to Berlin. It may be that early and tenderer memories were thus revived. "I find," wrote Elliot to his old playmate, "that nothing is so like an unmarried man as a married man." About the same time his wife discovered that a married woman's fancy is as liable as a spinster's to stray. There was a quarrel about her at Rheinsberg, Prince Henry's country seat, between Elliot and her cousin, Baron von Knyphausen, a dashing blade in his Royal Highness's service. Elliot's appointment to Copenhagen forced on the choice between husband and lover. The lady declined to quit Berlin, pleading ill-health. Elliot went alone and left his little daughter in her mother's custody. Presently he received a letter from Mme de Werelst announcing a change in his wife's sentiments: "I don't think she loves you as much as in the past—no; but I trust she has friendship for you." Busybodies reported that Knyphausen was making free with the absent ambassador's reputation, and credited him with a scheme for securing to his mistress the permanent custody of the child and the control of the child's fortune. Liston, whom Elliot had brought with him from Munich and had left behind at Berlin, forwarded a report which caused the irritated husband to return post-haste, without obtaining leave, from his new station to the old.

His first step on reaching the Prussian capital was to examine the evidence against his wife and her paramour.

Then, taking advantage of her absence at a party, he carried off his little daughter Isabella, and dispatched her to Copenhagen in charge of a nurse. His granddaughter's narrative of his movements is at points contradictory and unintelligible. For some reason he refrained from meeting his wife face to face. Having ransacked her papers, in accordance with custom, he possessed himself of a draft of Knyphausen's most scurrilous letter.

> Assembling the men-servants [the narrative continues], he positively forbade any one of them to cross the threshold during twenty-four hours, under penalty of being *haché en pièces*; which expression he accompanied with an *air d'Alexandre* and with his hand on his sword; and having thus secured himself against any immediate communication between his wife and Baron von Knyphausen [*sic*], he returned to his friends and spent the night examining the correspondence which they had seized.

Furnished by that time, one would suppose, with the means of procuring a divorce, the British minister then travelled back post-haste to Copenhagen.

It may be suspected he was as glad to be rid of his German wife as she of him. Sternly admonished by her mother and by her highly placed friends, the young woman avowed her passion for her cousin and went to live with him. In consequence the Baron was summarily discharged from the Prince's service. He had not left Rheinsberg more than two hours when Mr Elliot reappeared in search of him. "What?" exclaimed one of his friends, another of his Royal Highness's gentlemen. "Do we find you, a civilized man of the eighteenth century, seeking revenge on your wife's lover like some husband of the Middle Ages?" The British ambassador hastened to repudiate so ridiculous an attitude. The point was that Knyphausen had circulated damaging statements about him. That, of course, was a really serious matter, and he was put on his traducer's track. He overtook him at an inn upon the Mecklenburg frontier and incontinently broke a cane about his shoulders.

"Come out and fight," cried the Englishman. The Baron professed to be willing, and they went out in search of a spot where they could fight in peace. But the German raised difficulties. He wanted a distance of twenty paces, Elliot insisted on five. By this time the country people, scenting an encounter, had gathered round; and, rather than fight in the presence of two or three hundred clodhoppers, the two gentlemen agreed to meet four days later. The period expired, but Knyphausen, possibly because he could not find anyone willing to act as his second, continued to put off the encounter from day to day. Disgusted by what appeared to be cowardice, Lord Keith, a Jacobite exile high in favour at the Prussian court, threatened to shoot him if he did not give Elliot satisfaction, and to remove all further excuse for delay offered to act as his second. So the duel at last took place in the nearest village across the Saxon border. Three shots were exchanged without effect. Knyphausen declared himself satisfied. Not so the Englishman, who insisted on a further exchange of shots at ten paces, unless his adversary would sign an apology and retractation of his slanders. A long discussion between the seconds ensued, but, no agreement having been arrived at, the principals were again placed face to face at the original interval of twenty paces. "As soon as one of us is wounded I will sign the paper," announced the Baron, who seems not to have been so much a coward as has been represented. They fired. The German's bullet grazed Elliot's thigh. Thereupon the Baron wrote:

> Mr Elliot having been wounded at the third exchange of shots [*sic*] and having fired his pistol in the air [a statement which differs from our account of the affair], of my own free will I declare that I regret having done him wrong and beg to apologize, as well as for having written him an insulting letter on April 14th.

"Now our quarrel is settled," said Knyphausen, and he offered Elliot his hand. "No," said the Englishman. "I wish you every kind of happiness, but, as to friendship between you and me, there never can be anything of the sort."

All Berlin applauded Elliot; Old Fritz was delighted with his spirit. The affair, said some one, made more noise than the siege of Troy. Elliot had had a bad passage across the Baltic, and as the result of living on Norway smoked fish for four or five days found himself prostrated with fever. Meantime his lawyers hurried on his divorce, which, as is usual on the Continent, was conducted in private. The ill-matched couple were speedily disunited, and Charlotte was able to legalize her love for Knyphausen. Even so conjugal a monarch as George III could hardly condemn his envoy for dissolving his marriage in such circumstances; but there can be no doubt that in the King's mind the divorce appeared for ever afterwards as a black mark against Hugh Elliot's name.

II

Hugh Elliot relieved Morton Eden at Copenhagen on January 23, 1783. His mood must have corresponded to the melancholy atmosphere of the northern capital at that season. He had left behind an unloving and probably unloved wife. He entered upon his duties, as he afterwards averred, under a cloud, his removal from Berlin being generally looked upon as a proof of his own Government's displeasure.[1] But he soon had cause to chuckle over the irony of the event. Fox had recalled him because he was an obstacle to his pro-Prussian policy; Lord Grantham sent him to Denmark in order to countermine Prussian intrigues and to detach the little kingdom from the Armed Neutrality, which was supposed to be Frederick's own scheme.

Denmark, it may be worth while to point out, was at that time somewhat more important than it is now. To its crown was attached the kingdom of Norway as well as the duchies of Holstein and Schleswig. The king,

[1] F.O. 22/6. September 1, 1783. Public Record Office.

Christian VII, was, like so many despotic sovereigns of that century, an uncertified lunatic. Ten years previously the state had been very well governed by his queen, Caroline Matilda, and her lover, Count Struensee—an enlightened and well-meaning man. The substantial benefits the Count conferred upon them weighed little with the public against the facts that he slept with the Queen and that she was 'unfaithful' to a madman. Amid acclamations the minister was hurled from power and put to a most cruel death. The common people recovered from their jubilation to find themselves once more reduced to slavery. So let us waste no tears over the state of Denmark, which, according to Elliot's letters, was rotten indeed. The miserable sovereign was immediately taken charge of by his stepmother, Queen Juliana, a princess entirely devoted to the Prussian interest, by her son, and by the minister Guldberg, who supplied what brains there were in the triumvirate.

Virtue had triumphed, and there were no cakes and ale for the Danes. The new envoy extraordinary (to call Elliot by his official title) was at once aware of a growing opposition to the existing *régime*. Eyes were being turned upon the Crown Prince, or Prince Royal, Frederick, a towardly lad of fifteen, the son of the luckless Caroline Matilda. In true stepmotherly fashion he was being kept in the background by the Queen Dowager, and subjected to usage unfitting the heir to his father's throne. Burning for revenge on Prussia, the new British envoy inevitably sided with his Royal Highness, the nephew of his own king. He determined through him to create a pro-British party. From Count Schimmelman he learned that the boy had contrived a secret correspondence with Bernstorff, a statesman who had been exiled from Copenhagen on account of his opposition to the stepmotherly clique, and partly because of his sympathy with England. On his way back from settling affairs with Knyphausen the ambassador paid a secret visit to Bernstorff at his retreat in Mecklenburg. The two men came to an understanding. Elliot went back to Copenhagen, the confidant and intermediary of Bernstorff's faction, while careful to ingratiate himself with the party in power. Count Rosenkrone, among the ministers, was known to be anti-Prussian, and before long one of his more timid, vacillating colleagues, Schack-Rathelou, was seduced from the Queen Dowager's side. "Am I to respond to the overtures made me by the Prince's friends?" was in substance the question which Elliot put to his court on August 5, 1783. He got only a guarded and discouraging reply from Fox, who was once again in office. 'It was not the business of a British representative to meddle in the internal affairs of the country to which he was accredited. Counting on King George's detestation of the coalition Cabinet and knowing it would not last long, Elliot ventured, as he confessed on April 20, 1784,[1] to deviate in some measure from the letter of these instructions. He allowed himself to be guided by his feelings: there was no time to wait for instructions from home. Guldberg was growing suspicious. The Crown Prince manifested an increasing impatience of the tutelage in which he was kept. He had been taught to kiss the hand of his father's half-brother. In Elliot's presence he now dashed the outstretched hand aside with such violence as nearly to upset the balance of the misshapen prince. While Schack-Rathelou was talking State business with another member of the Government, a lackey indiscreetly brought him a packet of instructions from Bernstorff. Under curious and suspicious eyes the conspirator crammed the letters into his various pockets.

Meanwhile the young Prince himself had won over the support of the Norwegian Guards, of the artillery, and of the garrison of the citadel. On April 14, 1784, ten days after his confirmation—a particularly solemn event in Lutheran countries—he entered the council chamber and claimed his seat as of right. The old Queen

[1] F.O. 22/6. Public Record Office.

was not there. Her ministers were too much astonished at this display of resolution by a boy of fifteen to offer overt opposition. The King looked on bemused while his son, rising in his place, read a memorial drawn up for him by Bernstorff. His Royal Highness named certain people (among them, of course, the exiled statesman) who must be brought into the Cabinet, and wound up by demanding that no order signed by his Majesty should be valid without his own counter-signature. Christian was not so mad as not to be pleased at this show of spirit by his own son. No man cares to be ruled by his stepmother. Hastily he affixed his signature to the decree which virtually constituted the boy regent of Denmark. Guldberg resigned. The council broke up, and a messenger was sent to Bernstorff bidding him hasten to Copenhagen.

That statesman was incapacitated by gout. To Elliot it seemed not improbable that a palace revolution achieved simply by surprise might easily be undone by another. After all, the Prince was scarcely more than a child, living under the same roof as his enemies and without natural protectors. Fearing a counter-stroke by the Queen, the Norwegian officers began to show the white feather. Queen Caroline Matilda had been saved from death or lifelong imprisonment by the timely appearance of a British fleet. Now Elliot metaphorically waved the Union Jack above her son's head. The ambassador took an expensive house in order openly to entertain and provide a rallying centre for the Prince's party. The evening following the *coup d'état* he seated himself in the most conspicuous box at the theatre, and upon his Royal Highness's entrance paid him signal marks of respect. This demonstration was the more noticeable since the other members of the *corps diplomatique* had stayed away out of courtesy to the Queen. On his return to the palace the Prince discovered that the bolts had been removed from the inside of his bedroom door. His attendants cried out; it looked as if an abduction was contemplated. Young Frederick alone showed no fear and refused to have the bolts replaced. He had been assured, and no doubt his enemies had been warned, that Elliot had a force of British seamen, recruited from the shipping in the harbour, ready to move at once to his assistance and to protect his person.

Armed intervention by his Britannic Majesty's envoy was a bolder step than even Malmesbury had ever resorted to. It was not called for. The rejoicings of the people at their future sovereign's accession to power satisfied the Queen Dowager that her reign was over. Soon after she retired to the country-seat of Fredensborg. The arrival of Bernstorff to take over the direction of the Government confirmed Elliot's victory. He had safely reckoned on the fall of the coalition Ministry at home. The Marquess of Carmarthen relieved Fox at the Foreign Office. Writing to him on September 1, Elliot did not scruple to request an augmentation of his rank and emoluments in recognition of his services to British policy. In addition, he required payment of a bill for £1500, the cost of his intervention.

The men whom he had helped to place in power were grateful—for a time. Bernstorff talked of an alliance between Great Britain, Russia, and Denmark, or, if the Empress proved unwilling, between Britain and Denmark alone. The Prince at the age of thirteen had been coaxed into an engagement with a princess of the house of Hohenzollern. In his revulsion against all things Prussian the youth announced his extreme repugnance to proceed with the match. The court of Berlin remained bent upon it. Elliot was reminded by Count Rohde, King Frederick's ambassador, that his daughter had expectations in Prussia, which might be defeated if he continued to thwart Prussian policy. He shrugged his shoulders. The Empress Catherine also had her candidate for the crown matrimonial of Denmark in the person of a princess of Anhalt-Bernburg, or, if she were unacceptable, a Brunswick girl. In the background there was always the

Prince's cousin, Sophie Frederica, daughter of the Prince of Hesse-Cassel.[1] But the young man's fancy strayed towards the country of his hapless mother, and he employed a lackey to procure him a portrait of one of King George's daughters. His own sister's experience, however, hardly encouraged his Britannic Majesty to look with favour on the suit; and Elliot must have disposed of it finally when, on June 19, 1787,[2] he reported that there was that in the Prince's manner and gestures which led many to suspect that he had inherited his father's taint—a suspicion, it should be added, which was not borne out by the subsequent history of Frederick VI.

The next four years passed tediously and painfully for our envoy extraordinary at Copenhagen. Distastefully he gazed across the steely blue Sound, on the narrow, mist-encumbered streets, the copper roofs rusted green, the moist beech-woods and the damp verdure of the Danish landscape. He hated the climate, which for him spelt rheumatism; he hated the people. The Rev. Mr Johnstone, his secretary, "in the emphatic language of an author," called a Danish mission "a waste of life and an abbreviation of existence." At a ball at court a French officer, looking at the deformity of the fair sex, exclaimed, "En Dannemarcq il est possible d'avoir des besoins mais on ne sçauroit avoir des désirs." Elliot wearied of the pettiness of his situation. "Fearing that all our zealous efforts at Copenhagen to give a Bias to the round world, and all that dwell therein, will not have the desired effect," he resigns himself to retailing merely local events. Bernstorff has an idea that Elliot is not honoured with Lord Carmarthen's entire confidence. "Would to God," he exclaims, "your lordship had an opportunity of convincing them of their mistake by my removal to a better climate and situation!"[3]

Eventually he had reason to be glad his prayer was

[1] Whom he ultimately married in 1790.
[2] Add. MSS. 28062, f. 244.
[3] F.O. 22/8. September 1, 1786. Public Record Office.

not listened to. In the year preceding the outbreak of
the French Revolution Gustavus III of Sweden alarmed
old Europe by another display of that eccentric audacity
aptly described by a contemporary critic as his hussar-
like humour. The Empress of Russia was busy fighting
the Ottoman Turk. This, the Swedish monarch decided,
was an opportune moment to attack her on the side of
Finland. Behind him he left a bitterly disaffected
aristocracy and a distrustful people. Victory was dashed
from his grasp by a mutiny of officers, who declared they
would take no further part in a war which the Riksdag
had not sanctioned. At this time, as we know, the power
of Britain appeared to foreign observers to be on the
wane. It was to Russia that the court of Copenhagen
looked for protection; and now Bernstorff informed the
British envoy that by a treaty concluded in 1773 Denmark
was bound to furnish the great empire with a force of
auxiliary troops in case of attack. Thanks to Malmesbury, England was now in alliance with Prussia, and
neither Power wished to see the Baltic a Russian lake.
Equally dangerous would be the intervention of France
on Sweden's behalf. Keep Denmark neutral if you can,
Carmarthen directed Elliot, but the equilibrium of the
North must be maintained. The ambassador waited on
the Crown Prince with an offer of mediation by Britain
and Prussia. The Prince fancied himself as a soldier and
was anxious to flesh his sword. He treated the offer as
a mere device to procure a breathing space for Gustavus.
His chief minister would not believe in the existence of
a concert between London and Berlin, and suggested
that the proposal of mediation emanated from Elliot's
own fertile brain. On August 19, 1788, Denmark
declared war against her harassed neighbour, and an
army collected on the Norwegian frontier, under the
command of the Prince of Hesse-Cassel, was set in
motion towards Göteborg. With it rode the Crown
Prince himself as a volunteer.

"We are saved!" shouted Gustavus on hearing of the

invasion. His advisers thought him mad. The event proved he was right. The Powers would not tolerate the annihilation of his kingdom; his people, who would not help him in his unnecessary assault on Russia, would rise to repel the secular foe. He rushed back to Sweden to raise the martial peasantry of the Dales. From Ewart at Berlin Elliot received the advice that a body of 16,000 Prussian troops would enter Holstein simultaneously with the entrance of the Norwegian army into Göteborg. At this crisis the British legation at Stockholm was vacant. Upon Elliot devolved the burden of preserving the peace of the North. He was instructed from home to warn Bernstorff of the awful possibility of Britain's having to employ force to maintain the balance of power in Scandinavia.

Emboldened by the presence of a Russian squadron in the Kattegat, the Danish Cabinet closed its ears to these remonstrances. An agent of the King of Sweden passed through Helsingör on his way to invoke the intervention of the court of France. Gustavus had vanished from Stockholm.

> The pressing circumstances of his Swedish majesty [Elliot explained at a later date], and the immediate danger to which the balance of the North was exposed, left me no time to wait for further instructions. . . . Indeed, the very positive though general instructions given me, to prevent by any means a change in the relative situation of the northern nations, invested me, as I conceived, with full powers to act according to the exigency of circumstances.

On the pretext, by one account, of taking the waters at Medevi, Elliot, on September 17, 1788, crossed into Sweden. He travelled north, "though exceedingly ill of a sore throat or fever, and with a blister" upon his neck, as he wrote to Ewart from Jönköping on September 26.[1] Gustavus had met with a hearty response to his appeal from his people, but at Karlstad on September 30 Elliot found him

---
[1] Add. MSS. 28063, f. 28.

GUSTAVUS III, KING OF SWEDEN
From an engraving after a painting by C. F. van Breda

without generals, without troops, and devoid of every means of defence. . . . "You behold me," said the King, "in the same situation as James II when he was obliged to flee from his kingdom and abandon the crown. I am about to fall a victim to the ambition of Russia, the treachery of Denmark and the factious seditiousness of my own nobility.". . . In the sincerity of his distress the King added, "and to the mistakes of my own conduct." Backed as I presumed myself to be [continues our ambassador] by the joint concert of the Kings of Great Britain and Prussia, I replied with confidence: "Sire, prêtez-moi votre couronne et je vous la rendrai avec lustre" ("Sire, lend me your crown and I will restore it to you with lustre"). . . . All that could have been done had been effected in some measure by my arrival.

Elliot had addressed an appeal to the Prince of Hesse to suspend his advance, since the King of Sweden had accepted his mediation. He expected his reply, he wrote to Ewart, but he was not hopeful of success.

The King galloped on into beleaguered Göteborg, and was surprised to find it still flying the blue and yellow flag. "Evidently Elliot's courier must have had its effect," wrote his Majesty on October 4, "since it appears that the enemy have halted at Uddevalla." Two days later the ambassador rejoined Gustavus. With enormous gusto—and complete forgetfulness, it must be added, of his diplomatic character—he threw himself into the business of preparing the city for the defence. He boasted his early acquaintance with the art of war and the science of engineering.

The voluntary assistance of the English seamen then in that harbour, ready to man the batteries under my command [he says], would, I trust, have helped to render the Danish attack of a very doubtful issue, had not these very preparations had the more desirable effect of inducing the Prince of Hesse to treat for an armistice of eight days, in which interval the Prussian declaration arrived, and I was confessed to have been no less the saviour of Holstein than of Göteborg, Sweden and its sovereign.

Elliot somewhat underrates the King's own share in

staving off the catastrophe. He had with him now a force of hardy Dalesmen who clamoured to be led against the enemy and showed a disposition to turn the tables on his adversary. On the pretext that the seas were not mentioned in the armistice he seized on twenty Norwegian barques laden with supplies for the invaders. Exasperated by this and by the presence of Baron de Borck, the Prussian envoy, in the Swedish camp, the Danish prince talked of marching on the capital. "Stockholm vaut bien Altona" was his retort to the Prussian threat. Elliot promptly and decisively intervened. He reminded Gustavus that he had pledged his word for the observance of the armistice and insisted on the restitution of the ships. To save his face the King made the ambassador a present of his prizes, so the Norwegians got their sorely needed supplies. Soon after Elliot had to protest against a slanderous proclamation issued by his Swedish Majesty, designed to raise the peasantry against the Prince of Hesse's troops.

The armistice was ultimately prolonged till May 15 of the next year. The Danes, when the final convention was signed by Elliot at Uddevalla on November 6, were glad enough to recross the border. The Prince Royal in presence of his officers called the Englishman *l'ami commun du Nord*. Gustavus wrote, "I cannot praise Elliot too highly. He has accomplished a master-stroke which does as much credit to his judgment as to his courage, and which in saving Sweden will maintain the balance of Europe and cover England with glory."

It was a pity, wrote Elliot, that no one could restore the balance of the King of Sweden. He had been given to understand that the war originated in the fanatical and occult principles of Freemasonry, with which the King, like the Prince of Hesse, had been inoculated. The Pretender (Charles Stuart) had bequeathed to him the prophesied succession to Three Kingdoms, which the house of Stuart, had it survived, was to receive as compensation for the throne of Great Britain.

The King of Sweden has now, therefore, entered into the enjoyment of these Mystical Rites, by virtue of purchase and the complaisance of the whole tribe of supernatural agents, formerly attached to the Stuarts, but now performing spiritual duty near the person of the King of Sweden. . . . As there is another prophecy that the crimes of the King will be avenged by a Man upon a White Horse, with a red coat, the Prince of Hesse, mostly appears at the head of his troops in that tremendous form. Upon the first intimation of such nonsense [continues Elliot] I had the good fortune to leárn also that there was a prediction that the King of Sweden would be saved from a great perplexity by a stranger who was to bring him the most essential and unlooked-for assistance. No sentence of the Pythian Priestess ever fitted a public minister so exactly as that lucky prophecy did me. . . . Finding myself, then, armed with supernatural powers, I made the most natural use of them.

The Witches of Macbeth, so lightly thought of in Scotland, enjoy full credit with princely persons on the rocks of Sweden and Norway, and the diplomatist declares himself deeply indebted to them.[1]

Whether or not the King of Sweden and the Crown Prince of Denmark believed, as Elliot assured them, that the preservation of peace was the greatest glory of a prince, there was no kindly feeling in Copenhagen towards the foreigner who had destroyed Denmark's last chance—as it might have been foreseen—of territorial aggrandisement. The Empress Catherine's indignation at his interference found an echo in London through the mouth of her ambassador, Voronzov. Probably at his instance, the Danish *chargé d'affaires* addressed a protest to Lord Carmarthen, alleging that when the Prince of Hesse rejected his first appeal for an armistice Mr Elliot had declared that a state of war existed from that moment between Denmark and Great Britain. In a private letter to Bernstorff the envoy had said he was ready to take up arms on behalf of Sweden. The Foreign Secretary replied that he must suspend his judgment till he heard

[1] To Lord Carmarthen. F.O. 22/10; November 29, 1788; Public Record Office.

the ambassador's own tale. This was very vigorously worded. What he had said in a private letter, Elliot rightly argued, could not be quoted in an official complaint. He denied making use of the exact expression to the Prince of Hesse complained of, but insisted that he was bound by his instructions to warn that commander of the very serious consequences which would follow the rejection of his overtures. Carmarthen (who about this time succeeded to the dukedom of Leeds) did not send the letter endorsing his action at every point, which the indignant ambassador demanded; but he said sufficient.

> I have the satisfaction of acquainting you by His Majesty's command that he highly appreciates the zeal and ability which you have manifested. . . . His Majesty considers the general tenor of the instructions which you have received and the peculiar urgency of the situation as having fully justified you in the measures you adopted to prevent the extension of hostilities. . . . You may show this dispatch to Count Bernstorff.

This certificate of the royal approval is dated April 10, 1789. The delay was no doubt partly due to George III's temporary lapse into insanity, but an opinion subsequently expressed of Mr Elliot by the sovereign [1] hardly bears out the whole-hearted commendation which the King's advisers thought desirable. When, flushed with success, Elliot posted off to Berlin in the December following his return from Sweden, he appears again to have acted on the general tenor of his instructions, without asking for leave. At Berlin, at any rate, he was sure of a warm welcome by Frederick William. Elliot, said his Prussian Majesty, had conducted himself not only as an excellent minister but as a distinguished statesman. The grateful Gustavus told his cousin of Great Britain that his representative had acquitted himself with the loyalty and firmness of a true Englishman.

Having defeated Bernstorff's intrigues to foment a difference between the courts of London and Potsdam, Elliot went back to his station and succeeded in the

[1] See p. 113.

course of the year 1789 in preventing a renewal of the war between the two Scandinavian Powers. It was hard work to keep the Danes quiet while hostilities between their hated neighbour and Russia were still going on. A conspiracy was hatched by the Swedes to burn the Russian fleet as it lay at anchor in Danish waters. The ambassador was not helped by the impetuous truculence of King Gustavus, but on July 9 he was able to report that Denmark had bound herself to an unlimited neutrality on land and sea. His work, he said wearily, was now done. But Elliot always had a grievance. In the State Papers, under date August 6, 1789, he complains that Mr Liston, his ex-tutor and secretary, who had now been appointed minister to Sweden, while passing through Copenhagen, unfortunately conveyed to the Danish Prime Minister the impression that Prussia might be detached from Britain. Three days later he goes farther and hints that Liston is giving encouragement to the Russians and Danes and seeming to countenance the parties opposed to Gustavus. A year after the Convention of Uddevalla disquieting rumours reached Elliot. "I shall be very happy," he wrote to his chief, "to learn from authority whether there is any foundation for the ill-natured reports circulated here, with respect to the impressions entertained *in a certain quarter*, to which indeed it would be my duty to bow with deference."

Circumstances certainly lent colour to those rumours. No honour was conferred on the man who had preserved the peace of the North. His subordinate Liston was elevated to the same rank as his, and Alleyne Fitzherbert, who, as he complained, had been resident at Brussels while he was envoy extraordinary at Berlin, was given the Madrid embassy. No doubt the Danish prince had the ear of his uncle, George III, and Elliot's friendship with the Prince of Wales [1] would not have been mentioned to his advantage at Windsor.

[1] See a new letter quoted by Dr J. Holland Rose (*William Pitt and National Revival*, p. 396).

III

When Elliot returned home on leave in November 1789 he probably made it clear that he would not go back to "those dreary regions." But no eagerness was shown by the Foreign Secretary to find him employment elsewhere. Pitt and his colleagues were too much occupied with the clouds blowing up from the south and west to remember what he had done in the North. Spain, then very efficiently administered by Florida Blanca, was demanding the evacuation of our trading posts on Nootka Sound, on the Pacific coast of America. The dispute waxed fierce. Moodily the unemployed diplomatist watched events and wished he were in Fitzherbert's shoes to conduct the negotiations at Madrid. Unfortunately for him, his acquaintance was solely with the courts of Northern and Central Europe. Meanwhile he was also following with the closest interest the progress of events across the water. Day by day, at first with astonished amusement, soon with the gravest attention, he marked the emergence into fame and power of his old schoolfellow at the Abbé Choquart's—of Mirabeau, his lately bankrupt, persecuted, out-at-elbows friend. Yes, it was Mirabeau who towered above the new constitutional assembly of France and shielded the court against the Republican factions; and it was Mirabeau who advised the Assembly to honour the Family Pact with Spain in case of war between that country and England and to add another thirty ships of the line to the French navy. For this service he received a thousand louis d'or from the Spanish ambassador—so, at least, Pitt was informed by W. A. Miles, an amateur diplomatist whom he had employed to sound the feelings of the deputies towards Britain.

If Elliot heard the story, as seems probable, he would have credited it. In his acquaintance with the strange man dominating the new Parliament of France he perceived an opportunity. He wrote to Pitt, offering to approach Mirabeau as to the possibility of a better understanding with Britain. The offer was accepted. The King, later on, when informed by Pitt of his mission, grudgingly signified his consent, though not sanguine that Mr H. Elliot and his French friend were likely to succeed where caution and much delicacy were required. There was to be no intermeddling with the internal affairs of France, his Majesty insisted, and nothing was to be said which would commit the Government. Britain's attitude of non-intervention puzzled foreigners. Elliot's old enemy Voronzov believed that he was sent over to back the constitutional party against the Crown. What he did do and say and what he achieved is not known with certainty, for the papers relating to his mission are nowhere to be found. The recent investigations of eminent historians,[1] however, should satisfy us as to the nature of his activities and instructions, though minor doubts remain to tease us.

In October Earl Gower, our ambassador at Paris, announced that Mr Elliot's conversations with M. de Mirabeau had led to a good understanding with the dominant party in the National Assembly. Elliot himself wrote that the actual Government of France was bent upon cultivating the most unbounded friendship with Great Britain, that if they met with encouragement they would confirm the commercial treaty with us, and that they would place no obstacle in the way of the settlement of Europe on the most liberal terms.

The encouragement offered to the Diplomatic Committee of the Assembly may well have consisted mainly in appeals to their statesmanship. Spain, the British emissary adroitly insinuated (bearing out Voronzov's suspicions), sought for war in concert with the malcontents or court party. But when in the course of a long letter dated October 26, 1790, he tells us that "what has taken place in my more intimate conversations with

[1] Notably Dr Holland Rose, *op. cit.*, pp. 579–581. See also Ward and Gooch, *The Cambridge History of British Foreign Policy*, vol. i, p. 201.

individuals cannot be committed to paper," we seem to hear the chink of gold. Was it heard, too, at Brest, where a formidable naval mutiny paralysed the French fleet? "I am more master of the springs of action here than anybody else could have been," boasts Elliot, who is inclined to think that when the news of these disturbances reaches Madrid his Catholic Majesty will make peace rather than expose his fleet to the danger of any junction with French ships. The whole negotiation smells of corruption, but the tide of sentiment in France was in Britain's favour, and vanity would prompt Elliot to exaggerate the importance of his personal overtures.

No doubt Mirabeau took his money. It was wasted, since the great orator died too soon to cement the alliance between the two constitutional nations. As to Spain, as Elliot had expected, the court would have no truck with the National Assembly. Finding, apparently to his surprise, that Prussia and the Stadholder were prepared to stand by Malmesbury's treaty of alliance, Pitt, two days before the letter quoted above was penned, was able to extract from Spain a renunciation of the land which is now British Columbia.

Even so, Elliot, convinced that he had prepared the way for a good understanding between France and England, must have hoped for a substantial reward. His services were again ignored. Perhaps he had spoken a little too warmly of the new order of things over the water. He had to explain that his expression "the glorious Revolution" was meant only for the ears of Frenchmen. Far better qualified than Malmesbury to deal with the new diplomacy, he was left idle for nearly two years, then relegated to the electoral court of Saxony (1792). He would have been as useful at Cape Horn.

The second marriage which he contracted about this time did not make for his advancement. His wife was Margaret Jones, a lovely girl, we are told, of humble origin. Elliot's brother, Lord Minto, visiting him at Dresden, said she reminded him of Raphael's Sistine

Madonna, and their children of the cherubs in the picture looking up. His lordship continues:

> I find her sensible and pleasant, and they are generally liked and on the best footing here. Hugh's extreme good humour and temper and his affectionate and cordial manner to every creature that approaches him, in whatever shape, are captivating qualities.

Good temper we should hardly have expected of our disappointed diplomatist. We recognize him more distinctly under the description supplied by Mrs St George, an Irish visitor in the year 1800:

> Mr Elliot is a very pleasing man, about forty; his style of conversation and tone of voice are highly captivating. . . . He is wonderfully amusing. His wit, his humour, his discontent, his spleen, his happy choice of words, his rapid flow of ideas, and his disposition to playful satire, make one long always to write shorthand and preserve his conversation.

His spleen and disposition to playful satire were just then powerfully stimulated by a visit from the "Nelsonians"—Lord Nelson and Sir William and Lady Hamilton, who were slowly progressing across Germany on their way home from Sicily. How sorely these boisterous guests affected the ambassador's nerves may be inferred when, having with infinite relief seen them depart, he thus adjured his family: "Now don't let us laugh to-night; let us all speak in our turn; and be very, very quiet."

At his next post Mr Elliot was to hear a great deal more about the Nelsonians.

THE FIGHT FOR SICILY
Hugh Elliot and Lord William Bentinck

THE peace which had been denied Britain at Lille and conceded her at Amiens by the Consul Bonaparte lasted nineteen months. On May 18, 1803, the two nations were again at war—as they were to remain another twelve years. The same date heads the instructions issued by Lord Hawkesbury to Mr Hugh Elliot, then on leave from Dresden, upon his appointment as minister to the court of the Two Sicilies. This was, in fact, promotion, if only from an electoral to a royal court, but we may believe Elliot when he told Fox three years later that he accepted it much against his inclination. He was now in his second half-century; ambition no longer tormented him; at Dresden, during the last eleven years, he had led a happy, peaceful life, devoted to his family. Now, at forty-eight hours' notice, he had to sail for Naples, and as ill-luck would have it aboard the ship of the great Admiral from whom he had parted with so much relief on the quays of the Elbe, two and a half years before. Nelson's ceaseless belauding of the royalties of Naples would already have prepossessed the envoy against them. Gloomily throughout the long voyage he no doubt reflected that from their court Sir William Hamilton had been recalled in something like disgrace, and that his successors, Paget and Drummond, had left it without having in any way enhanced their reputation. The King of the Two Sicilies (as Ferdinand IV was officially styled) was placed between the devil in the form of Napoleon, controlling the land, and the deep sea controlled by Britain. It might be concluded that the unfortunate monarch would follow the line dictated by his immediate interests, and it was the difficult task of an English envoy to persuade or coerce him to sacrifice those interests to Great Britain's.

THE FIGHT FOR SICILY.

News had already reached London that the French were summoning the Neapolitans to make common cause against the British and to close their ports to our shipping. Elliot's instructions were brief but explicit. If his Sicilian Majesty were constrained to admit French warships to his ports and to exclude the British, his Britannic Majesty's Government would not tolerate any such exclusion from the harbours of Sicily. "His Britannic Majesty," runs the instruction, "feels himself called on to garrison the forts of Messina as a temporary measure."[1] We had broken with France rather than surrender Malta, and we regarded the larger and adjacent island as equally necessary to our control of the Mediterranean. Napoleon, on the other hand, was pushing down troops to occupy the Neapolitan province of Apulia, the heel of Italy, as the most convenient jumping-off ground for Egypt and the Levant.

Thanks to the loyal devotion of Emma Hamilton and Nelson's inexplicable attachment, the gross, pusillanimous, beast-killing Ferdinand and his unloved consort, the masterful, headstrong Maria Carolina, have become as well known to British readers as any characters in history. Shaking in his shoes, his Sicilian Majesty heard that war had broken out again. He lived over again the horrors of that flight to Sicily in the December of 1798 and cursed himself for ever having recrossed the seas. From his windows at Portici he might have seen some French craft laden with oil seized and carried off by an English frigate, and this prior to any declaration of war. The prizes were released upon the remonstrances of the nominally neutral Government; but the English did the same thing again (as they had done constantly during the period before the Peace of Amiens) on June 6. Daily the tone of Charles Alquier, regicide and ex-*conventionnel*, who represented France at Naples, became more threatening. His anger was not likely to abate now that he was to be faced by a duly accredited ambassador

[1] F.O. 70/21. Public Record Office.

from Britain instead of a *chargé d'affaires*. His Sicilian Majesty sought to avoid trouble by delegating the responsibility of receiving Elliot to his son. But the new envoy would not submit to that. He refused to present his credential letters to any but the King; and Ferdinand had to come back from his retreat at Caserta to receive him.

"The presence of a British minister in his capital, of a British man-of-war in the harbour, and of Lord Nelson's fleet in the offing," were, in Hugh Elliot's opinion, "calculated to restore confidence in the King." He was right in a measure, since Ferdinand was less concerned for the safety of his kingdom than for his own, and it was the sight of that man-of-war which emboldened him to reject the proposals for an alliance with France, to be paid for by an augmentation of his territory at the expense of the Pope. The Marquis di Gallo, his ambassador at the Tuileries, advised acceptance. "Rather death than that I should sully my lips by acceding to such an abomination!" wrote his Majesty to his Prime Minister. "The opposite sooner at any cost." Informed how the King had in former years vowed to die at the head of his troops and then abandoned his capital when no man pursued him, Elliot could not have attached much value to this protestation. He had more reason to be pleased by the warm welcome he received from the Prime Minister. This was General Acton, the veteran English baronet born in France, who had for decades steered the ship of State on its zigzag course. Bonaparte's determination to quarter his troops in the Adriatic provinces, despite the protests of the Russian and Neapolitan ambassadors, made the old man apprehensive of a sudden raid upon Naples itself. He arranged with Elliot to keep a frigate close at hand, in readiness to take off the royal family. They concerted measures for the security of Sicily. The small force of Neapolitans at Malta was to be sent to Messina; the citadel of that port was to be re-armed and to be provisioned for six months.

THE FIGHT FOR SICILY

That Sicily might be held when Naples was lost, while Naples could not be held if Sicily were lost, was an axiom of British statecraft. It was an axiom to which King Ferdinand warmly assented; but his queen and the power supposed to be friendly to Great Britain saw in it something more than a determination to provide an asylum for him and his family. The Tsar was loth to see Malta pass permanently into English hands. Even the Duke of Serra Capriola, Ferdinand's ambassador at Petersburg, was infected by the Russian suspicions. Writing to his court on December 7, 1804, he describes our Secretary of Legation there as

> a firm supporter of the English system of embroiling the Continent in a war to make a diversion for itself, but without any view for the benefit of the allied powers. . . . He defends the whole of the English system with all its pretensions, to keep Malta whatever it may cost, to commence hostilities in the kingdom of Naples with the forces already there, because provided the citadel of Messina is in English hands whatever happens to the kingdom of Naples will only be a signal for England to turn Sicily to what end it pleases, and as the island is near to Malta, the two possessions will become one dominion.

Before this letter was shown to Elliot by the Queen he learned that his old enemy Voronzov had warned his colleague at Naples to put their Sicilian Majesties on their guard against him as a hothead who would land them in scrapes.

They had good reason, on the contrary, to be grateful to the British representative for taking thought for their interests as well as his own country's. The decision to throw a British garrison into Messina, announced in his instructions, had not so far been carried out. When Nelson and Sir Alexander Ball, the Governor of Malta, proposed to act upon it, Elliot was therefore able to restrain them. He argued that by way of reprisals Bonaparte would inevitably occupy Naples itself. Moreover, the blockade also contemplated by Nelson would only afford the French an excuse for spreading themselves over the whole kingdom in order to find additional areas of supply for their troops, and would besides deprive the British themselves of the use of the ports. Elliot refused to be scared by the rumours of an immediate French advance. "Don't listen," he advised Nelson, "to our merchants, who are excellent dealers in Newfoundland fish but bad newsmongers, and who will continually harass you with the same absurd stories with which my table is also covered until I get a proper opportunity of consigning the intelligence and alarms of these deep politicians to their proper place." [1]

What is strange is that Elliot was for a long time unable to credit those most concerned with the single aim of keeping Naples out of the war. With a curious and a jaundiced eye he first studied the Queen, whom he had heard so fulsomely extolled at Dresden by her forgotten favourite. The story of Nelson was fresh in his ears. He forgot that the spell laid by Maria Carolina on the Admiral was woven solely in the interests of her husband's kingdom—he missed the significance of the fact that she had callously thrown aside her minion, Emma Hamilton, as soon as she had served that purpose. The Queen was now fifty-one years of age and the mother of seventeen children. But Elliot at his first approach conceived her as subordinating her interests to her passions—a thing which a man does very often, but a woman at any time of life and in any class of society very rarely. The event shows that he greatly exaggerated the depth of her so-called love affairs. Speaking of her fancy for the Marquis de Saint-Clair, one of a colony of French royalist *émigrés*, he writes: "That title no longer denotes any real hostility towards the government of Bonaparte. I must confess the First Consul cannot make use of any better channel to forward his own purposes at foreign courts than that of French emigrants." "The Queen," he tells Lord Nelson (of all men!) "is well inclined to us; yet she is continually drawn into scrapes

[1] The Countess of Minto, *Memoir of the Right Hon. Hugh Elliot* (1868).

and inconsistencies by these designing people who are in their hearts equally hostile to Great Britain and to General Acton." Another and unprejudiced witness,[1] however, states that Saint-Clair was always considered to steer clear of her Majesty's political measures; and, so far from regarding the *émigrés* as useful auxiliaries, Alquier more than once demanded their expulsion from the kingdom. At this distance of time it is easier to disentangle the cross-currents swirling round the court of the wretched Italian kingdom. Elliot wished generally to keep the country neutral for its own sake and the benefit of British shipping. Acton and the King entertained a deadly fear of the French and always had an eye on the back door, held open by Nelson. The *émigrés*, for the most part, wished for peace with France at any price, so that they might stay where they were, and for that reason they viewed the aged minister's British sympathies with alarm. Russia, though drawn towards Britain by her dread of Napoleon, distrusted her ulterior designs, as we have seen. Queen Maria Carolina, the daughter and mother of Austrian empresses, the sister of Marie-Antoinette, could never be suspected of a predilection for France, but she remained steadfastly and all the time Neapolitan, equally desirous to keep the French out of Naples and the English out of Sicily.

Thus is explained the appeal to Napoleon, written in her own hand, to spare her unfortunate country and at least to relieve it of the burden of supporting the French army of occupation commanded by Gouvion-Saint-Cyr. Elliot knew of this when two months after his arrival he was sent for by the Queen. He found her in her private room. "She was much agitated and it was some time before she could speak on public affairs. At length, however, she did so, with more than usual animation, and having occasion to mention Bonaparte, his name was always accompanied by some appropriate epithet."

[1] Sir Henry Bunbury, *Passages in the Great War with France* (ed. 1927), p. 148 *n*.

Caustically Elliot expressed his surprise, since Bonaparte had graciously condescended at her request to bear a part of the expenses of his own troops quartered in her kingdom. "I have sent for you," said her Majesty, "to show you a letter from him which has not yet been communicated to General Acton." Napoleon expressed his desire to consolidate peace and to aid a weaker kingdom, the well-being of which was useful to French commerce. He wished well to Naples, but how could he consider it dispassionately when he descried at the head of its administration a foreigner who had centred in England his wealth and his affections? Here, he frankly declared, was the reason for those hostile measures which provoked her Majesty's complaints.

"If Acton sees this," said the Queen, "he will hand in his resignation." Elliot asked leave to consider the matter and returned to his legation through the reeking streets of Naples. His conclusions he states in his dispatch of August 28, 1803.

> Her majesty has so many irons in the fire that the natural consequences must inevitably ensue. There are, both in France and Germany, many individuals in habits of intimacy and correspondence with the Queen, who conceive that if General Acton was removed and the French influence established here, they would be put in possession of the Government.

People aware of the Queen's infatuation for Saint-Clair, he thought, had put it into Napoleon's head that she would be glad to get rid of Acton. At this view he hinted in his advice to the Queen. The implied demand for the General's removal emanated from other minds than Napoleon's, and she should ignore it. The letter should be shown to Acton. Being English (*sic*), he would not second the aims of the First Consul by deserting his post in the hour of danger. Comforted by promises of British and Russian assistance, Ferdinand showed the letter to his old counsellor and bade him continue in office.

It was a mere respite. No intrigue need be imagined

to explain Napoleon's objection to the control of a Bourbon kingdom by a man of British origin. Put on his guard, the old man tried for some time longer to keep an even course. In October 1803 he refused permission for a number of foreign-born mercenaries, discharged from the British service, to be landed at Naples *en route* to their respective homes. His refusal resulted in a gain to the British, for Elliot's son rowed out to the ships, took off eighty-four of the men who were willing to re-enlist and embarked them on a British warship for Malta. To this feat his father proudly calls his Government's attention. In the following spring the French ambassador had a more serious complaint. A Maltese recruiting officer was enlisting French deserters —deserters, alleged Elliot, who had been directed to him purposely by the complainant. Alquier discussed the affair with Acton. He used such violent language that the Anglo-Italian statesman declined to continue the conversation. The Frenchman, of course, considered himself insulted, and vowed he would withdraw to Rome unless General Acton was dismissed. This came ominously near to a declaration of war. King Ferdinand temporized by relieving Acton of his functions as Foreign Secretary and entrusting them to Micheroux, a courtier of known French sympathies.

Alquier's resentment was not to be so easily disarmed. His distrust and contempt for the Bourbons of Sicily is expressed in all his dispatches. His report reached Paris. Gallo took fright and wrote post-haste, declaring that war could only be averted by Acton's removal from all his offices. Elliot scoffed at the warning. News had reached him that a Russian squadron was under sail in the Black Sea. Stay, he advised Acton. But the old man was prevailed on to think it more dignified to resign than to be dismissed. He handed over the seals and sailed aboard the *Archimede* for Palermo on May 25, 1804. Eight days later, says Elliot, the dreaded dispatch from Paris was received and turned out, as he had predicted, not to be an ultimatum after all. Instead, he goes on to say, his master told Alquier not to carry the quarrel too far.[1] No dispatch conceived in these terms has been traced.[2] Elliot, one must suppose, thus freely interpreted a verbal summary given him of Talleyrand's note to Gallo, dated May 7. Therein Napoleon, busy about his approaching investiture with the imperial purple, contented himself with the strongest possible recommendation to the King of Naples to get rid of the objectionable minister and with the assurance that there existed, and could exist, no real cause of discord between the two nations.[3] In the absence of a positive threat of war Maria Carolina generously admitted that she had been overhasty. "Vraiment, M. Elliot," she confessed, "je suis au repentir, et nous avons été trompés."

Deceived by Gallo and Micheroux, the British envoy believed; assisted, he would have added, by the *émigrés*. Alquier and Gouvion-Saint-Cyr had been bribed, so he asserted, to frighten the court; the Queen was blinded by her passion for Saint-Clair; Acton himself was induced to leave by the promise of a pension of £6000 a year, etc. It is safe to say that this plot against the aged minister existed only in our envoy's perfervid imagination. On May 15 we find the Queen writing to Gallo of "the honest, worthy, incorruptible Acton." "It is we," she says, "who are the anti-revolutionaries, the anti-usurpers, not Acton." "I do not deny," she writes on May 27, "that his departure is extremely painful to me."[4] She has no confidence in Micheroux. As to Saint-Clair, what he stood to gain by the minister's departure Elliot does not pause to ask himself. The flamboyant background of Naples disposed him unconsciously towards romantic theories.

As every one might have foreseen, Acton's influence

[1] F.O. 70/22. June 15, 1804. Public Record Office.
[2] C. Auriol, *La France, l'Angleterre, et Naples*, vol. i, p. 617.
[3] C. Auriol, *op. cit.*, vol. i, p. 601.
[4] *Correspondance inédite de Marie-Caroline avec le Marquis de Gallo.*

was not immediately extinguished by his departure from the seat of government. From his distant retreat he continued to advise the King, who acted upon his counsels, while the Queen acted on her own or other people's. So now it was the British ambassador who became restive under the hidden hand of the pro-British minister. He was "lost in a labyrinth of contradiction and inconsistency." To clear matters up he insisted on a private audience of Ferdinand, a privilege hardly ever accorded by that timid monarch. After moving the envoy almost to tears by his lamentations and heroic sentiments his Majesty told him, in effect, never again to bother him about matters of State, but to discuss them with the Queen. The Government, Elliot soon reports, is entirely in charge of the Queen. Now he has nothing but praise for her diligence and efficiency. On June 24, 1804, he writes:

> Her majesty has permitted me to wait upon her every day between the hours of one and three and communicates to me all the dispatches received by the court without reserve. Her professions of attachment to England are as strong as those of General Acton; but I mistrust the impetuosity of her majesty's feelings which will ever betray her into acts of imprudence.

Six months later he is able to announce that her Majesty's confidence in him is unbounded. In proof of this she gave him copies of Serra Capriola's letters which voiced the Russian court's suspicions of Britain.

Bonaparte made himself Emperor of the French in 1804, and announced his intention of being crowned King of Italy. Princes stand much by styles and forms. The new title exasperated Ferdinand as implying an overlordship of the whole peninsula. Maria Carolina talked and, what was worse, wrote of organizing a new Sicilian Vespers to get rid of the French. She soon saw reason to curb her fury. In vain she scanned the horizon for those Russian sails. Desperately she made a bid for Napoleon's friendship by offering a tribute of six million French livres. At the end of January 1805 she sent a copy of the Emperor's reply to Elliot. She could not, she wrote, bear to witness his perusal of it. This letter has often been transcribed. None knew better than Napoleon how to breathe flame and fury into the written word. He told the Queen plainly that he had before him several of her letters which left no doubt as to her secret sentiments and which it was impossible to reconcile with her assurances of friendship. He accused her of fomenting war, and warned her that she was bringing her husband's kingdom to ruin and herself and her children to beggary. He would spare her if (among other things) she dismissed the French, who excited her against her own country, and Elliot, who busied himself with plots for his assassination and was behind all the Neapolitan manoeuvres.

With the inconsistency common to Christians Elliot would, of course, have shrunk from killing the man he held responsible for the slaughter of thousands, while he would have had no scruple about killing his helpless minions; but to this imperial blast he responded with all the pugnacity of his nature.

> The first feeling of a gentleman on reading such a letter addressed to a princess, the wife of a sovereign, the daughter of Maria Theresa [he wrote], must be a strong desire to inflict personal chastisement on the writer. The arm and not the pen would give the fittest answer.

Maria Carolina wept at the humiliation she had brought on herself. In justice to her Elliot apprised his Government that the idea of a tribute had been approved by Acton. "I have but too much reason," he added, "to observe that both his temper and judgment are impaired from the mortification attending the decline of his influence at this court." We see that Mr Elliot, now he enjoyed the confidence of the Queen, thought better of her judgment.

All that the Emperor achieved by his bluster was to throw the terrified Queen almost literally into the arms of the British representative. "He spent hours with her and her ministers, and not a day passed without her writing to him." So writes Elliot's granddaughter, who goes on to comment on the Queen's letters which lie before her.

> In almost all, there are some characteristic traits which account for the influence the Queen obtained over those she could not dupe. She carried into her intercourse with the person in her confidence the charm of a kindly bonhomie, of a high spirit, and of the indiscretion which looks so like, and is not, trust.

The high spirit is not always noticeable. Multitudes of this queen's letters to Gallo and others are as lachrymose and dismal as any Mrs Gummidge could have penned.

One must suppose it was against Elliot's advice, as it was contrary to common prudence, that another *émigré*, Count Roger de Damas, was placed in command of the Neapolitan forces. Damas had served in Condé's army and fought in almost every war against his own countrymen since the outbreak of the Revolution. The French instantly took up the challenge. On February 16 a French officer presented himself at the court bringing with him an ultimatum from General Saint-Cyr. The levies in the provinces must be disarmed, recruiting must cease, Damas must be dismissed and deported from the mainland, and Mr Elliot directed to repair to Sicily. Failing compliance with these demands the General would take steps to enforce them and would seize the *émigré* wherever he could find him. At this moment, and for a few weeks longer, Austria was at peace with France. The Austrian ambassador, Count Kaunitz, interposed his good offices so far as Elliot was concerned, and by pointing out, as one supposes, that the Neapolitan Government's expulsion of her representative would mean instant war with England, persuaded Saint-Cyr to waive that particular demand. Meanwhile Prince Cardito was dispatched by the Queen to the French headquarters. He was so far successful that the irate commander agreed to postpone further action till he had received orders from Paris. In the end only one of the points was insisted on. Damas, of course, had to go. Loaded with honours, he departed for Sicily. Further to humour the tyrant, the Sicilian ambassador in London, Prince Castelcicala, was instructed to ask for the recall of Elliot. As it had been hoped and expected by the Queen, the request was refused by Lord Mulgrave, the Foreign Secretary. Mr Elliot's conduct, he said, had earned the entire approbation of his Britannic Majesty. There could be no doubt at whose dictation the demand for his recall had been formulated. Nor could his lordship see his way to placate a nation at war with Britain by acquiescing in the exclusion of British warships from his Sicilian Majesty's ports.

These impudent demands made in the name of a sovereign who was at that moment drawing an annual subsidy of £150,000 from the British Treasury showed how little reliance was to be placed on his steadfastness. Pitt got ready a force of 3400 infantry, 300 light dragoons (without horses), and a large proportion of artillery, for dispatch to the Mediterranean, under the command of Sir James Craig. But on April 11, 1805, Britain entered into a coalition with Russia directed against France, and the sound design of securing Sicily was complicated with vague and ill-considered projects. Although Sir James's instructions did indeed state that the defence of the island was to be his principal object, he was also ordered to co-operate in the defence of the Continental dominions of the King of Naples if called on to do so by Mr Elliot or the Russian commander-in-chief. Since the Russians had already collected a force of 12,000 men at Corfu, it should have been obvious to the men at Downing Street that they would certainly avail themselves of Craig's assistance and that the secondary object of the expedition would become the major. The adhesion of Austria to the Coalition was anticipated, and some idea of a diversion in her favour in Northern Italy haunted the minds of the

MARIA CAROLINA, QUEEN OF THE TWO SICILIES
From a contemporary engraving

Allies. No one seems to have measured the distance from Naples to the Brenner. It was unfortunate that Pitt did not study the map of Europe more closely before he rolled it up.

While Craig's little armada was on the water Elliot stretched out a hand to steady the distracted Queen. By an unlucky chance now, when the two Russian generals, Lacy and Oppermann, were on their way to her court to concert measures for her defence, Prince Sherbatov, another of their countrymen, landed at Naples and was recognized as having killed the Chevalier de Saxe in a duel in Bohemia several years before. The dead man had been loved by Maria Carolina. Straightway she ordered the slayer to be seized and put across the border. Karpov, the Russian *chargé d'affaires*, threatened to demand his passports. Elliot succeeded in talking him over, pointing out that this was an affair of police, not of policy. It was not so easy to persuade the Queen that the Russians had abandoned all thoughts of reprisals. When the British frigate usually stationed for her protection off Naples put to sea in order to exercise her crew, she flew into a panic, concluding this had been done to give a Russian warship liberty to seize the Sicilian frigate *Archimede*. Her Majesty was in a fair way to rejecting the Tsar's help when Napoleon once again blew her into his enemy's camp by an explosion of temper. Because Naples still waited on Austria to recognize the new Kingdom of Italy, the newly fledged Emperor covered the unhappy Queen with abuse; he held her up to odium as the Messalina and the Frédégonde of her age and charged her with homosexual practices, possibly because of her politic friendship with the buxom Emma. Napoleon, as the Duke of Wellington once remarked, was no gentleman. "Don't be frightened," said Hugh Elliot, "stand firm. The more you yield, the more he will ask for."[1] The clear-sighted diplomatist knew that, with three great empires on his hands, Napoleon would

[1] F.O. 70/25. Public Record Office.

not seek to raise up a new enemy in the shape of Naples on his right flank. A neutral Naples would best serve his purpose, and Britain's too, as it seemed to Elliot.

But, cut off though he was from all communication with his Government except by the months-long sea-route, Elliot was no longer the man to play a lone hand. He had learned his lesson at Berlin and Copenhagen. His independence and initiative, however successful in their immediate results, had won him no favour at his court—not so much as a knighthood. It behoved him to act warily. In the mission of the Russian generals, followed by the arrival of the new Russian ambassador, Tatishev, he could not fail to discern a scheme to drag the Kingdom of the Two Sicilies into war. He had no reason to like or trust these allies of Britain. From the first he held aloof from them—from the moment of M. Tatishev's arrival, we are told, his influence at the court of Naples waned. Mr Elliot, we fancy, let it wane. Nevertheless, the Tsar was now his King's ally, and duty bound him to support his agents. Even, at certain conjunctures, he appears to have tried to persuade himself and to persuade others of the wisdom of the Russian policy. When Alquier, justly suspicious of the northern strangers, began bullying the Queen once more and declared his master was ready to supersede King Ferdinand by the Hereditary Prince, we find Elliot writing to the Governor of Malta, "The attitude of Bonaparte is such that only if the Russians are enabled to carry out their plans can the kingdom be preserved. At this juncture, moreover, everything must be done to humour the Czar."[1]

Lacy, a Livonian of Irish extraction, was a genial veteran, clear-headed, in Elliot's opinion, but curiously inarticulate. He was able, notwithstanding, to express his indignation upon being told by King Ferdinand to discuss his plans with the Queen—a woman. Gulping down his wrath, the Muscovite first insisted upon her

[1] F.O. 70/25. July 19, 1805. Public Record Office.

Majesty recognizing Bonaparte as King of Italy. This was to gain a breathing space. He next tackled the British minister. Had Mr Elliot received any orders directing the expeditionary force now on its way to co-operate with the Russian forces? Elliot had not. His last letter from home, dated March 20, gave him to understand that the principal object of the expedition was the defence of Sicily. But on being shown a letter from Voronzov, who apparently commanded quicker means of communication than Downing Street, he was obliged to admit that close co-operation between the allied forces was contemplated, and announced himself ready to second Lacy's efforts as far as he could. In the letter to Ball at Malta, already quoted, the Governor was asked to collect transports sufficient to convey the Tsar's troops from Corfu to Italy.

Truly, the persistence of men in their petty quarrels has in it something of the sublime or the ridiculous! Such time as princes and diplomatists and generals were taking counsel how to thwart the imagined designs of Napoleon, their chairs reeled and their ears were deafened by the crashing of houses and the screams of the populace. In that earthquake (July 26, 1805) upwards of four thousand people perished. The tremors of the earth having subsided and the work of burying the dead and searching for those buried alive having begun, the statesmen again took up their pens—only to find their paper blotted by the hot ashes of Vesuvius. The fiery mountain did its worst. It abated its fury till another day; and, a little envious perhaps of the destructive powers of nature (which science has since helped us to surpass), the soldiers got to work again.

By the end of July Elliot received news of Craig's arrival at Malta, together with a copy of his instructions from Lord Mulgrave. Those instructions, the general wrote on July 20,[1] had been superseded by others issued on April 22 by Lord Camden, the Secretary of State for

[1] F.O. 70/25. W.O. 6/56, p. 35. Public Record Office.

War, and sent after him by a fast sailing vessel. He was not in any case (unless, of course, the King of the Two Sicilies should close his ports against British ships) to occupy Sicily without the consent of the Russian general, and it was his Majesty's pleasure that he should co-operate with the Russian commander-in-chief in any requisition he might make for the defence of the Neapolitan dominions. Elliot must have breathed a sigh of relief. He had done right, at all events, in crediting Voronzov's intimation. He found himself coming round to his Government's ideas. Now that the Russians and Austrians were mobilizing Napoleon might profit by the interval to invade the Neapolitan provinces. Backed by Russian troops before it was completely overthrown, the kingdom might prove a useful ally. So much to Lord Mulgrave. To Craig he sent greetings as an old acquaintance of his Berlin days; then, getting down to the matter in hand, said he had deemed it part of his duty to represent to General Lacy that the security of the island of Sicily should not be exposed by any enterprise unconnected with it—this he said though he was not supposed to be informed of the plan of operations. To expel the French altogether from the kingdom would no doubt be the most effective means of preserving the island, but, in addition to that extensive project, it might be advisable to place a body of 1000 or 1500 foreign troops, principally British, in the fortress of Messina. This, however, was a very delicate subject, owing to the jealousy of the friendly Powers.[1] Probably at the moment the British envoy was writing, Tatishev was warning Maria Carolina to beware of the British designs on Sicily.

There was also the possibility of Ferdinand's betraying his new ally as well as his old and closing his ports against British ships. For, as Elliot had anticipated, the Emperor of the French had changed his tone and was anxious now only to keep the southern kingdom quiet. To Gallo, in Paris, he proposed a treaty of neutrality. The Italians

[1] F.O. 70/25. August 4, 1805. Public Record Office.

showed themselves at once alive to their advantage. How could the kingdom profess neutrality, was the reply, so long as French troops occupied part of its territory? Not the logic of the query, but the need of all his troops determined the Emperor's rejoinder. The Marquis di Gallo was able to announce that his Imperial Majesty would withdraw every one of his soldiers from the Neapolitan dominions upon the conclusion of a treaty of neutrality between him and his Sicilian Majesty. To the man on the spot it must have seemed that the Colossus in Paris had temporarily lost his head. Alquier saw the goings and comings of the Russian agents. He guessed what was afoot. His dispatches to Talleyrand warn his Government that no confidence whatever can be reposed in the Bourbon king and his Habsburg wife. Thinking to sow dissension between the allies, he named Elliot as the authority for the rumour that a Russian landing was contemplated. Elliot, in a note to the Neapolitan minister Luzzi dated August 23, denied ever having spread such a report. Artfully, yet truthfully, he declared that since his arrival at Naples he had never ceased officially to assure that court of his Britannic Majesty's desire to respect its neutrality. Three days later the French ambassador categorically inquired whether his Sicilian Majesty was willing or in a position to oppose a disembarkation of foreign troops. Luzzi and his colleague Circello did not hesitate to assure him of their pacific intentions. On the same day they were given powers to negotiate a treaty with Tatishev.

That treaty was signed on September 11, 1805. The safety of his kingdom being endangered by the presence of French troops (so it was declared in the first article), his Sicilian Majesty entered into an armed alliance with his good friend and brother the Tsar Alexander. The British are not named as parties to the convention but only as auxiliaries. Elliot's attitude and misgivings are expressed in detail in his letter to Lord Mulgrave, dated the following day:

The Russian ambassador was at first inclined that I should take a part in this instrument. [He declined.] First, because the more I favour the very marked inclination the Russian minister has manifested . . . of taking the lead, the more likely he is to commit his court to the protection of this kingdom without having it in his power to repeat a language respecting the endeavours of the British Government to draw this country as a party into the war. I have therefore thought it advisable not even to see the convention before it was concluded. . . . My second reason . . . is that the above mentioned convention could not be carried into effect without a considerable augmentation of pecuniary assistance. My third motive was that hitherto all my efforts since I have been alone and unsupported at this court by the ministers of any other foreign power have been calculated solely to maintain the security of the Two Sicilies by yielding as much as possible in every instance which might have committed its neutrality and by encouraging on the other hand the adoption of every secret means . . . with a view to their own defence. From the conversation of the Russian minister and the Russian general, it appears to me that their conduct is now to be regulated by very different principles. They expect to bring the country forward as an active member of offensive war against France, in order that it may make an essential diversion in favour of . . . the Austrians in the north of Italy. I shall not attempt to discuss how far so extensive a project can be considered as expedient or practicable. I confine myself therefore to repeat that it can in no case be carried into execution without the previous adjustment of a considerable subsidiary arrangement.

He leaves it therefore to his Government to decide whether it would be better to favour the continued neutrality of the country or to grant such pecuniary aid as might enable his Sicilian Majesty to take the field with a specific number of regular troops.[1]

In blissful ignorance of what was being done at Naples, Gallo accepted with enthusiasm Napoleon's unexpectedly liberal proposals for confirming the neutrality of his master's realms. He set his name to a treaty, dated September 22, by the first and second articles of which King Ferdinand bound himself to defend his neutrality

[1] F.O. 70/25. Public Record Office.

by force and specifically to resist the disembarkation in his territory of any forces belonging to the belligerents. The command of his armies was not to be entrusted to any officer of British, Russian, or Austrian nationality or to any French *émigré*. His ports were to be closed to the fleets of the belligerents. By a secret article the King was pledged not to acknowledge the sovereignty of the English over Malta or to admit General Acton to his counsels. In return the Emperor recognized the absolute neutrality of the kingdom and bound himself to withdraw the last of his troops from Neapolitan soil within one month of the ratification of the treaty. The document was forwarded by Gallo for his master's signature.

Enormous was the embarrassment of the Neapolitan court. To reject the treaty would be to declare war against France with a French army within a few marches of the capital. Certainly, Luzzi or whichever minister acted as mouthpiece to the Queen might have reconciled her conflicting obligations by pointing out to the Russians that the *casus fœderis* stipulated in the convention of September 11 could not now arise, since the Neapolitan territory was to be completely evacuated by the French troops. Tatishev should have been politely bowed out, with heartfelt thanks for his offer of service. For a moment, there seems reason to believe, there was some probability of this course being followed, for the angry Russian envoy talked of asking Elliot to stop the subsidy. The British ambassador meanwhile looked on, one suspects, with a sly smile. Her Sicilian Majesty had elected to follow the Russian counsels, and must extricate herself from this dilemma without his help. Alquier, marvelling at his master's trustfulness in these people, sternly pressed for the ratification of the treaty, under threat of leaving Naples.[1] King Ferdinand washed his hands of the whole matter. Such time as he could spare from killing animals he was now devoting to the cultivation of the vine. It was in the vineyard that his wife's

[1] C. Auriol, *op. cit.*, vol. ii, p. 601.

messenger found him, and in the vineyard that he carelessly signed his name to the treaty with France negotiated by Gallo. He was the man who had torn up the capitulation concluded in his name by Ruffo with the Neapolitan revolutionaries in 1799, and had sent hundreds of them to their doom in defiance of that pledge. The day he wrote his name on the treaty of neutrality (October 8, 1805) he sent a note to Tatishev, declaring that his signature had been extracted by force and calling on the Russians and British to aid him. "We have obeyed as one might obey a bandit who holds a pistol to one's head," wrote the daughter of Maria Theresa to her daughter at Vienna.

Mr Elliot did not see things in the same light. He called on Count Roger de Damas, who had stolen back from Palermo. "It is a shameful proceeding which I should never have advised," he said.[1] The high-born *émigré* was not of that opinion. To Lord Mulgrave our ambassador wrote communicating the ratification of the neutrality treaty, with the mere observation that it did not appear to contain anything prejudicial to our country: British transports had been sent to Corfu to embark the Russians. He saw no reason to contradict the suspicion entertained by the French that the expedition was destined for Ancona, a port outside his Sicilian Majesty's dominions. Having only two very old ciphers in his possession, he did not think it proper to communicate any more political or military intelligence of a more secret nature. Craig on receiving Lacy's orders to join him at Naples, in flat violation of the treaty, stigmatized the business as perfidy; but both Englishmen were bound by the orders of their Government. Elliot busied himself buying horses for Craig's unmounted light dragoons.

Alquier warned his Government of what was going on. Nevertheless France complied with the terms of the treaty. On November 5 the last French soldier crossed

[1] *Mémoires du Comte Roger de Damas* (1912), vol. i, p. 397.

the Tronto, and the kingdom was free of foreign troops. At this juncture Napoleon wanted soldiers. He did not trust the Bourbons any more than his ambassador did, but he could afford to leave them rope enough to hang themselves. Yet even now the perfidious monarch might perhaps have steered between the rocks. It was on the Adige that the Austrians, under the Archduke Charles, were fighting Masséna and his Frenchmen. Moved by obvious strategical motives and perhaps by some faint tinge of commiseration for the country he was dragging to its doom, Tatishev two days after the completion of the evacuation proposed that the allied Russian and British force should be landed in the north of Italy, outside the Neapolitan limits. Terrified lest the French should return, the besotted court rejected the new plan, although by this time they were aware of the capitulation of the Austrian army at Ulm. The die was cast. On November 17 a combined Russian and British fleet cast anchor in the bay. Alquier instantly demanded his passports. He left Naples on November 20, 1805, from which date the Kingdom of the Two Sicilies continued in a state of war with France. Frantically Luzzi tried to save his master's face. He tried to make Gallo believe that the disembarkation of the foreigners was unexpected, and that, in any case, his king could not resist it, since he had so long tolerated the presence of a French army within his dominions.

Elliot pursued what is now called a policy of masterly inactivity. Writing home on November 13, he complains of Tatishev's unfriendly attitude and puts his Government on its guard against Voronzov. On December 10 he announces that the Allies have disembarked and are now taking up positions near the frontier. The Russians numbered nominally 13,000, the British 6000, and there were with them some 6000 Neapolitan troops. What they were supposed to be doing is not very clear. On November 22 the Archduke summoned Lacy to land near the mouths of the Po and attack Masséna in the rear, but the message was not received, or at any rate not communicated to Craig, until December 13.[1] It was then too late. The Austrians, so Elliot reported, were in full retreat towards Hungary. On Christmas Day Maria Carolina, turning once more to her English friend, informed him of the final catastrophe of Austerlitz. Napoleon, now fully apprised of the treachery of the Neapolitan Bourbons, decreed their doom. Masséna, no longer needed to rout the Austrians, was ordered to march on Naples.

At this crisis Elliot's dispatches become less frequent. The whole continent was overspread by the enemy, and he could communicate with his Government only by sea. In London, one supposes, not much anxiety was felt about the Italian kingdom. Nothing that happened there could materially affect the course of events. Thus Lacy may have reflected when he determined to withdraw his army from the frontier and retire into the mountains of Calabria. Craig had despaired of success on learning what had happened at Ulm. Now, mindful only of his original instructions to secure Sicily, he insisted on the total evacuation of the mainland. Against this abandonment the Queen passionately protested. She was sending emissaries to the French headquarters and to Paris with abject proposals for peace. Ferdinand would abdicate in favour of his son, Francis. Old Lacy, alarmed by the advance of the French, yet reluctant to abandon the kingdom he had come to save, was relieved of his perplexity by the Tsar's command to evacuate the country and take his troops to Corfu. In a dispatch dated January 13, 1806, Elliot announces that Sir James Craig and the British auxiliaries have that day crossed the Maddalena bridge, in the suburbs of Naples, *en route* for Castellammare, where they were to embark for Messina. This measure the minister pronounces the wisest that could have been taken, and he gives Sir James the credit for it. Elliot's attitude in the midst of these

[1] Sir Henry Bunbury, *op. cit.*, p. 138.

events is dubious and contradictory. His approbation of the evacuation is hard to reconcile with other of his utterances. Perhaps he did not wish to harass his Government by admitting any differences of opinion between himself and the military commander. Certain it is that in a later letter to Fox (of June 3) he puts forward the view that so narrow a country as Naples, lying between two seas, and with ample resources of population, not without military value and very strong positions, might have been contested step by step against an advancing enemy. His granddaughter admits that he supported the Queen in her demand that the allied force should cover the capital in order to reinforce her peace offers. According to Bunbury, an unfriendly witness, Mr Elliot, either seduced by the court of Naples or possessed by some vain hope of baffling the French by diplomacy, protested against our repairing to the ports of Sicily and had even undertaken for the Queen the management of a negotiation with the approaching enemy. "Mr Elliot persisted obstinately in his wild scheme of negotiation."

Our military authority exaggerates. Elliot was certainly not entrusted with the management of the negotiations. His advice no doubt was asked, but it is clear from her letters that her Majesty did not look on him as a wholehearted partisan.

> Come whenever you choose [she writes (January 19)]. Proceedings are of too much importance for me not to wish to see you. I see the fleet is under sail. I hope that to all the execrable conduct held towards us there is not to be added an attempt to enter Sicily by force—to render all compromise impossible, to ruin us and our family beyond redemption. I have received letters from Rome of the 18th. We must look for every sort of insult as the result of this short-lived and costly Anglo-Russian visit. Certainly, our hearts have been revolted; nor has anyone been so loyal and honourable as we have been.

One can but smile. A week later the Queen complains of the distressing silence and absence which Elliot has observed both in his private and official characters. She had heard of the death of Nelson, her old and devoted friend, and inquires anxiously as to the whereabouts of Collingwood's squadron.

Not unnaturally, the British minister took refuge in silence. The Queen had acted throughout the last desperate venture upon the advice of the Russians. On the other hand, he could not openly condemn Craig's withdrawal, however much he may have privately disapproved it. It is impossible to acquit this country of all responsibility for the entry of Naples into the war. Nor could Elliot have dissented from the Queen in holding that the occupation of any part of her husband's dominions by the British would destroy any chance of an accommodation with France. His part was a difficult one. To a man of his chivalrous nature the abandonment of the kingdom without our firing a shot must have appeared more or less disgraceful. He did not know when he received the Queen's letter of January 19 that her envoy, the Duke of San Teodoro, in an interview with Alquier in Rome had announced the readiness of his court to purchase peace with France by entering into an alliance against the British and by placing all the means of injuring them which the Two Sicilies afforded at the disposal of the Emperor.[1]

Napoleon knew their Sicilian Majesties better. His answer to their appeals and pourparlers was an order to his brother Joseph to advance upon Naples and make an end of the perfidious dynasty. Ferdinand fled, as he had fled in 1798, but this time without any effort on the part of his subjects to restrain him. The country, Elliot admits, was tired of the Bourbons. There were many in Naples whose fathers, sons, and husbands—and wives and mothers—had perished cruelly on the gallows at their hands. Amity with Britain certainly secured the people the supply of some commodities by sea; against this advantage had to be set the high-handed interference of the British with the coastal trade, the

[1] C. Auriol, vol. ii, p. 792 (Alquier to Talleyrand, January 16, 1806).

frequent seizures of Neapolitan vessels on the charge that they came from or were bound for ports held by French garrisons. The ruler whom the mighty Emperor was sending them was, after all, a sort of Italian—no more a foreigner than the Bourbon king and his Austrian wife.

That "Austrian hen," as her consort unlovingly called her, waited on till the invading army of Joseph Bonaparte had crossed the Garigliano. Then, without a godspeed from the Neapolitans, she set sail for Palermo. Never again did she look on the lovely city to which she had come as a bride thirty-eight years before. The passage was as stormy and painful as was that other, more than seven years earlier, when her boy Leopold had died in Lady Hamilton's arms. By the time she reached Sicily, not less than five days later (February 11), half the ships that had sailed with her had put back into Neapolitan ports, their masters gladly availing themselves of the foul wind as an excuse for surrendering to the conquerors.

Hugh Elliot, of course, accompanied the Queen in her flight. He had striven for the preservation of the Sicilian kingdom almost, as we have seen, to the detriment of Britain's interests; now he could apply himself wholeheartedly to the preservation for England of the Sicilian island. The first news that greeted him on landing was that Ferdinand, now restored to the influence of his old adviser Acton, had invited Craig to disembark his little army at Messina, off which port he had been lying since January 22. On February 17 the soldiers, heartily sick by now of their confinement on shipboard, took possession of the citadel. Their commander was ailing and about to return to England. The Neapolitan ministers, he complained to Elliot, had suspected him of the intention to land and take the citadel without the consent of the Government.

> It has seemed to me [went on the General] that you were under the same impression. How that has arisen I cannot tell. . . . I undoubtedly remember having mentioned in private conversation with you that circumstances might arise that would

make such a step necessary, and I may have enlarged a little on that subject, but certainly not with a view to leading you to suppose and still less to communicate to the court that such was my intention.

To this Elliot replied on February 28:

> Nothing can be more unjust than to suppose for a moment that I could have suggested to the Neapolitan government that it ever was your intention to take possession of the citadel of Messina by force of arms . . . although it was very evident that such an idea did prevail with some of the Neapolitan ministers.[1]

The idea was always present to their minds and to that of their mistress. There is no need to suppose that Elliot put it there, or that it was encouraged to any great extent by reports from other mouths than his of indiscreet talk in which Sir James Craig admits he indulged. In their haste to charge the ambassador with undue zeal for the interests of the court to which he was accredited, the General and his lieutenant Bunbury appear entirely to forget the solicitude he expressed for the security of Sicily when he first heard of the British force being destined for service on the mainland. During the brief remainder of his mission he ceased not to urge all possible measures for the defence of the island upon the court at Palermo and his own Government. Money must be sent to Acton to enable him to raise a local force and put the fortifications in order. He gave notice that he would draw on the Treasury for the needs of the Sicilian court to the extent of £25,000 a month. To guard against a surprise by the French a powerful British fleet must be maintained in those waters. He hoped that the naval command would be definitely entrusted to an officer not liable to supersession at any moment by the chance appearance on the scene of a senior in rank. Failing to secure for the British general the entire military command of the island, he secured him at least the command of the north-east corner, including Messina and Milazzo.

[1] F.O. 70/27. Public Record Office.

Stuart, who relieved Craig, landed in Calabria and signally defeated the French at Maida.

Meanwhile the Queen was quarrelling furiously with Acton. She had found, as she believed, another Nelson in Sir Sidney Smith, that erratic seaman who deluded her with hopes of an early reconquest of Naples. Sir Sidney made himself a nuisance to the commander of our land forces and insisted on communicating directly with the court. Elliot, in what he termed the hardest letter he had ever written, refused to finance the sailor's harebrained projects. His attitude was courageous, for he knew by now that he could expect little support from home. Pitt was dead, and Fox and Grenville governed England in his stead. The Marquis of Circello, a former Sicilian ambassador to London, having received a friendly letter from Grenville, the Queen delightedly took advantage of it to secure the dismissal of Acton and to appoint the Marquis in his place.

The sight of Fox's signature at the foot of a Foreign Office dispatch could have left no doubt in Elliot's mind that his days as an ambassador were numbered. As may be seen to this day by his summary of the year's events in the *Annual Register* for 1806, the Whig leader regarded the expedition to Naples as utterly stupid and ill-conceived. Elliot, as we know, thought not very differently, but he loyally defended his former chiefs. Writing on June 3, he held the British Cabinet guiltless of the harm done to Naples. The responsibility rested with the Russians, who had led the Neapolitans to expect a larger army than the Tsar could spare.

> I am now told [he said] that in virtue of a secret concert between the courts of London and Petersburg, the Neapolitan troops, in conjunction with those of the allied powers, were to have acted offensively against the French beyond the limits of the kingdom. . . . To this part of a general plan, as far as it regarded his Sicilian majesty, I must still plead ignorance.

Here it seems at first sight that the defendant is lying. But Lord Camden's orders to Craig of April 22, 1805, went no farther than directing the General to comply with any requisitions made by the Russians for the defence of the Neapolitan kingdom. In his own letter home the envoy treated the report that the allies were going to Ancona as a mere blind. It is very unlikely that Lacy's proposal to land in Northern Italy or the Archduke's appeal was ever communicated to him. His is a good answer. He is on still firmer ground when he calls Fox's attention to his careful and deliberate abstinence from any participation in the shameful business of the treaty repudiation. The Kingdom of Naples, he maintains, could and might have been defended.

At this moment—June 1806—Fox was making another bid for peace. His agent, Adair, found it necessary on June 18 to reassure Vienna that Britain had no idea of getting Ferdinand to exchange Sicily for some other principality.[1] Elliot's defence, therefore, was listened to by unsympathetic ears. On August 10 he received the expected letters of recall. Fox had decided to combine the offices of minister to the court of Palermo and commander-in-chief of the British forces in the person of his brother. "I should have been very happy to co-operate with Major-General Fox," says the dismissed diplomatist. He is in the thirty-fifth year of his service abroad, and probably the *doyen* of the European *corps diplomatique*. He hopes for further employment. Meanwhile he throws himself at his Majesty's feet and solicits his consideration for the oldest, one of the most faithful and zealous, and certainly the most needy of his servants abroad.

His last dispatch is dated from Malta on December 1, 1806. Though death so soon removed the unfriendly Fox, no fresh embassy was found for Hugh Elliot. But, as one not very well-informed biographer puts it, the brother of the powerful Earl of Minto could not be

[1] Sir Robert Adair, *Mission to the Court of Vienna* (1844), p. 15. On July 6 Oubril, the Tsar's ambassador, agreed to enforce the cession of Sicily to France in exchange for the Balearic Islands.

altogether neglected.[1] In 1809 he was sent as governor to the Leeward Islands. Far more than for his diplomatic victories he is entitled to honour as a staunch friend of the slaves. Severity is an unusual title to respect, but nothing in his whole career became him more than his refusing, in spite of threats and contumely, to pardon a white scoundrel named Hodges, who had murdered half a dozen slaves. In 1814 he returned to England and was immediately appointed Governor of Madras. This sign of ministerial approbation was accompanied by no higher honour than a Privy Councillorship.

> His government at Madras [writes Lady Minto] was unmarked by any events of conspicuous interest or at least by any in which he individually took a part; for the period of his government was that of the close of the Mahratta war. His private life, however, was brightened by the acquisition of many valued friends, some of whom bore names which, as those of Munro and Malcolm, will live in the history of India.

But these gains counted little against the loss of his wife, the pretty Margaret, in the last year of his term.

He came home in 1820, and died on December 2, 1830, aged seventy-eight. Burial in Westminster Abbey was a tardy expression of national gratitude. Hugh Elliot deserves well of his country and of humanity. An earldom was conferred on Malmesbury, whose one diplomatic success was the short-lived Treaty of Loo; a peerage was conferred on the irrelevant and ridiculous clergyman brother of the victor of Trafalgar. Elliot, who forced two warring kings to sheathe their swords, who kept the honour of England untarnished, yet staunchly upheld her interests, in that maelstrom of perfidy, the Neapolitan court, lived and died a commoner. No stars or garters came his way. That unfortunate matter of the Americans' dispatch-case at Berlin, his divorce, his indiscreet testimony to the new order of things in France—all these, no doubt, as has been hinted,

[1] *Dictionary of National Biography.*

tended to lower him in the esteem of his sovereign. But, these things set apart, the macaroni of the 1770's never became exactly like his fellows. His personality was decided and original. He made up his mind and acted in the right way, but an unusual way. And the incalculable is not a desirable element in one whose duty it is merely to voice the views of a far-away master.

II

From 1806 to 1815 the foreigner ruled over Naples, and Ferdinand of Bourbon reigned and sometimes ruled in the island of Sicily. Joseph Bonaparte in due time was promoted to the Spanish throne, and his sister's husband, Joachim Murat, became king of Naples in his stead. Pass the narrow seas he could not. Still the Union Jack fluttered over the citadel of Messina, and British cruisers forbade the passage of the Faro. Meanwhile at Palermo Circello held the seals of office, taking his orders from the Queen. Never could the woman divert her longing eyes from the mainland. She hated Sicily, where everything was otherwise than at Naples. There was an ancient Parliament without whose consent the sovereign could not get a soldo. Even the system of justice was different.

At least, her Majesty might have consoled herself, the constitution of the island was feudal and by no means democratic. The national assembly was composed of three estates, "without any particle of the elective franchise." The baronage was represented by 227 members against 104 representatives of the clergy and the towns. Nevertheless, all ranks were united in their hatred of the Neapolitans, and the constitution was looked on by the ministers of George III as a powerful check on the Queen's conspiracies with the enemy. In April 1809 her granddaughter, Marie-Louise, married Napoleon. She had made allies in another French camp by marrying her own daughter, Marie-Amélie, to the Duke of Orleans (afterwards Louis-Philippe). With such connexions, she could not have appeared to the English Government a trustworthy custodian of Sicily. Though we bound ourselves not to conclude peace without safeguarding her husband's rights, it suited us very well to keep the island under our thumb. As the years went by without our making any very strenuous efforts to unseat Murat, the Queen alternately cursed us for lukewarm allies and for usurpers of Sicily. The repugnance of the court of Palermo did not, however, extend to our money, which they pocketed to the extent of £400,000 sterling a year. Though only a part of this sum was actually expended on maintaining a force of 10,000 men and keeping the island in a state of defence, his Sicilian Majesty was soon at shifts for money, and tried, like our Charles I, to levy it without the consent of Parliament. There was reason to fear a conflict in which incalculable elements might rise to the surface, to the advantage of French-ruled Naples and the undoing of British policy in the Mediterranean.

A stronger man than Lord Amherst or his predecessors was needed to restrain the ageing but indomitable Maria Carolina. The Marquis Wellesley, who took over our Foreign Office in 1809, was no friend of despots. His choice fell on Lord William Henry Cavendish Bentinck, the second son of the third Duke of Portland. In the course of his thirty-seven years Bentinck had seen a great deal of warfare. He had served with the Duke of York in the Low Countries and with Sir John Moore in Spain. As Governor of Madras he failed to score a success, but the mildly Liberal sympathies he had manifested there and in Ireland, taken with an inflexible character, designated him, in succession to Amherst, as the champion of constitutional Sicily against an untrustworthy ally and would-be despot.

His instructions from the Marquis would have imposed firmness even on a weaker man. His attention was directed to the neglect by his Sicilian Majesty of the insular Parliament, to his imposition of vexatious taxes, especially on British merchants, and to his partiality for Neapolitan interests; also to the vexations caused by the persistence of feudal rights and privileges. A revolution was averted only by the presence of the British forces. The Queen suspected the British Government of a readiness to sacrifice the kingdom in order to make peace with France and of trying to foment a revolution. On Bentinck, as formerly on General Fox, was conferred the supreme command of our forces in the island. His mission was to strengthen British authority. He was to explain that it was never contemplated in 1806 to infringe the rights of King Ferdinand without his consent. The Government bound itself to secure the restitution of all his dominions, but the promise was conditional on his observance of Bentinck's counsels. The British Government had no idea of promoting a revolution. Discontent, it was to be pointed out, must be allayed by giving a share in the administration to native Sicilians. If this advice was followed every assistance would be rendered the Crown by British troops, but they were not to be used to oppress the people of Sicily. In addition, the new envoy was to arrange for the supply of corn to our Mediterranean fleet, and to see that the number of Sicilian troops was increased in proportion to the subsidy.[1]

The event proved that at Downing Street they were very well posted as to the situation in the Mediterranean kingdom. No sooner had the ship conveying the new ambassador cast anchor in the bay of Palermo, than Rear-Admiral Boyle, commanding the British naval forces on the station, came on board, accompanied by Douglas, the chief clerk of the legation, to inform him that three days before five of the leading barons had been deported by royal decree to the islands of Marittimo and Ustica in punishment of their opposition to the court. On July 25, 1811, Bentinck presented his credentials. His first talk with Circello satisfied him that the Sicilian

[1] F.O. 70/44. May 30, 1811. Public Record Office.

LORD WILLIAM CAVENDISH BENTINCK
From an engraving after a painting by Sir Thomas Lawrence

royalties had not forgotten or forgiven what they believed to have been Fox's willingness to abandon Ferdinand's claim to Naples in 1806. Nelson and Sir Sidney Smith were the only British officers in whom they had had confidence. It was precisely the news of Bentinck's appointment which had stimulated the barons in their resistance to the King's will. They had been abetted and countenanced by Viscount Valentia, "a person full of vanity and self-importance," who had very nearly shared their fate. From the first the Sicilian minister took a firm stand. He would not recognize the right of the British Government to interfere between King Ferdinand and his Parliament, and asked whether the British were going to help his Majesty recover Naples.

Substantially the same rejoinder was made to the written note, embodying his instructions, sent in by Bentinck a few days after this interview. The court, he perceived, was relying on an army of some 10,000 or 15,000 men, made up for the most part of deserters from Napoleon's foreign contingents and of Neapolitans. This force, his lordship did not fail to point out, could be of no use to his Sicilian Majesty or his ally. The men would go over to the enemy as soon as they set foot on the mainland. While notes were being exchanged a privateer carrying a British licence was seized by the Queen's orders and brought into Palermo. Our consul, Fagan, for protesting was suspended from his functions, although he was somewhat a favourite of her Majesty. The Sicilian court, wrote Lord William on August 3, can only be frightened into doing its duty. On the 14th he called on Circello and announced that he would return to England immediately in order to seek further instructions and wider powers. Alarm was painted on the Italian's face. He promised to restore Fagan's exequatur; but, backed probably by the Queen, he made no further concessions. A month after landing in the island the British envoy was on his way back to London.

Not improbably the Queen hoped that his return

would be taken by his Government as a confession of failure. Her relationship with the French Emperor and the apparent tightening of the French grip on Spain towards the middle of the winter, she would have reckoned, should make Britain chary of exasperating her nominal ally. We can thus imagine her Majesty's chagrin when Lord William reappeared at Palermo on December 7. Circello came running to his mistress. The subsidy had been stopped; part of it, upon the detested envoy's recommendation, was to be given to Sardinia. Ferdinand, skulking in his remote country seat at Ficuzza, twenty miles from his capital, of course declined to see the Englishman and delegated the duty to his wife. The Prince Regent, his lordship began, had no other object in view than the honour and independence of his Sicilian Majesty and his family. "How can you, as an honest man, make use of such language?" interrupted the Queen; for six years past it had been the settled policy of Britain to get possession of the country—the lively Fox had said so; Moore, who was a *jacobin enragé*, did not deny it; Drummond (*qui parle comme un fou*), Stuart, and Bentinck himself,[1] were all working to the same end. She had always seen it, and now her ministers had come round to her view.

Then, countered Bentinck, we have abstained from doing what we might have done at any time the past six years. "No," said the Queen, "that would have been too much like Bonaparte. You have tried to gain your end under the cover of forms, in order to save your reputation. When the Spaniards invited my son, Prince Leopold, to Spain Admiral Collingwood kept the letter in his pocket nine months under the pretence of having forgotten it, and when the Prince did go he was detained almost as a prisoner at Gibraltar. . . . Stuart had twenty thousand men at Ischia. The French had only three thousand men at Naples, but he would do nothing."

[1] Those named were all British ministers or officers employed at one time or another in Sicily.

To these not ill-founded reproaches Lord William returned no direct answer. He passed on to complain of the influence of the King's favourite, the Duke of Ascoli, and the exclusion of Sicilians from the Council. "I and Ascoli are not members of the Council," protested the angry woman. "It is composed of Butera, Cassaro, and Paessi, who are all Sicilians, of Circello (*qui est un bête*), Medici, and Arriolo, another fool, who is Minister for War. The difficulty is that so few Sicilians can read or write. Cassaro, for instance, has singular notions of geography. He would think it quite natural if he were told that the British fleet had anchored in the roads of Vienna. As to Prince Belmonte, I should like to see him in the administration; it is he who in this very room warned us long ago against the designs of the British." As to giving the command of the Sicilian army to Lord William, as she understood he demanded, to that she would never consent. Why did he require the repatriation of the barons? Was he supporting rebels?

Her Majesty's tone became warmer as the altercation proceeded. Furiously she denied ever having had any correspondence with that *coquin*, Napoleon, or with his Empress. Of course, she had occasionally been in communication with Naples. She was sick of the whole thing. She would leave Sicily to go back to Germany. She did not propose to beg her bread in England or Italy. The King could do as he pleased. He had thoughts of abdicating in favour of his son. His lordship expressed the hope that the Queen would give him no such advice. The Queen scoffed at the British Government's assurances of friendship, and declared that she had positive proof of their schemes to raise a rebellion. Bentinck, at an end of reasoning, took his leave with the warning that the subsidy would not be resumed unless the conditions contained in his instructions were complied with.

"With exceeding good abilities," wrote the envoy, "the Queen probably never had any common sense. Enfeebled by age, she had been brought to the verge of insanity by the operation of violent passions and by consuming vast quantities of opium." Fagan, the painter-consul, succeeded hardly any better with her. The English, she knew, were preparing to send her in a ship of war to England, to murder her *en route* or to lock her up in the Tower. She would like to see Bonaparte dead at her feet, but she hated the English still more. The Sicilians were ready to massacre them. "Fagan," she said, "if your Government wishes to get rid of me, why don't they have me poisoned or stabbed?" This display of temper Bentinck attributes to the false report that we had landed another 3000 troops on the island.

That the Queen had been in correspondence with Murat, the usurper of her husband's throne, was positively affirmed by General Goldemar, an officer sent by that prince to discuss an exchange of prisoners with Donkin, Bentinck's Quartermaster-General. "She lies when she contradicts it," shouted the veteran; "*la vilaine menteuse, la fière putain!*"[1] At the end of December Bentinck was put in possession of the details of the method of communication adopted by her Majesty. Packets of letters in the hand of Circello's secretary were frequently sent from Palermo to Ustica, thence to Pantellaria, and thence to the Continent. The boat from Palermo generally conveyed an officer attached to Castrone, the Sicilian Minister of Police. There was often a priest on board. The letters were addressed to Gallo and Lusciano. Roquet, a French officer, had stayed twelve days in the Marquis Saint-Clair's house at Palermo. Later on came another French officer, who was lodged with the Cavaliere Brisach, another *émigré*. There were continual secret conferences between him and the Queen and Circello. Castrone carried on a constant correspondence with Murat's ministers. More serious were the efforts to tamper with the foreign troops forming part of the British garrison. A spy named Jacobi, arrested on this charge, implicated two Austrian officers and told a confused

[1] F.O. 79/51. February 25, 1812. Public Record Office.

story of a plot to place the Archduke Charles on the throne of Sicily in exchange for Naples, which was to be given by France to old Ferdinand. Jacobi said he was moved to take part in this conspiracy by musing upon the prophecies of Sant' Eustachia, according to which a German king named Carlo Berry (!) would one day rule over Sicily. One man was actually hanged for corresponding with the enemy. At his trial, so Bentinck alleged, the judge abstracted the papers incriminating the Queen.[1]

Manifestly the court of Sicily, an independent sovereign state, was within its legal rights in entering into negotiations with any other Powers. But while those rights were no more respected in 1811 than were the rights of Belgium and Greece little more than a century later, Britain had an obvious right to dictate the conditions under which she would resume payment of the subsidy to her disloyal ally. These, as the Queen knew, were, first, the admission of Sicilians to the administration; second, the handing over of the command of all the troops in the island to the British commander-in-chief; third, the recall of the exiled barons; fourth, the exclusion from any share in the government of persons suspected of anti-British tendencies. The first and second points were conceded by Circello, if only in principle. The King, he said, had withdrawn from any participation in affairs and sent back his letters unopened. His Majesty was understood to have said that those who had made the pie could jolly well eat it. Whether he had in fact abdicated Bentinck was unable to find out. The Italian was asked, if he was sincere in deciding to form a Cabinet acceptable to Britain, to furnish the names of the proposed members. The British naval commander became impatient. He entreated the ambassador to take immediate action. At any moment now the French

---

[1] Bentinck's Diary (existing in manuscript at Welbeck Abbey), cited in "Mémoire de la Reine Marie Caroline," by R. M. Johnston, *Harvard Historical Studies*, vol. xvi.

squadron might come out from Toulon. In view of such a contingency, his Royal Highness of Orleans also came out—on the side of the British. Pressed hard, Circello named two Sicilian barons, Butera and Cassaro, to be joined with him and four others in the Government. It was obvious, wrote Bentinck, that the Queen was seeking to cajole him into acquiescing in an arrangement which would leave everything the same as before. Circello, of course, was himself unacceptable, but, not caring to tell him so, the diplomatist advised him to confer with Cassaro. The Marquis agreed to do this, and next day reported that his list met with Cassaro's approval. Unfortunately for the Prime Minister, Bentinck had seen Cassaro and knew that, so far from approving the names submitted, he had spoken unfavourably of nearly all. Annoyed at being found out, the Marquis stiffened, and on January 9, 1812, announced the formation of the ministry as objected to, with the single addition of one, Gargello, a creature of the Queen's.

Lord William's answer was an order to the British garrison at Milazzo to embark at once for Palermo.

This threat brought the Hereditary Prince Francis upon the scene. In an audience with Bentinck on January 10 his Highness intimated his dissatisfaction at what had been done, but alas! he was limited in his own course of action by the profound respect he owed to his father. Nor would he admit that his mother's distrust of the British was unjustified. This brought up the demand for the reconquest of Naples. Bentinck's answer proves him to have been a statesman as well as a diplomatist. Murat was more popular than the sovereign he had dispossessed. The only way of driving the French from Italy (not merely from Naples, it should be observed) was by holding out liberty and a constitution to the nation; the recovery of Naples must be achieved by a regard for the rights and happiness of the Sicilian people. This must have sounded strange doctrine in the ears of a Bourbon prince. Whatever repugnance he felt, he succeeded for a moment in hiding from the Englishman who preferred to see him in the place of his father.

Upon his promise to see the old King Bentinck countermanded the order for the troops to march. Maria Carolina's anger flamed up anew. She reproached her son for his disloyalty; she spread abroad a rumour that the British intended to change the religion of the country by force. Sending for Lord William, at last she pretended to seek his advice. She did not wish her husband to abdicate. At this point she became very violent. The English, she knew, were seeking to dethrone King Ferdinand and his family. It was true she had thought of selling Sicily—not to France but to Britain. Now the King could save his honour only by putting himself at the head of his army in a last effort to reconquer Naples. He could at least die, like Tippoo Sahib, in the breach. The idea of old "Nosey" pitting himself against Murat struck the Englishman as so absurd that he asked the Queen if she was serious. "Yes," she replied, holding up her hand. "*Je vous le jure!*" She asked the minister to express his disapproval in writing. Since he declined to do this, she wrote down herself, "Lord William Bentinck declares that he does not object to the expedition to Naples. It must depend upon the Admiral to give convoy." "This," she said, "will leave you in complete possession of Sicily, which you will not dislike."

Ferdinand, all this time, was by no means deaf to what was passing outside the walls of his hunting-lodge. His detested wife was going too far. His Majesty feared the French more than he did the devil. If he resisted the demands of the English they might withdraw from the island, and the very next day Murat would land. By a decree dated January 16, 1812, he conceded certain of the imperious envoy's demands. The Hereditary Prince was designated Vicar-General and his Majesty's *alter ego*, his powers being limited by the important reservation that no engagements with foreign Powers should be entered into without the King's consent. Lord William was appointed Captain-General of all the forces in Sicily, and the five barons, it was announced, were at liberty to return to the island. One is moved to smile on learning that the ambassador declined a seat on the Council on the ground that it was contrary to the policy of the British Government to interfere in the domestic affairs of their allies. The Duke of Ascoli, regarded by him as the sovereign's evil genius, was honourably relieved of his commands and sailed for Cagliari, accompanied by his politically minded mistress, Donna Flavia. Belmonte and Villa Hermosa, two of the barons, were met outside Palermo by a large concourse of lords and commoners and escorted back to the capital. The hurrahs of the crowd might have been heard by Maria Carolina, quivering with rage in her palace. Castrone, the Chief of Police, notorious for his anti-British activities, was dismissed, and fifteen of his minions were arraigned before a military commission at Messina for conspiring to attack the British garrison and seize the forts.

For a short while all went well. The Hereditary Prince made a great show of devotion to his father's allies and of friendship for Bentinck. His Royal Highness would be glad to see the English troops in the neighbourhood of Palermo. Loyally Bentinck resumed the monthly payment of the subsidy. Thus encouraged, the Prince once more mooted the question of the recovery of Naples. By now the pettiness of his actual mission was apparent to the man who had governed Madras and was one day to govern India. The restoration of the Bourbon brood was an act of treason to humanity. Insisting that the time was not ripe for a descent upon the mainland, Bentinck continued (January 27):

> I should feel myself authorized to afford the utmost assistance of the British troops to any endeavour of the whole Italian people. . . . To recover Italy from the French must be the first and only object. To require this or that form of government, to parcel out the country beforehand into separate governments

would have the appearance of conquest rather than of assistance to a great nation to its independence.

If the Italian people did succeed in driving out the French they would be too strong to accept dictation. "Speaking for myself alone I could only pledge myself to use my best endeavours to drive the French out of Italy. I cannot undertake *to force* the Neapolitans to receive their former government," but would use every other means in favour of the Bourbon family.

> Sicily can contribute most powerfully to the conquest of Italy not by arms but by the example of its happiness. The Italians are an intelligent people. They have long desired a constitution which should give them national liberty. . . . If by the desire of the Prince, a constitution is given to Sicily, which shall assure a moderate and reasonable freedom to its people and shall promote its happiness and prosperity, I shall consider the conquest of Italy and the restoration of Italy as half achieved. All eyes on the Continent will be turned to Sicily as the model of their happiness and security, and possibly not only Naples but many of the surrounding states may desire the blessings of the same chief and the same government.[1]

And *possibly*, Bentinck may have thought, even Francis de Bourbon might develop into a blessing if subjected to a rigorous constitutional discipline. But, writing on March 16, he admits that he is very sadly disappointed in the Prince. The convocation of Parliament, the formation of a satisfactory ministry, were adjourned from week to week. Though never a favourite of his mother, Francis remained completely under her influence. When Bentinck wrote to the Queen charging her with corresponding with the enemy, and suggesting that it would be prudent for her to withdraw from Palermo before her proceedings became the subject of further discussion and irritation, the Prince challenged the ambassador to produce the proofs of her treachery. He was referred to the testimony of various persons arrested and examined by the British and Sicilian authorities. One, Cassetti,

[1] F.O. 70/51. Public Record Office.

said he had been employed to negotiate with Murat, who had suggested the Ionian Islands as compensation for Sicily. The Queen rejected the offer, saying she would prefer the Low Countries. The same agent had been entrusted with a letter to the Empress of the French. Our envoy, though he spent over £58,000 in espionage in the year 1812 alone, was unable, it must be confessed, to produce evidence which would have weighed in a British court of law. In his presence the Prince opened an intercepted letter from his mother to a person in Naples. It contained nothing criminal. A new ministry composed of Belmonte, Villa Hermosa, Cassaro, and Aci, all men acceptable to Lord William, was formed, but his Highness, with a firmness for which one likes him, flatly refused to be a party to any persecution of his mother.

Thus rebuffed by the son, the implacable Englishman turned to the husband. The old man, he was told, had himself ordered the Queen to go. "Andate via, andate via," he repeated wearily. He had been married forty-four years, and every year had been a year of martyrdom. Despairing of otherwise piercing the cordon by which the monarch was encircled, Bentinck entrusted his letter to Fra Caccamo, the royal confessor. The next day the letter was shown by the Queen herself to Fagan. Another monk, whom Bentinck had employed to convey his letters to the confessor, refused in future to undertake such commissions; upon which the Englishman lost his temper and, contrary to law and fairness, compelled the Prince to banish him to the Liparis. The royal family, his lordship reminded Saint-Clair, stood little chance of getting an increase of revenue from the Parliament unless her Majesty withdrew to the interior of the island. To this threat the lady replied in those dignified terms which seldom conformed to her behaviour.

> If Lord William imagined that such sordid considerations would induce her to submit to a vile slander, he was mistaken. She was prepared to suffer violence. . . . Lord William Bentinck should be at last convinced that the daughter of Maria Theresa

may be oppressed and calumniated but never dishonoured. He could address his letter to the King if such a step suited his delicacy.

It may have been that Lord William recoiled before the thrust. Reporting a woman to her husband and ordering him to separate from her is a proceeding from which the chivalrous would shrink. Bentinck himself was aware "how soon compassion takes the place of hatred in the public mind," and that "pushing things to an extremity would have an appearance of cruelty." He knew also that the King had sent Prince Medici to London to protest against the attitude of his Britannic Majesty's representative. But we can believe him when he says it was mainly because he fancied the Prince Vicar was capable of adopting an independent line that for the moment he held his hand. Parliament had been summoned. Both the King and the Prince dreaded the introduction of a new constitution. There had been some talk of proposing one on the new-fangled Spanish model. In his alarm Prince Francis sought to throw the responsibility on the British ambassador. "The sole merit of deciding on a new constitution belongs to your highness," was the dry reply. Finally, when the speech from the throne was drafted, the states were recommended to adopt the Constitution of Britain if that of Sicily proved unsuited to the needs of the times. In a letter to Castlereagh, who had succeeded Wellesley at the Foreign Office, Lord William professed to approve the alternative, on the ground that the two constitutions were the work, as he erroneously supposed, of the Normans. To Belmonte, however, he said frankly that no one had ever been able to understand or define the British Constitution. A subtler mind than the Bourbon's should have welcomed it on that account; but when it was adopted, in principle and with certain important modifications, by the Parliament of Sicily on July 20, 1812, the old man vowed he never would sanction it, chiefly because it cut down his civil list.

Bentinck was sent for to Ficuzza. No doubt he read with interest, and perhaps amusement, the Queen's account of his behaviour at the audience which she communicated to Fagan and which the consul loyally passed on to his chief.

> He continued mute as a stone. At last, I said I had a right to expect he would converse with me on friendly terms. He then loosed his tongue and in the most bitter manner, with a sarcastic smile, he assured me that he had never expected and certainly never wished either to see me or converse with me, and this he urged with a tone and manner which was not customary even between equals before the general revolution of Europe.

Before the terrible envoy the King gave way. His son was allowed to sanction twelve out of the fifteen articles voted by the Parliament. Maria Carolina in her chagrin cried out for a frigate to be got ready to convey her to the nearest port to Austria. The Englishman did not suffer her to forget that demand.

Assured by now of the full support of the Prince Regent and of Castlereagh, he redoubled his pressure on the miserable court. Fagan, whom the Queen perhaps trusted because he was a Roman Catholic, listened to all her confidences and betrayed them to his superior. The day the treaty was signed he warned Bentinck that the King and Queen were coming back to Palermo and might attempt something desperate. By a new military convention 7000 Sicilian troops were placed at the disposal of the British, to be employed if necessary in Spain, and Britain renewed her previous pledges to the dispossessed monarch of Naples. Ferdinand not unnaturally objected to the employment of his soldiers in a foreign country. The Queen has been at him, thought Bentinck, and he sent Captain Milner to Ficuzza to inquire of the King when her Majesty proposed to carry out her intention of leaving the country. Ferdinand was at dinner. He refused to see the messenger. On the following day he requested Lord William, through the mouth of Cassaro, not to send him any more impertinent messages. The Queen declared that Bonaparte was a *joli enfant doux* in comparison with his Britannic Majesty's minister.

This brought his lordship once again to the door of their frightened Majesties' retreat. He was at first denied admission, and then kept waiting in an antechamber. He saw the Queen go into her husband's room. She offered to receive him. He had nothing to say to her, he answered, and if the King did not receive him he would certainly resort to extreme measures. He would await the King's decision in the village inn. On the morrow Circello and Cassaro presented themselves and showed him, scanning his face anxiously, the draft of a letter which they promised their master would sign. "The Queen," read the ambassador, "is determined to pass the winter at Santa Margherita until the spring when she intends to set out for Vienna, there to remain so long as the state of her health requires."

With this intimation Bentinck had to be content. If we are to believe Maria Carolina he dashed into the stable, saddled his own mare, and rode away, his mouth full of imprecations and the most terrible threats. As he had not been offered even a glass of water at Ficuzza he was compelled to stop at a wretched village tavern, to munch some black bread and drink some glasses of wine; on reaching Palermo his mare fell dead on passing his gates, "such had been the strain which in his fury he had put upon her." And such was precisely the story which a Sicilian lackey would certainly have had ready on such an occasion to gratify an enraged and mortified mistress.[1]

The place selected by the Sicilian royalties for their retirement lies not very far from Palermo, in the valley of the Belice, on the south-western slope of the island.

---

[1] "Mémoire de la Reine Marie Caroline," *Harvard Historical Studies*, vol. xvi, p. 160. The memoir is undoubtedly the work of the Queen herself, and, brilliantly edited by Professor R. M. Johnston, is a valuable source of information.

Their ears, as the year 1812 wore away, were gladdened by reports of acrid dissensions between the detested Autocrat and the ministers who owed him their appointment. To Sicilian nobles the domineering foreigner's conception of efficiency and plain-dealing was incomprehensible. They forgot all too soon that by his timely aid he had saved the State from a welsher's bankruptcy when the odds in the national lottery turned surprisingly against them; they forgot that he purchased the freedom of 400 Sicilian slaves from the Barbary corsairs, and that his wife, the daughter of the first Earl of Gosford, went in Admiral Fremantle's ship to bring them back. Maria Carolina sneered at Lady William's efforts to win the people's regard and ignored her ladyship's invitation to a garden-party, although she grudgingly admitted that she was not altogether without talents or manner. At Christmas Bentinck was startled by the arrival of the old King at La Favorita, in the immediate neighbourhood of Palermo. "I never thought he would dare to come," exclaimed the ambassador. "If the King resumes the government," he warned Cassaro, "I am determined to *enlever* the Queen." The Sicilian doubted whether his Excellency had authority to go so far. "I give you my word," came the stern assurance, "that I shall do what I have said. We shall only have peace in this kingdom when she has quitted it."[1] Upon this being repeated to her Majesty she exclaimed, "Bonaparte never went so far as to force a husband to separate from his wife!"

There could be no doubt as to Ferdinand's intentions. He proposed to brush aside his feeble son and regent and to put an end to all projects of constitutional reform. For some weeks he dallied, sounding the sentiments of his ministers, while his agents went about striving to rouse the masses in his favour. On March 9, 1813, he set out for his palace in the city, where the Cabinet had been summoned to meet him. The Prince was ill. There were rumours, started it would be unsafe to say by whom,

[1] Bentinck's diary, cited by R. M. Johnston, *op. cit.*, pp. 199–200.

that he had been poisoned by his mother. "I determined," writes Bentinck in his journal, "to go personally to the King and see if I could frighten him." This time he was admitted to an audience. Ferdinand was informed that the Prince Regent of Britain would not permit the constitution to be destroyed. The King took fire at the word "permit." "Permit, permit!" he repeated. "England has no right to interfere." "I am a plain man," said Bentinck as the altercation developed. "I am a plainer man than you, and more honest," retorted outraged Majesty. The diplomatist bowed. Ferdinand corrected himself by adding, "You may also be honest." Finally he refused to listen any longer to his taskmaster and asked him to say what he had to say in writing. On his return to the legation the ambassador was told that the people were shouting, "Viva il Re!" and that shouts of "Down with England!" had also been heard.

Next day the monarch's reappearance was celebrated by a *Te Deum* at the church of St Francis. Ferdinand stayed at the palace. He was roused from a nap by the Governor of Palermo with the news that the British were under arms and awaiting the command to enter the city. Bentinck declared that he was prepared to set aside the King by force and nominate a council to govern the kingdom till Parliament could be assembled. He would regard the alliance as at an end if all necessary guarantees for the security of the constitution were not at once given. The time-serving Duke of Orleans went to and from the palace and the legation, working on the fears of his wife's father. Belmonte and his fellow-ministers appointed by the Prince Vicar resigned, and without their counter-signatures the King's letters were refused consideration by the ambassador. In this extremity Ferdinand sent word to Fagan that he would appoint Bentinck his Chancellor for life, if he would seat him on the throne again. Without his wife to support him the old man gave way. He left the city and shut himself up at La Favorita. Bentinck sent some troops to frighten him, but quickly recalled them, out of respect, perhaps, to the protests of Lord Mahon and other British visitors. "I was fully prepared to have made the King a prisoner," writes Lord William in his diary. This extreme measure his lordship would have been at pains to justify. The King had not abdicated, and was legally and morally entitled to resume the powers which he had in vague terms lent to his son. Happily, perhaps, for both parties, the Augustinian friar Caccamo now intervened. The ambassador came to the palace. The King met him and said, "I promise not to interfere with the government of my son. I promise not to remove from here, and if you like it you may place sentries at the gates." His lordship assured him he was not the spiteful person he was represented to be. The King took his hand, and said he felt sure of him. He hoped he would guarantee his personal security. Bentinck said he would. The authority given to the Hereditary Prince was not to be revoked without the consent of England. The rest of the day the old monarch paced his room, muttering, "Sanctus Deus, sanctus fortis, sanctus et immortalis, miserere mei, fiat voluntas tua." [1]

The Queen had returned to Ficuzza on March 8, hoping to be recalled to the capital. Hearing that all was lost, she retreated, crying out upon her husband's weakness, first to Santa Margherita, then somewhat farther still to Castelvetrano, on the other side of the mountains. With the King virtually his prisoner, Bentinck hastened to get rid of the mainspring of the opposition. He had heard, he wrote to Ferdinand's henchman, the Duke of Sangro, that her Majesty proposed to cross the island in order to embark at Syracuse. Since so lengthy a progress might be the occasion of disturbances, he preferred that the embarkation should take place at the port nearest to her Majesty's actual retreat. On March 25 General Macfarlane waited upon the Queen to announce that he was the forerunner of a small British

---

[1] Fagan to Bentinck (April 8, 1813); quoted by Johnston, *op. cit.*

column which would escort her to the coast. But her Majesty was not to be got rid of quite so cheaply. She had no money. By a stretch of his authority Bentinck pledged his Government to pay her debts and guaranteed her an annual pension of 12,000 Sicilian *ounces*, to be paid in advance. She pleaded illness, she produced medical certificates. Bentinck sent the British Inspector of Hospitals to examine her, and he reported that her health was more likely to be benefited than impaired by a sea voyage. On May 24 the ambassador ordered Macfarlane to put her on board so long as this could be done without endangering her life, in which eventuality she was to be kept encircled by a close cordon of troops. In desperation the Queen appealed to Murat. If he would send 6000 men to Sicily she could raise another 6000, and they could drive out the English.

Unluckily for her, the French King of Naples, upon his return from the snows of Russia, had decided to save his crown by negotiating with the British and Austrians. He threw Maria Carolina's messenger into prison and revealed her proposal to Bentinck.[1] By that time her Majesty was at last on the water. She arrived at Mazzara, where two British frigates awaited her. In vain she complained of a severe toothache and demanded a day's grace for the attendance of the dentist. Captain Duncan took out his watch and allowed her thirty minutes in which to embark. So, on June 14, 1813, the Queen of the Two Sicilies sailed away for ever from the kingdom to which she had come as a bride forty-five years before. Her husband, who had never loved her, grunted with satisfaction on hearing she was gone. Her eldest son came not to bid her farewell. One is glad to know that she was accompanied on this, her last, long journey by her best-loved son, Leopold. Changing ship at Zante and Constantinople and Odessa, and subjected to long delays at each of those ports, the Habsburg

[1] Letter from Robert Jones to Bentinck (June 22, 1813); F.O. 70/57. Public Record Office.

princess at length reached the home of her ancestors on February 2, 1814. The sun of her arch-enemy, Napoleon, was setting, but her own nephew, the Emperor, was conniving at the settlement of her husband's crown on Murat. The part of Maria Carolina was played. She died on September 7 at Hetzendorf, near Vienna, at the age of sixty-two, four months before that Emma Hamilton who had so much loved her.

III

In a dispatch to Lord Castlereagh dated May 19, 1813, Bentinck announced the approaching departure of the pestilent Queen. On the following day he wrote apprising the Foreign Secretary of the beginning of a negotiation with Murat. Napoleon, driven out of Russia, was rallying his forces. His ruin, which posterity regards as by that catastrophe accomplished, appeared by no means complete or irretrievable to his contemporaries. Bentinck himself believed that the Emperor's genius would restore his fortunes. Francis of Austria hesitated whether to forsake his son-in-law. But Murat, who had with his own eyes seen the Grand Army perish beneath the Russian snows, asked himself whether the time had not come to emancipate himself and his kingdom from the galling yoke of the man who had made him a king. He hastened back to Naples, to read the censure publicly inflicted on him by his terrible brother-in-law and to endure the reproaches of his wife.

In the month of February Bentinck had sent a small British force commanded by Lieutenant-Colonel Coffin to occupy the islands of Ponza, a few leagues from the Neapolitan fortress of Gaeta and not much farther from the capital itself. At this point it was easy to keep in touch with the mainland. The Russians reached the Vistula on January 22, but the Italians showed no impatience to rise against the kings and viceroys set over them by Napoleon or to recall the old brood of Bourbons and Habsburgs.

Even when, at the beginning of May, a man named Giuseppe Palombo approached Coffin with proposals for a rising at Naples, he declared he was willing to bring the kingdom in subjection either to its legitimate sovereign or to the British Government. The commandant suspected a trap, set possibly by Maria Carolina. He discouraged any premature attempts which might result in a useless effusion of blood, adding that Great Britain cherished no schemes for her own aggrandisement, and that while her good ally King Ferdinand showed himself desirous of promoting the happiness of his people, as he had done by the acceptance of the new constitution, she could wish for nothing better than to see him re-established in the Kingdom of Naples.

Despite this assurance, Coffin, like his commander, was fully alive to the advantage to Britain and her allies of detaching the French King of Naples from his master's cause and inducing him, if possible, to stab that master in the back. He had made a number of prisoners in capturing the islands. One of these, a Frenchman named Bosset, he allowed to return to Naples. Taking him aside on the moment of his embarkation, Coffin remarked that the English would be happy to come to some understanding with Murat, who was a brave man and a good soldier. He hoped he might be made the channel of a communication. Bosset replied that nothing could be more agreeable to King Joachim than such a proposition, and he would certainly enter into some commercial arrangements with Britain if this could be done without the knowledge of the Emperor.

This overture resulted in the appearance at Ponza of Don Giuseppe Cerulli, an official in the Neapolitan Ministry of Police. He was charged, he said, to open up a method of commercial intercourse with Sicily. Told by Coffin that he would be given an opportunity of discussing this with a leading British merchant of the island, he disclosed the real purpose of his visit. There was bad blood between Napoleon and Murat. An alliance between Britain and Naples was hinted at. The English must, however, understand that King Joachim would lay down his life for his kingdom, and that, though Cerulli's countrymen admired the British, they would never hear of the restoration of the Bourbons.

These negotiations were communicated by Coffin to his superior at Palermo. His lordship told the Hereditary Prince that the usurper was willing to treat, but that he would certainly not give up the kingdom of which he was in actual possession. To Coffin he wrote approving the negotiations. In another private dispatch he reminded him that their official correspondence must be shown to his Highness. He doubted Murat's sincerity. The French King was not threatened by the disaffection of his army or his people.

> The finest part for Murat to play [went on Lord William] would be that of champion of the trampled liberties of the world —to place the lawful sovereign upon the throne—to establish a constitution (and upon the negotiator, if a Neapolitan, liberty and the example of Sicily should be strongly enforced) and retaining his command of the Neapolitan army, to unite with us for the liberation of Italy and France itself. . . . If one could depend on him, our mutual interests might be reconciled. Whatever plan might be agreed upon, the cession of Gaeta to us should be the pledge of his sincerity and of our security.[1]

The idea at the back of the Englishman's mind was disclosed to the Hereditary Prince in writing. Murat should resign the Kingdom of Naples to Ferdinand on condition that he should receive an equivalent and that he should keep Naples till he received that equivalent. To this the Prince replied that he would never renounce his rights to the Kingdom of Naples or to a proportionate compensation (May 18, 1813). Bentinck did not stay to elucidate this ambiguous answer, which appears to have been framed in order to keep open the negotiations. Our ambassador was thirsting for military glory and

[1] F.O. 70/58. Public Record Office.

embarked for Spain with a mixed force of British and Sicilians. The ship in which he sailed arrived off Ponza in the night of June 2. On the island he found a Mr Robert Jones, an English merchant long resident at Naples, and one Nicolas, who brought with him an authority from Murat's minister, the Duke of Campo Chiaro, to treat with the British ambassador. Nicolas had been secretary to Acton under the old *régime*, and now held a nominal appointment in connexion with the fine arts.

Bentinck landed on the 3rd, and had a very long interview with these delegates. He made an unpromising beginning by intimating that he was not furnished with powers actually to treat with the existing Government of Naples, and that the whole subject was one of extreme delicacy in view of our friendly relations with King Ferdinand. A deadlock presently resulted on an approach to the claims of the two kings. Lord William asked for a few hours for reflection. Before retiring he was reminded by Nicolas that King Joachim could attack Eugène Beauharnais, Napoleon's viceroy in Northern Italy, with an army of 40,000 men, and if provided with English muskets could raise another 10,000. Bentinck thought this force inadequate to exercise a decisive influence. Resuming the discussions, he put in as a basis for further negotiation the propositions already laid before the Hereditary Prince. This the delegates accepted and departed for Naples. Since Murat had proclaimed his attachment to the kingdom over which he reigned, he could hardly have announced his readiness to exchange it for some other dominion unspecified. It is not surprising, therefore, that the delegates came back two days later to announce that they could proceed no farther at the moment, on the ground that Lord William had not full powers and that the attitude of Austria was still doubtful. King Joachim in the meantime had refused to send 20,000 Neapolitans to co-operate with the French fleet at Toulon. It was a pity, said his lordship; precisely because the outlook was doubtful he would have taken it upon himself to sign a military convention with Murat there and then. The turn of events might not dispose him again to such favourable terms. He re-embarked and sailed away to Spain, leaving Coffin with full powers to resume the negotiations. Murat, he thought, had counted upon our being thoroughly disgusted with the bad faith of the Bourbons. Robert Jones, writing to his Excellency on June 22, bore out this suspicion by expressing the hope that consideration for an undeserving royal house should not be allowed to stand in the way of a settlement.

The news from Sicily which reached him in Spain should have shaken Bentinck's faith alike in constitutions and constitutional sovereigns. The quick-witted Sicilians were not long in perceiving the opportunities for obstruction and factious opposition which their constitution, modelled on the British, afforded. The partisans of absolutism vied with extreme radicals, such as Emmanuele Rossi, in making government impossible. The constitutional ministry was driven to adopt unconstitutional methods. Parliament was illegally prorogued while Lord Montgomery, left in charge by Bentinck, cleared the streets of Palermo of rioters. Lord William, who was defeated by Suchet at the pass of Ordal, determined to return to Sicily, in spite of the Duke of Wellington's well-known dispatch that he conceived the island to be in no danger whatever. It was certainly in danger from its own people. The King's party, profiting by the new liberty of the Press, assailed the British in a score of gazettes and broadsheets. The Government was charged with having introduced the plague from Malta. On October 31 Bentinck issued a threatening proclamation. The authors of the slanders were prosecuted and thrown into prison. The Sicilians evidently knew not how to enjoy political liberty. Old Ferdinand looked on derisively, and waited for his hour.

The imperious Captain-General seems about this time to have despaired of his experiment. Possibly it had become clear to him that English institutions could only be worked by English rulers. In a note to the Hereditary Prince (December 4) he predicted that the reunion of the two halves of his father's realm could only be accomplished at the cost of much blood. The island, he continued, had never been of much advantage to Naples. It would be well if the King could be persuaded to hand Sicily over to Britain. Territorial compensation might perhaps be found for him on the mainland, and, failing that, Britain would engage to double his civil list and to go to his support on any occasion with a powerful army. In this astonishing proposal his Highness must have perceived confirmation of his mother's reiterated suspicions. Hotly he rejected the suggestion. Bentinck shrugged his shoulders. His Highness was not to take the note as official—it reflected simply the dreams of a traveller, a mere philosophical idea. But the Prince not unnaturally took alarm. His ambassador in London brought the matter to the notice of Castlereagh, observing that if Lord William was prone to dreams of this kind he was not a fit person to be accredited to the court of the Two Sicilies.[1]

By that time Bentinck appears to have banished the idea from his mind. Napoleon's new successes in Saxony, and his reappearance so soon after the Russian disaster at the head of another powerful army disposed the courts of London and Vienna to welcome assistance from any quarter. Metternich turned a willing ear to Murat's offers. The Earl of Aberdeen, our representative at Vienna, was instructed to support the Austrian Chancellor. While in Spain Lord William was accordingly ordered by Castlereagh to conclude a convention with the King of Naples on the basis which he had discussed with the Hereditary Prince. In his reply, dated December 26, 1813, the ambassador hardly concealed his disgust.

[1] Weil, *Prince Eugène et Murat*, vol. iii, p. 181.

In this letter, Naples is left to Murat,[1] he being required to find for the King of Sicily an equivalent. Your lordship directed me to ascertain the disposition of the family to such an arrangement. But as Murat, who was then with the main army of Napoleon, had made no reply to my previous propositions, and seemed to have taken a decided part, I refrained from renewing with the Hereditary Prince a discussion which was unnecessary and not likely to be well received.

Stung by the reproaches of his high-spirited wife, Caroline Bonaparte, Murat had, in fact, returned to his old allegiance. But when the eagles were again overborne at Leipzig he hurried back to Naples, cursing his quixotism and wondering how to excuse it to the victors. Resuming the negotiations interrupted at Ponza, he sent the Cavaliere Schinina to sound Bentinck. His lordship received this new emissary at Syracuse. If King Joachim had placed himself again at his master's side, said the Neapolitan, it had been only at his wife's entreaty. Did he fight at Leipzig? inquired the English general. The Cavaliere replied that he did not know. His lordship was asked to look at a note which confirmed King Joachim in possession of his kingdom on condition that he joined the Allies. Bentinck observed that it was dated October 7 and had not been accepted prior to the battle. Murat's situation, he said, appeared to him desperate, and he could not see he had any claim on the allied Powers. Therefore he (Bentinck) would be no party to a convention which gave up the rights of the legitimate sovereign. On December 14 Schinina returned to Naples without having secured a suspension of hostilities—which were not, indeed, very active. General Manhès, who had been sent by the Neapolitan Government to confer with Sir Robert Hall, Bentinck's representative, on the beach opposite Messina, had no more success. To his lordship's contemptuous message that he regarded the fate of Italy as settled, and that it mattered little which

[1] In accordance with Castlereagh's instructions to Aberdeen, dated August 6, 1813.

side Murat espoused, the Frenchman hotly replied that when a man of his master's stamp put a crown on his head the crown and the head must fall together. The pronouncement was prophetic.

As he had been of the opinion, said our ambassador to the Hereditary Prince, that Naples should be given up to save the rest of Europe, so he was now of the opinion that the necessity no longer existed. Napoleon's sun had set. Strong in this conviction, he postponed obedience to his Cabinet's orders to the last moment. Like Stratford Canning, that bold diplomatist of the succeeding generation, Bentinck held that an ambassador is justified in disobeying instructions if circumstances have materially altered between the date of their issue and the time appointed for their being carried into effect.

To the court of Austria the assistance of the King of Naples appeared, however, of more moment than that of Lord William Bentinck, with his 15,000 British and Sicilian troops. Animated mainly by the desire to keep his kingdom, but professing to have the interests of the Italian people at heart, the crowned cavalryman joined the coalition against his wife's brother. The loyal Eugène Beauharnais, the Emperor's viceroy, was holding Northern Italy against the Austrians under Bellegarde. The Neapolitans marched northward to take him in flank. Bentinck was informed by the Duke di Gallo, Murat's Foreign Secretary and formerly King Ferdinand's ambassador to Paris, that Lord Aberdeen was authorized to sign conjointly with Austria a treaty with the King of Naples. Ferdinand could hardly believe his ears. An alliance between Austria and the bold trooper who had usurped his dominions sounded indeed incredible. Bentinck sent his secretary, Graham, to Naples, ostensibly to facilitate the convention, but with secret instructions in no circumstances to sign an armistice till he had personally communicated with the Allies. He was to proceed to the Austrian headquarters if he could, and there explain that there were enough troops in Sicily to keep Murat occupied, in case fear of an attack by him should have dictated the treaty. To Castlereagh the irate envoy wrote:

> Upon Murat no reliance can ever be placed. Austria by the terms of this treaty will have created not only a rival but a master in Italy. When Beauharnais is beaten, the relics of his army will not rally to Austria but will prefer Murat, become an Italian prince and declaring himself the champion of Italian independence. If the British protection and assistance had happened to be within their reach, that great floating force would certainly have ranged itself under their standard. That great people, instead of being the instruments of one military tyrant or another, or, as formerly, the despicable slaves of a set of miserable petty princes, . . . would become a powerful barrier both against Austria and France, and the peace and happiness of the world would have received a great additional security.

Lord Castlereagh may be pictured reading this protest with lifted eyebrows. The reference to miserable petty princes he no doubt deemed to be in execrably bad taste. The Whig general's dreams of an independent Italian people savoured of Jacobinism. If the Foreign Secretary also disliked Murat it was for other reasons than those held by the ambassador. To his colleague Lord Aberdeen Lord William expressed himself in terms equally strong:

> In point of fair dealing, I consider Prince Metternich and King Murat upon a level. They have for the moment a common object of interest, but each proposes to take for himself as much of Italy as he can, each evidently sets out with the intention of deceiving the other, and each probably foresees their early disagreement.

At last orders came from Castlereagh which left no choice to our representative in Sicily. The armistice had to be signed, and the Government of his Sicilian Majesty was to give its adhesion. Bentinck had the disagreeable task of stating the wishes of the British Government to King Ferdinand. In a discourse "of the nature of a religious rhapsody" the monarch refused to enter into any transaction as to his claim to his ancestral dominions.

The Englishman said he could not but admire feelings which would sacrifice interest to honour. Having touched heights of such sublimity, his Majesty came down to earth, asking his lordship when he went to Naples to take with him a pheasant pie as a present to an old sporting companion whom cowardice alone had prevented from following the court to Palermo.

Bentinck landed at Naples on January 31, 1814, the armistice having been signed on his behalf by Graham. The ambassador made no secret of his ill-humour. He rode into the courtyard of the royal palace, walked about the gardens whip in hand, and made no attempt to pay his respects to the Queen. For that matter, Caroline Bonaparte, though she may have shared his opinion of her absent husband, would not have extended the hand of greeting to an English ambassador. Baron Neipperg, the Austrian delegate, who became not many years later the second husband of the Empress Marie-Louise, very reasonably complained of Lord William's devotion to the supposed claims of a useless monarch. But old Ferdinand, if he could be kept in the constitutional path, appeared to the devotee of Italian independence a more useful stalking-horse than Napoleon's nominee. On February 2 Bentinck had perforce to put his name to a military convention, defining the part allotted to each of the allies in Italy. He would have preferred to confine himself to an attack on Corsica, in order to avoid contact with Murat. It was determined instead that he should threaten Beauharnais's rear from the side of Leghorn and Genoa. The Apennines were to be the boundary between the British and Neapolitan zones of operation, and the base of the British was to be Tuscany and the Riviera of Genoa, "countries which they were to occupy exclusively and from which they would draw their supplies." The stipulation proved crucial.

When Bentinck landed with his little army at Leghorn on March 12 he was met by Murat's general Lechi. Stores had been accumulated for the use of the Anglo-

Sicilian force, but King Joachim had found it necessary to occupy the grand duchy. The Englishman, it may be suspected, was not too sorry to have his forebodings confirmed. He was less pleased to discover that Murat had also made a bid for the support of the Italian people generally. Proclamations in his name had been circulated exhorting all Italians to achieve their independence by rallying to his side and that of the allied sovereigns. To this Lord William at once issued a counterblast.

> Italians [he called], hesitate no longer—be Italians! Soldiers of Italy, we do not demand that you should unite yourselves with us. We summon you only to assert your own rights and make yourselves free. Call on us and we shall not fail you. Thanks to our united efforts, Italy will one day become once more what she was in her happiest days and what Spain is to-day!

Two days later he met Murat at Reggio nell'Emilia. He behaved, it is admitted, with the utmost rudeness. Studiously he avoided addressing the sovereign, whom Austria, if not Britain, had recognized, by any royal title. To his demand for the fulfilment of the convention the King of Naples rejoined that he held Tuscany by right of conquest. The British were free to use the duchy as a base. "In other words," growled Bentinck, "we have to ask alms of the Neapolitans." Murat had half of the peninsula to draw upon, but his ally was expected to confine himself to a single province. The altercation grew fierce. Bentinck refused to march unless Tuscany was given up, and threatened to take his troops to Naples and reinstate King Ferdinand. Failing, somewhat to his surprise, to move Murat, whom he had always looked upon as a weak character, he posted off to Verona to lay his case before Bellegarde, the Austrian commander-in-chief. He found every one against him. The soldiers cared little about the eventual distribution of the Italian lands, but they were very anxious to hasten the Neapolitans' advance against the French. Bentinck, happening to be also a statesman, insisted on the danger of leaving the renegade lieutenant of Napoleon in possession of half

JOACHIM MURAT
From an engraving after a painting by François Gerard

Italy. Spies reported that Murat was negotiating with Eugène. Since he had not received the ratification of the treaty with Austria, and England had concluded merely an armistice with him, he could hardly be blamed for his double-dealing.

A further attempt to patch up the quarrel was made at Bologna on March 29. Sir Robert Wilson, the British military representative at the Austrian headquarters, a man of agreeable manners, was left to approach the King of Naples. His impressions of him were favourable. He credited his excuse for deserting his benefactor by the plea that Napoleon had actually drafted a decree incorporating the Neapolitan states with France or the Kingdom of Italy. The great cavalry leader's appearance was a shade too picturesque for Wilson's liking, but he thought him the best actor that had appeared "on the royalty theatre." Castlereagh had directed Lord William to inform the King of Naples that

> the British government entirely approved the treaty made between the Austrian and Neapolitan governments and consented to the addition of territory therein specified, upon the condition of the immediate and active co-operation of the Neapolitan army, and that the refusal to sign a treaty *ad limine* proceeded from feelings of delicacy and honour which forbade that the hereditary possessions of an ancient ally should be sacrificed without an indemnity, and he was instructed to invite the Neapolitan government to exert its utmost efforts for the same object.

These instructions, says Sir Robert Wilson, were candidly and liberally worded as written in the public dispatches, but they were not so given by Lord William. Obliged with an ill-grace to communicate them, he chose to tack on a long statement that in his opinion the Neapolitan Government had not fulfilled the hopes on which the treaty was founded. There had been no loyal co-operation with the allied armies. His lordship recommended the King of Naples to cede a part of Tuscany to the British, to take vigorous military action against the French, not to pursue any isolated political activities, and to reinstate the Pope. His Holiness, having been released by Napoleon, had entered Bologna amid the acclamations of the people. His return was decidedly embarrassing to King Joachim, whose claims for territorial expansion included part at least of the Pontifical States. By Bentinck, of course, his Holiness was welcomed as a friend, though it is not clear how the Papacy would have fitted in with his scheme of an independent and united Italy. Learning that the Pontiff was in sore straits for money and had only four shirts in his wardrobe, the Englishman on taking his departure left behind him on a piece of furniture a sum of money amounting to over £1200 sterling.

He acted less tactfully by Murat. His message was, indeed, so offensively worded that the King declared that if he were still only a Field-marshal he would call him to account. Wilson noted the change in his Majesty's expression when he read the charge of disloyalty. He allowed no exclamation to escape him, but handed the message to Gallo. That minister neatly replied to Bentinck that his message conflicted seriously with the tenor of conversations held at Chaumont between Lord Castlereagh and Prince Cariati, his Neapolitan Majesty's ambassador. Therefore he proposed to resume the discussion through that channel.

The news of the fall of Paris acted on Murat as a more powerful stimulant than any of Bentinck's protests. He set his troops in motion and marched with them. But it was said by the Austrian officers that he was never in action for so much as two hours. It is to his credit that to the last he refrained from staining his sword with French blood; it is also to Bentinck's credit that he recognized Murat as a dangerous time-server. Had Napoleon driven Schwarzenberg out of France, it is beyond all reasonable doubt that the Neapolitan forces would have joined hands with Eugène Beauharnais and fallen on the flank and rear of the Austrians. Very wisely the English commander had taken what territory he could. He marched along the Riviera di Levante and entered Genoa. His dream of a united Italy could not be realized for want of a leader. Moreover, there was no Italian feeling. Milan set up an independent Government upon the departure of the French Viceroy, and Bentinck sent an officer to encourage the movement. But the Genoese, far from proclaiming themselves citizens of a new kingdom of Italy, petitioned Lord William to reconstitute their ancient republic. To this demand, he informed Castlereagh on April 27, he had no hesitation in acceding. By a proclamation dated the previous day he restored the constitution of 1797. He sent officers to Corsica in support of an insurrection against the French flag.

All this was viewed by the British Foreign Secretary with grave disquietude. It was evident that Lord William was getting out of hand. He had been asked to refrain from those confidential insinuations about the fate of Sicily which had alarmed the Hereditary Prince (April 3); on the same day he was directed to co-operate more cordially with Murat and to inform King Ferdinand that if he attacked that prince the Sicilian troops would be ordered back to their own island and Britain would conclude a treaty with the actual Government of Naples. In conference with the representatives of the allied Powers at Chaumont, Castlereagh bound himself to that policy of concerted action which left the final settlement of Europe to the Congress of Vienna. He admonished the headstrong ambassador in mild enough language:

> In your lordship's proclamation [of March] there may perhaps be found an expression or two, which, separately taken, might create an impression that your view of Italian liberation went to the form of government as well as to the expulsion of the French. . . . [His lordship would realize] how necessary it is, surrounded as your lordship must be by individuals who wish for another system to be established in Italy, not to afford any plausible occasion or pretext for umbrage to those with whom we are

acting. . . . It is not insurrection we now want in Italy or elsewhere—we want disciplined force under sovereigns we can trust.

His lordship, it was supposed, had already been informed of the appointment of Mr À Court as *chargé d'affaires* at Palermo during his absence. It was the Prince Regent's desire that he should accept the sword of honour which King Joachim of Naples had sent him. Grinding his teeth, Lord William took it, saying that the sword of a great captain was the most flattering present which a soldier could receive. He asked for leave and got it. His vision of a strong, united Italy had faded. Clearly he foresaw the fate reserved to Italy by the allied despots. Genoa was to go to Sardinia, Austria had her eye on Venice and Lombardy, the miserable petty princes were to be reseated on their thrones. He made a last-minute effort to save the fabric of constitutional liberty. On June 8 he reappeared at Palermo and informed the heads of the different parties that Britain's interest in Sicily was now at an end. Ferdinand, emerging from his retirement, took over the reins of government. His exultation was somewhat dashed by a letter from Tsar Alexander, imputing the loss of his Continental dominions to his own bad behaviour and enjoining on him a more humane and liberal treatment of his subjects. His Majesty was reminded that the fate of his kingdom would be settled at Vienna. Bentinck urged the old man if he returned to Naples not to re-enact the bloody scenes of 1799. There was no love-besotted Nelson at hand now to violate armistices, and do the Bourbon's dirty work. Ferdinand not only promised an amnesty, but expressed in the strongest terms his determination to maintain the constitution. In his last dispatches Bentinck at least affected to believe him.

The minister left Palermo on July 20, 1814. For thirteen years he was not employed by his Government. Part of the time he spent at Rome. He saw Murat finally dispossessed by an Austrian army, and heard of his execution in Calabria upon the failure of his desperate attempt to recover his throne after Waterloo. In July 1828 he turned his back on a Europe given over to despots. He was appointed Governor-General of Bengal, to become five years later the first Governor-General of India. His career in the East lies outside the province of this volume. He there found vent for that active philanthropy which in Italy had come so near to thwarting the illiberal, narrow policy of Metternich and Castlereagh and Talleyrand. As a Whig, he believed himself bound to respect the wishes and customs of the majority. Yet the greatest service Bentinck rendered to humanity was to defy the tradition of countless ages by forbidding Hindu widows to mount their husbands' funeral pyres. He was the first Governor-General to promote the admission of educated Indians to the Government service, the first to declare and act on the principle of governing India in the interests of the Indian people. Macaulay wrote the inscription which is to be read on his monument at Calcutta. James Mill admired him. Returning home in 1835, he died in Paris on June 17, 1839. His wife, the Lady Mary who had sailed across the Sicilian sea to bring back the captives from Barbary, survived him.

They left no children. This the believer in heredity must regret. William Bentinck was a great man. He was too great a man for a mere diplomatist, too great to serve the mean designs of his employers and their confederates. In Southern Italy the tender tree of liberty which he planted took at least as deep a root as that other planted in more northern soil and watered by French blood. To the present writer it appears that Bentinck's great mistake was his refusal to co-operate with Murat. In King Joachim's hands any constitution would have been safer than in Ferdinand's. But even had he hated the Frenchman less the Englishman would still have been bound by what he deemed his honour not to abandon the Bourbon to his enemies. In the end Italy was left to save herself. Whether she has yet done so the men of this generation are not agreed.

STRATFORD CANNING, VISCOUNT STRATFORD DE REDCLIFFE
(1786–1880)

IF Stratford Canning, better known, perhaps, under the title bestowed on him late in life, remains the most generally famous of British diplomatists, it is for the wrong reasons. He is supposed to have been the author of the Crimean War and the staunch upholder of the Ottoman Empire. But of direct responsibility for the war he has been acquitted by all serious historians; and in the red light of Abd-ul-Hamid's reign his undoubted zeal for the Turk is hardly likely to be accounted to him as merit. Unfortunately, if the ambassador towards the end of his ninety-three years ever half suspected that his policy was like to prove futile, it was too late to revise the memoirs which, like the first Lord Malmesbury, he had taken care to bequeath to posterity and on which his more doubtful titles to fame have been built. Those memoirs have now disappeared, probably within the darkest and dustiest recesses of a country-house library. With such corrections as official documents afford, they constituted very much more than the skeleton of the diplomatist's most authoritative biography.[1] By now we know as much as we are ever likely to know of the facts of his career; but, taking a fresh view of these, we perceive that Stratford Canning did things very much more worthy of remembrance than bolstering up a decaying empire and setting Christian nations at each other's throats. The defender of the Turks helped to call dead Hellas back to life.

Stratford, born in the City of London in the year 1786, was equipped with no more than the qualifications ex-

[1] By Stanley Lane-Poole. The edition of 1888 is here used. A shorter life, bringing out new facts, is Malcolm Smith's (1932).

pected in his day of an aspirant for the diplomatic service (or "the foreign line," as it is frequently described by the diplomatists themselves). At Eton he learned Latin and Greek and the history of the Jews. He could, indeed, write verses in Greek, but it does not appear that he could converse in that language with the many Greeks he was destined to meet; and when at Vienna he was driven back on Latin as the only medium of communication with the Abbot of Saint-Gallen, he found great difficulty in the prelate's pronunciation. Possibly he derived much inward refreshment from his study of the Hebrew chronicles (though not, as he certainly supposed, his strict notions of sexual behaviour); but a more intimate acquaintance with modern history and modern languages might have been more useful. However, he was by birth and education an English gentleman, and an uncommonly handsome man to boot, so by all the standards of his time his cousin, George Canning, soon after he became Foreign Secretary, was justified in sending him as second *attaché* on a mission to Scandinavia in the year 1807. At twenty-one Mr Canning surveyed the world outside Britain with a supercilious and generally disapproving eye. Swedish royalty in the person of Gustavus IV he held cheap; he cared for Copenhagen as little as Hugh Elliot had done twenty years previously. A political career at home, he decided, would suit him better than "lying abroad." His powerful cousin had other views for him. The young man dared not disobey, and in 1808 he was sent on an embassy with Robert Adair to the city in which was laid the fabric of his renown.

Stratford lived to know a time when the Ottoman Empire was regarded by millions of his countrymen as chiefly a field for reform and missionary endeavour. When he first set foot in Istanbul it is safe to say that no English statesman's slumbers were disturbed by the sufferings of the Grand Signior's Christian subjects. I do not suppose that anyone in Downing Street (unless he had read Gibbon) had heard of the Bulgarians. And it was Stratford himself who trained his Government to look on the maintenance of the empire as essential to British interests. Turkey in these days of his youth was regarded as a possible thorn in the side of the common enemy, Napoleon. Britain had been at war with the Porte in order to oblige our doubtful ally, Russia. So when the Tsar Alexander fell under the Corsican's spell, naturally enough we held out the hand of friendship to his enemy. Adair's mission was to make peace with the Sultan and to keep him from following Russia's pernicious example. In this he succeeded with no great difficulty. The Turks, one thinks, must have been bewildered by the rapid and repeated reversals of policy among the Giaour Powers.

The envoy remained eighteen months at Constantinople. It was longer than he intended. He had been instructed to proceed to Vienna to concert another alliance with Austria. The defeat of the Archduke Charles at Wagram put an end to that scheme. No road across Central Europe was safe for a British envoy. In the winter of 1809 Bathurst, one of our agents, vanished suddenly and inexplicably for ever from the sight of man in the dark innyard of a posting station in Brandenburg. Young Canning was safer at Pera, in sight of the Seraglio where Sultan Mahmud had but two years before destroyed all the members of his house in order to make himself the indubitable heir. The memoirs reveal a mode of existence which most people would describe as thrilling. But assistance at splendid and barbaric ceremonies, excursions on horseback into Asia Minor, even a visit from Byron, merely varied an existence which to the taste of a young sprig of twenty-three compared ill with life led in the precincts of Pall Mall. Only at the Swedish embassy could he find what he would call society. "A lady according to our English standards" was unknown. "One might as well speak of a red goose." As to the French, in the opinion of Stratford Canning they were "the vilest scum that ever fell from the overboilings of the pot of

Imperial Jacobinism." He yearned for home. But a letter came from his cousin, dated July 30, 1809, informing him that he was designated to succeed Adair as minister plenipotentiary to the Sublime Porte. Stratford shut himself in his room and wept.

In the following October George Canning fought his duel with Castlereagh and resigned office. Stratford eagerly sought to avail himself of this excuse for escaping from the exile to which he seemed doomed. He proposed to relinquish his appointment so soon as he had taken it up. He could not, he alleged, live on a minister plenipotentiary's salary. His pleadings and proposals were swept aside by the man on whom his advancement depended. No gentleman in those days ever lived within his means. He was sternly told by the ex-Foreign Secretary to renounce all idea of a career at home and to persevere in the path in which he had been set. There was no help for it. When Adair at last took his leave in July 1810, the young man had perforce to present his credential letters and to step into his shoes.

> In after-years [writes Lane-Poole] one who knew Lord Stratford intimately remarked that much of his exceeding masterfulness was due to the misfortune of having had things made too easy for him in early life. . . . He was pushed up the easiest possible incline to the top of the ladder of diplomatic rank before he was twenty-four, and to this premature elevation must be traced in a large degree the faults which have been remarked by his contemporaries. Had he been compelled to work under taskmasters in youth, he would probably have learned the lesson of submission. He was impatient because he had never known what it was to wait in despair of advancement; he was suspicious because he spent his early youth in a nest of intrigues. Of all schools for his nature, Constantinople was the very worst. There he was compelled to deal in menace and high-handed authority, and the necessity created a habit. Circumstances strengthened the natural bent.

In such surroundings, too, he was cut off from intercourse with men of wit and culture. He had few opportunities of revising the narrow and fanatical ideas instilled into him in childhood. Lady Hester Stanhope, one of the few choice spirits with whom he came in contact, spoke of him as a political and religious Methodist. He was well fitted, she thought, to be the head of a society for the suppression of vice. He was furious with her for meeting Latour Maubourg, the brilliant French envoy, on terms of civility. In the metropolitan circles for which he longed he would have been voted a prig. It is recorded with approval by his Victorian biographer that he once ordered a young *attaché* out of the room for laughing at a smoking-room story retailed by a diplomatist present. A Muslim vizier would have taken the same stern view of such levity. It is droll to hear Stratford accusing the Turks of pride, ignorance, and obstinacy. He was no doubt better read, but not much more enlightened than the bearded statesmen of the Divan. On one notable occasion the Reis Effendi, or Ottoman Foreign Secretary, complained of his bad manners—of his interrupting debate by speaking in too loud a tone, and by showing sometimes "a ruddy face, sometimes a yellow." Yet, perhaps because of his likeness to them, no other envoy from a Frankish nation was ever able to bend the Turks so completely to his will. George Canning's selection of his kinsman one might imagine to have been inspired, not by unblushing nepotism, but by an insight, not gained by contact, into the Turkish character.

That selection evidently occasioned no disquietude to Wellesley, the new man at Downing Street; for he left British interests at Seraglio Point entirely at the discretion of the twenty-four-year-old ambassador, sending him only sixteen dispatches, and those of no diplomatic significance, within a period of twenty months. All the overland routes were closed to British messengers; Constantinople was three thousand miles by sea from London. Such isolation would have pleased Malmesbury and Bentinck, but it was hard on a diplomatic fledgling. It was displeasing, one suspects, to Stratford chiefly because his prestige suffered. The Turks compared his scanty mail with the heavy bags from Paris almost every day delivered to his French rival. But Wellesley's neglect might very well have secured Napoleon a new ally. While Latour Maubourg paid assiduous court to the Sultan, the Englishman, having no instructions from home, thought he could best serve his country by bullying the Porte and picking quarrels with the ministers. French privateers, he insisted, were not to be allowed to take their prizes into Ottoman harbours. On the other hand, he was always prepared to justify the most high-handed infractions of international law by our own seamen. Captain Hope, encouraged by him, pursued a Frenchman into Turkish waters and fired on him under the guns of a Turkish fort. The patient Osmanli were exasperated. Latour Maubourg watched, smiling. That Sultan Mahmud did not throw in his lot with France was due, I suspect, to the tactful rendering by Pisani, the dragoman, of the ambassador's haughty message. Our representatives' ignorance of the language of the courts to which they are accredited has not always been a disadvantage. But some credit must be allowed to the Sultan's statesmen. They were not diverted from their interests by the impetuosity of one whom they looked on as a beardless boy. By the end of 1811 it was plain to all men that the short-lived friendship between Napoleon and Alexander was near its breaking-point. The Powers were setting to fresh partners. The Turks were weary of the war with Russia. Stratford was asked by the sage Reis Effendi whether, instead of pursuing trivial disputes, he might not more usefully exert himself to bring about a peace.

Stratford might retort that nothing which affected the honour of his master was trifling and press for the redress of the privateering grievances, but he perceived the greatness of the chance offered him. It was his duty to strengthen Russia's hand. We were still nominally at war with that Power, so while Turks and Muscovites wrangled over the conditions of peace in Wallachia he got in touch with that Duke of Serra Capriola, the Sicilian minister at Petersburg, whose anti-British bias had been reported on by Hugh Elliot.

> I rather think [he wrote] the Porte is disposed to cede as far as the Pruth—provided Russia will give some certain proof of her having no further designs upon the Turkish territory. And even this Russia will not obtain but by retaining the present military advantage during the negotiation—nor will she if the Porte can see the least chance of continuing the war without greater danger than at present exists.

The giving of this warning strikes one as a little less than fair to the Turks who had invited his mediation. And though Stratford later on requested Serra Capriola to remind the Tsar of the danger of driving Turkey into an alliance with his French rival, the Reis Effendi was not without grounds for attributing to the mediator a readiness to sacrifice Turkish interests to Britain's. To reassure him Stratford wrote directly to Italinski, the Russian delegate at the peace conference, urging that "the conclusion of a peace between Russia and the Porte would be one obstacle the less to a peace between England and Russia, and consequently to that peace which alone can assure the repose of the universe." Nevertheless, he was required to submit his correspondence to the Divan. "As if," said Stratford scornfully, "a double correspondence could not be maintained!" He showed three of his most important letters to the Sultan himself, who, without presuming any unselfishness on the part of England, was inclined to trust to her more than to France.

It was now that Stratford produced his trump card—a paper obtained by secret means from Vienna and left with him by his predecessor, Adair, the purport of which was that Austria was preparing, with the concurrence of France, to invade the Ottoman Empire. Even now the Reis Effendi persisted in his doubts of the Englishman's entire good faith. Canning was, in fact, playing on the fears of both sides. By a secret agent he transmitted to the Russians another paper which he declares to have been an authentic intimation of a proposal for the cooperation of Turkey with France and Austria in the coming struggle. Both sides were now frightened into coming to terms. On May 28, 1812, Ghalib Bey, the Ottoman delegate, signed the Treaty of Bucharest, which put an end to the war with Russia.

Since this settlement enabled the Tsar to move his forces from the Danube against the flank of Napoleon's retreating host, an important share in effecting the Emperor's downfall may be claimed for Stratford Canning, then only twenty-five years of age. No one at Downing Street was entitled to dispute that share. On April 21, 1812, we find the young ambassador writing to his Government, only five weeks before the treaty was signed:

> The conclusion of peace with Russia is the first remedy. I am doing all I can to bring it about, but my means are very scanty. Both parties are obstinate. I am very much in need of instructions. Even the smallest communication direct from his majesty's government, if greater means cannot be employed, would be of great service. The French are making every possible exertion. Courier after courier arrives from Paris.

By now Castlereagh had taken charge of the Foreign Office. Not perhaps expecting that Stratford's efforts would be crowned with success, he granted his repeated prayer for recall. Two days after the ratification of the Treaty of Bucharest (June 28) Robert Liston landed in Constantinople to supersede the man who had practically imposed peace on two reluctant belligerents. But no expression of his country's gratitude could have been more grateful to the homesick diplomatist. On July 12 he joyfully turned his back, as he hoped for ever, on the Ottoman capital, speeded by a kindly wind towards the winding Dardanelles. He did not present his letters of recall too soon. Within a month of his going the distrustful Reis Effendi was informed of the treaty between France and Austria which guaranteed the integrity of the Sultan's dominions. The Turk was angry. His apprehensions were justified—Turkey had been jockeyed by that pestilent Englishman into concluding a disadvantageous peace. Fiercer still would have blazed the Moslem's wrath had he known that Mr Canning was congratulating himself on having saved the Treasury a cool £300,000, which he had been empowered to pay the Porte in the last extremity by way of bribe. As it was, wrote Liston, evidently somewhat doubtful of the ultimate value of his predecessor's methods, the most that could be hoped for was that the Turks would persevere in their neutrality. They did so. Sultan Mahmud knew he had more reason to be wary of his foes round the Seraglio than of those across the frontier. According to a Turkish historian,[1] the Peace of Bucharest is generally considered disastrous by his countrymen. By holding out while the Grand Army pressed farther and farther towards Moscow the Porte might indeed have wrung better terms from Russia, but by that time the British Government would probably have resorted to the "greater means" hinted at by Stratford and ordered the fleet to the Dardanelles. Whether or not the release of the Russian army of the Danube had the decisive effect claimed for it by Stratford Canning's admirers, it is hard to see how in the long run Turkey would have profited by the triumph of Napoleon.

The backwash of the war swept westward, leaving the Padishah to brood on his divan. While by one by one the nations forsook the falling star of Bonaparte, and British agents hurried from court to court composing mutual rivalries and concerting a common action, Stratford Canning rested on his laurels. He was glad to be home again. He was happy in the company of his sisters and his old schoolfellows. He waxed lyrical over the charms of Tunbridge Wells and of Wordsworth's country. He tried the handles of back doors to the House of Commons. Happily his dream of a public life in his own country was never realized. Those accustomed to managing Orientals seldom succeed in managing Europeans. In 1814 all

[1] Halil Ganem, *Les Sultans ottomans* (Paris, 1902).

eyes were turned on Paris. Monarchs and ambassadors were busy at the council board, preparing to erase by strokes of the pen the boundaries which Napoleon had traced with the sword. Stratford followed his elders. In Paris he met Castlereagh, whose lucky shot had driven George Canning for the time being out of politics. They liked each other. Stratford was offered and accepted the legation to Switzerland—a strange mission for the late envoy to Istanbul! The appointment is dated June 28, 1814.

The alpine scenery enraptured the diplomatist. He was proportionately bored by Swiss society; which was ungrateful, for his handsome face and cold, haughty bearing captivated the girls of Bern and Zurich. Upon the break-up of Napoleon's system all the lumber of the Middle Ages floated to the surface. The excellent constitution with which the Emperor had endowed the Swiss people was set aside; and those cantons, like Bern, which had lost territory under it, and those, like Unterwalden and Fribourg, which honestly preferred darkness to light, were straining to restore the ancient order of things. The Powers required the Switzers to put their house in order and draw up a new federal constitution without delay. Baron Schraut, the Austrian minister, was all for reaction. The hopes of the Liberal elements were placed in that demi-semi-liberal Alexander I. His representative was Kapodistrias the Confiote, that remarkable man who had won the confidence of the Autocrat and was to die President of Greece. Before the newly appointed British minister left Paris he received a visit from an old gentleman, who inquired, "Perhaps you have heard my name. I am General La Harpe—one of the people you call Jacobins." Canning bowed. He recognized his visitor as a former President of the reformed Confederation, and as the educator of the Tsar in the views which were giving so much trouble to Castlereagh, Metternich, Talleyrand, and the other powers of darkness. Nevertheless, the Englishman listened to what he had to say about Switzerland, and was perhaps so far affected that during his short embassy at Bern and Zurich (the alternate capitals) he followed a middle path between his two colleagues. The peasants of Aargau, he wrote, had just grievances,[1] but a month later he spoke of "the unquestionable abstract justice" of Bern's claim to their territory. He advocated the admission of Geneva to the confederacy, and was disappointed when the Powers gave Chiavenna, Bormio, and the Valtellina to Austria. Thanks largely to him, the Bernese were compensated for the loss of Vaud and Aargau by the addition of part of the bishopric of Basel. He tried to modify the reactionary constitutions of Bern and Fribourg. Kapodistrias was so far pleased with the moderation of his British colleague that, on taking his departure for Vienna, he asked him to act as his *chargé d'affaires*. Canning soon followed him to the gathering Congress, and claims to have defeated his efforts, or his master's, to abate the pretensions of Bern and to liberalize the federal pact still more. Finally the articles of confederation, as voted by the Diet, were approved by the Powers. Without the interference of the British representative the Swiss people might have fared worse or better. It certainly cost Stratford Canning no pang to see the constitution he had sponsored swept away in 1848.

Vienna in those days of the Congress ever remained for Stratford "the greenest spot in mem'ry's waste." To the day of his death, we are told, there hung by his bed a sketch executed by Isabella Waldstein, the wife of a count to whom Beethoven dedicated a sonata. She was not very beautiful, but "virtuous" and so clever and "amiable" that it was impossible not to be fond of her. Thus the busy diplomatist in a letter to his sister. The Englishman and the Polish countess vowed an eternal friendship. One day they joined with eighteen others in a pleasure party to the woods. Dreading, after the manner of lovers, lest her happiness should be forgotten,

[1] F.O. 74/40. August 12, 1814. Public Record Office.

STRATFORD CANNING (AGED TWENTY-NINE)
From an engraving after a miniature by A. Robertson

Isabella proposed they should all meet again at the same spot that day twenty years on. All promised. The war clouds rolled away; Napoleon died and receded into history; one throne at least re-erected by the Congress collapsed. The autumn of 1834 came round. Stratford Canning sat in his country-house in England, preoccupied with the coming election. If he remembered that appointment he had no heart to keep it. One man only, von Hammer, the historian of Turkey, was true to the tryst. It must have been a mournful moment for the scholar. The lime-tree round which they had gathered had been cut down. And the Countess Isabella had been laid sixteen years before in the grave.

The loving and dancing at Vienna was cut short by the descent of Napoleon upon France. Stratford hastened back in five days to his station. It was not impossible that the liberal elements in the ramshackle Confederation might reassemble round their old champion. The Tsar, so La Harpe informed Stratford, would have preferred Switzerland to remain neutral. Canning was alarmed by the weakness of the reconstituted republic. Each canton jealously maintained the control of its own army. The ambassador claims to have proposed and laid down the basis of a federal force. He called on the Swiss commander-in-chief, whom he found in his night-cap, and unsuccessfully invited him to attack the rear of a French contingent directed against the Simplon. A defensive alliance, he thought at one time, was the most that could be expected of the little republic. However, the old-fashioned cantons were eager to hire their men out to the Bourbons, as in the good old days, and a Swiss force was sent to besiege the Alsatian fortress of Huningue. In recognition of this goodwill the Powers declared the perpetual neutrality of the Confederation on November 20, 1815, and forced the French to pay the Swiss an indemnity for the depredations of the year 1798.

The remaining four years of Stratford's mission were but a long holiday, the climax and anticlimax of which were his marriage to Harriet Raikes in 1816 and her death at Lausanne the following year. The widower stayed on in Switzerland till August 29, 1819, when he went home on leave with no intention of returning. He expected that a post would be found for him in England or that he would be advanced in the diplomatic service. Accustomed to look his gift-horses very closely in the mouth, he declares that he accepted the legation at Washington "only because there was nothing to count upon at home." On what principle diplomatic appointments are distributed nowadays we do not know. It may be that special qualifications are taken into consideration. Experience gained mostly at Constantinople would not be likely at any time to prove valuable to an envoy at Washington. Yet Castlereagh on announcing the new appointment to Rush, the United States minister to London, scrupled not to say that Mr Canning "possessed every qualification for treading" in the path of conciliation which the two countries were so happily pursuing.

Stratford arrived in Washington, still an uncompleted city, on September 28, 1820. A hardened Tory, he looked with no kindly eyes on a nation which believed itself to be democratic and which harboured a deep dislike of Britain as one of the effete European tyrannies. By a dangerous conjuncture the office of Secretary of State under President Monroe was then filled by John Quincy Adams. He was pugnacious, loving controversy and pursuing contention to the point of offence. The inevitable clash between him and the arrogant British minister was not long in coming. By the third article of the Convention of London, signed in 1818, it had been agreed between Britain and America that the Pacific coast north of the Mexican frontier should be left free and open to the citizens and vessels of both contracting parties for ten years, without prejudice to any claim which either of them might have to any part of that country. At the beginning of the year 1821 Stratford learned in conversation with a Congressman and from a letter by a senator published in the semi-official *Public Intelligencer* that it was proposed to strengthen and increase a settlement already formed by the Americans upon the Columbia river within the area specified. "Notwithstanding the peculiarities of Mr Adams's character," [1] writes Canning under date January 28, 1821, "my intercourse with him had hitherto been so satisfactory, I might almost say of so confidential a description, that I felt myself at liberty to call at his official apartment without any previous intimation." The accounts of the interview given by the Englishman in his dispatches and by the American in his diary do not differ materially, though each, of course, imputes blame to the other. Adams has it that, on being questioned by his Excellency as to the letter published in the *Public Intelligencer*, he said he had not read it, but thought from the prevailing disposition in the country that the settlement on the Columbia would at no remote period be increased; Canning says that Adams, replying to his question in the most determined and acrimonious tone, declared that the United States did propose to make a new settlement and had a perfect right to do so, the territory being their own. Both men took a sharper tone. Asked if this was the determination of the American Government, "No, sir," said Adams, by his own report, "you are to understand nothing that I say to you without consultation with and directions from the President. What I have now said is merely an opinion of my own." Canning called his attention to the convention of 1818. Adams looked for the book and read the article aloud. He then said, "Now, sir, if you have any charge to make against the American Government for a violation of this article, you will please to make the communication in writing."

This intimation, says Canning, was conveyed with an impatience and rudeness which he was at a loss to understand. He tried in vain to soothe him. The Secretary of State blamed him personally for stirring up trouble and

[1] F.O. 5/157, Part I. Public Record Office.

questioned his right to ground his inquiries on anything that might pass in Congress. But, if we are to believe Adams, the Englishman demanded, "Do you suppose that I am to be dictated to in the manner in which I may think proper to communicate with the American Government?"

"No, sir," said Adams, "but you will give me leave to determine what communications we receive and how we will receive them; and be assured that we are as little disposed to submit to dictation as to exercise it."

Notwithstanding Canning called again the next day. He found Adams in no better temper. The American scoffed at the claims put forward or that might be put forward under the convention of 1818 as a mere chicane. "What," he asked, "would England grasp at yet? What if Mr Rush were to question Lord Castlereagh on the occasion of a regiment's being sent to New South Wales or to the Shetland Islands?" The altercation, following the American version, proceeded:

> *Canning.* Have you any claim to New South Wales or the Shetlands?
> *Adams.* Have you any claim to the Columbia river?
> *Canning.* Why, do you not know that we have a claim?
> *Adams.* I don't know what you do not claim. India, Africa——
> *Canning.* Perhaps a piece of the moon?
> *Adams.* I have not heard that you claim the moon, but there is no place on earth which you could not claim with as much colour of right as you have to the Columbia. We know of no rights you have on the shores of the South Sea.
> *Canning.* And if we made a settlement there?
> *Adams.* I have no doubt we should object to it.

He asserted, says Canning, the undoubted right of the American Government to settle where it likes on the coast of the Pacific. "He seemed determined to show claws on the subject of the Columbia river—there was an evident determination to browbeat me." So wrote our envoy to his friend Joseph Planta at the Foreign

Office. The letter betrays his apprehension lest their chief should lay the blame on him. He doubted whether he possessed the exquisite humility and patience for enduring another such scene.

Castlereagh doubted it too.

> His Majesty [he wrote on April 19] does full justice to the zeal which dictated the proceedings. . . . But in the present state of the question, it is not the King's pleasure that you should renew the discussion. . . . You will avoid any step which may either compromise your Government or lead the American Government to infer that it is the intention of His Majesty's Government to take up this question.

Towards the end of the year Stratford fell foul of the French minister at Washington. "I laid down at night," he tells us, "under an engagement to exchange shots next morning with my colleague, but before daylight an arrangement volunteered by friends . . . was made, to my great relief." On the question of the slave trade a man of much meeker temper than Stratford Canning's could not have failed to irritate the slave-owning Americans. Canning, says Adams in his diary, was very earnest about this. The American Secretary of State abhorred slavery as heartily as the Englishman; but his Government would not help to put an end to the infamous traffic by granting to our cruisers the right to search vessels suspected of carrying slaves under the American flag. Hotly Canning demanded of Adams if he could conceive of a greater or more atrocious evil than the slave trade. "Yes," replied the professed abolitionist; "admitting the right of search by foreign officers of our vessels upon the high seas in time of peace; for that would be making slaves of ourselves"—an assertion so silly and so much at variance with the speaker's avowed principles that it could only have been inspired by personal hostility towards the Englishman.

The wonder is that two such men should have remained in touch with each other close on three years without dragging their countries into war. Not too soon Canning took leave of absence on the ground of ill-health and bade farewell to Washington on June 24, 1823. The estimate of him by his antagonist is not unfair:

> I shall probably see him no more. He is a proud, high-tempered Englishman, of good but extraordinary parts; stubborn and punctilious, with a disposition to be overbearing, which I have often been compelled to check in its own way. He is, of all the foreign ministers with whom I have had occasion to treat, the man who has most sorely tried my temper. Yet he has been long in the diplomatic career, and treated with Governments of the most opposite character. He has, however, a great respect for his word, and there is nothing false about him. This is an excellent quality for a negotiator. Mr Canning is a man of forms, studious of courtesy, and tenacious of private morals. As a diplomatic man, his great want is suppleness and his great virtue is sincerity.

II

Castlereagh had died by his own hand, which was one of the few services to humanity it ever rendered. George Canning, happily for mankind, was back at the Foreign Office. Stratford's hopes of a career at home revived. His cousin would have done much for him, but the most that could be extracted from the Prime Minister, Lord Liverpool, was the probable succession to the office of Vice-President of the Board of Trade when it should be vacant. For this not very brilliant opening the returned diplomatist was apparently willing to sacrifice the magnificent opportunities which awaited him abroad. Absence made his heart grow fonder of his native country to an unusual degree. Expecting and half-dreading orders from Downing Street, he passed his time mostly between London and "that refreshing place, Tunbridge Wells." At leisure, he turned his thoughts again to love. At thirty-eight he paid his court to Miss Alexander, a girl of eighteen. She was coy or she thought him too old for her. He pursued her even to Holland, but he could not change her mind. Duty called him back to England, his resolution to make her his wife unabated.

Unless he secured the coveted office in London, he could have had little doubt as to the quarter of the world in which he would presently be employed. Studying the development of the newest of nations, he had heard of the resurgence of not the least ancient. Greece had risen from the dust. Undismayed by Ypsilanti's failure in Moldavia, the Archbishop Germanos raised the standard of the Cross on April 2, 1821, at Patrai, in the Peloponnesos. Europe and the Sultan were astonished. Throughout four hundred years the Greeks had been the most submissive and, in many respects, the most favoured of the rayahs, or subject-races of the Turk. At Constantinople they had been the confidential servants rather than the slaves of the Porte. The furious Mahmud hanged the Grecian Patriarch from the doorpost of his own cathedral. The Jews, to gratify their ever-smouldering hate against their fellow-rayahs, dragged the prelate's body through the streets under the derisive gaze of their Moslem masters. A shudder, unfelt by the statesmen, passed through Christendom. Orthodox Russia lifted expectant eyes towards the Tsar.

> As a matter of humanity [wrote Stratford from Washington to his cousin (September 29, 1821)] I wish with all my soul that the Greeks were put in possession of their whole patrimony, and that the Sultan were driven, bag and baggage, into the heart of Asia, or as a provisional measure that the divided empire which existed four centuries ago could be restored.

The jealousy of the Powers, he well knew, made both solutions for the moment impossible. By Castlereagh and Metternich this rising of Christian against Moslem, of Aryan against Turanian, was strangely regarded as another of the revolutionary and purely political movements which had lately convulsed Europe. They trusted that the insurrection would burn itself out beyond the pale of civilization; but before Stratford Canning set foot again in England the Hellenes, supported by the sympathy of all that was best in Europe, had made themselves masters of the Peloponnesos, of a large part of continental Greece, and of the Ægean Sea.

The diplomatic history of this period is intricate and obscure. On March 25, 1823, Britain, to the dismay of Vienna, recognized the Greeks as belligerents. The sword of the Orthodox Tsar still rested in its scabbard. English statesman and Russian Autocrat alike wished well to the Christian cause, but each suspected the other of pursuing it to his own country's advantage. Between the two stood Metternich, the evil genius of Europe, equally distrustful of the aims of either and hating freedom in any form. On January 12, 1824, Alexander invited the Powers to a conference. The Porte, he proposed, should be forced to recognize the autonomy of the Grecian people, which was to be organized in three separate principalities. Metternich was in favour of a congress, at which he no doubt hoped to checkmate Russia's ambitions and to stifle the Greeks' hope of independence. The Sultan instantly protested. He denied the right of any other Power to interfere between him and his rebel subjects. The Greeks hoped to achieve more for themselves by force of arms than the Powers would ever concede to them. The British Foreign Secretary declared that it was not for a Christian Government which ruled over millions of Mohammedans to coerce the Turks, and he was even less disposed to force a settlement on the Greeks. His attitude was influenced by the memorandum on Greece which Stratford addressed to him about this time.[1]

> It is presumed the British Government would hail the complete independence of Greece, effected by the Greeks themselves, as the best solution. . . . [But, such a solution being impossible] It is therefore manifest that in the conference at Petersburg there can be no question of the complete independence of Greece. But it would be unfair to force such a solution on the Greeks. To induce the Porte to abandon the conflict, something more to be dreaded than an insurrection of the Janissaries must

[1] F.O. Stratford Canning Papers, 352/10. Public Record Office.

be presented to their imagination. War, though not actually menaced, with some of the principal Powers of Europe, or at least with one of them, must be made to appear the probable consequence of protracted hostilities between the Porte and her Greek subjects. If Russia is designated as the mandatory of the Powers, England cannot intervene. If England acts collectively, she will risk being committed to all the principles of the Holy Alliance. Ambassadors might present similar notes to the Porte simultaneously with the Russian proposals.

It might be worth while breaking off all friendly relations with European Turkey. In this way the supply of grain to the capital would be stopped. An armistice should be proposed, and an offer of mediation on the basis of suzerainty by the Sultan made to both parties.

The two Cannings understood each other so well that Stratford was sent in the autumn of 1824 as special plenipotentiary to Petersburg. Britain would not take part in the conference unless all idea of armed coercion of Turks or Greeks was abandoned, and till the Tsar put an end to his ambiguous relations with the Porte by sending a duly accredited ambassador to Istanbul. Stratford travelled by way of Vienna in order to sound the slippery Metternich.

> My first conversation with him [says our representative] took place at an evening party. The same sofa held us both, and I had not long been seated when he said rather curtly, "You have a bug on your sleeve." Whether he meant to try me or to provide for his own security, I do not know, but the remark was not pleasing, and I could only defend myself at the expense of the hotel.

He found that Austria was, in principle and in fact, the ally of Turkey. The Emperor Francis II was convinced that the Greeks were excited by Jacobins, and "he had no feeling for rebels." The Christian in his Apostolic Majesty, one sees, was entirely obscured by the sovereign. He thought Canning had gone much too far in recognizing the Greek Government. Certainly Austria was in favour of the congress proposed by Tsar

Alexander. Without reflecting on Stratford personally, Francis could not help regretting he had not chosen to go to Petersburg by some other road.

There was nothing more for the ambassador to do at Vienna. Casting a sad backward glance perhaps at the spots associated with Isabella Waldstein, Stratford on January 7, 1825, set out for the Russian capital. It was a grim journey of twenty-two days. The roads were bad, the inns worse, the cold severe. Colder still was his reception by Alexander. A dispatch was then on its way to London to inform George Canning that all conversation between Russia and Britain on the subject of Greece was to be considered closed. So of course his Imperial Majesty said no word on the subject to the British envoy. He would be damned, said George Canning, if he would speak Greek to us! If, hinted Nesselrode, the Russian Foreign Secretary, Mr Stratford Canning came with instructions to take part in the conference which was about to open, his lips would be unsealed. Instead, the British envoy turned the conversation to the claims of Russia in North America, which had caused a sensation at Washington. A treaty signed on February 28 limited Russia's monopoly of the Pacific seas to a distance of thirty miles from the coast and secured the seaward slope of the Rockies and the mouth of the Mackenzie river to England. The treaty was of more material importance to Britain than the questions which preoccupied the chancelleries of Europe, but Stratford will always be better remembered for having bolstered up the Ottoman Empire than for having opened up the North Pacific to our trade.

This agreement at least put Canning and Nesselrode in a good humour with each other. The conference plainly would lead to nothing. At an audience in April Stratford was assured by the Tsar that his only motives were humanity towards the Greeks, concern for the welfare of Europe generally, and anxiety to remove all causes of irritation between himself and the Sultan. This was probably true; but the Englishman was unable to gather what exactly were the advantages which the Greeks were to enjoy subject to the sovereignty of the Porte. At this distance of time we can but wonder why our representative was not empowered to offer the co-operation of Britain on condition that Greece was definitely emancipated and the Ottoman dominions otherwise left intact.

Stratford's mission was, in fact, not to do much. He profited by his leisure to observe the country and the people. He visited Moscow and met a few superannuated servants of Catherine II. The Russians he pronounced to be a people of lively imagination and deep feeling. "Many a page of history," he prophesied, "has yet to be filled with their exploits." Lane-Poole, writing in 1888, remarks that he lived long enough to realize the truth of his prediction. How far the event surpassed his expectation-we who live to-day have seen. The imagination of Stratford Canning never compassed the creation of an entirely new civilization in Russia within less than a hundred years of that desultory and futile conference of Petersburg. It would have been hard for him to conceive a Russian Government which despised territorial acquisitions and which deemed the welfare of the Russian people to be its primary and almost exclusive concern.

"While the kings rave the Greeks weep." The old tag was verified under the eyes of the statesmen and diplomatists to whom it was familiar in their schooldays. Stratford was still manœuvring for openings against Nesselrode when Sultan Mahmud called on his powerful vassal, Mehemet Ali, the Pasha of Egypt, to stamp out the revolt. In February 1825 Ibrahim Pasha landed in the south of the Peloponnesos with an Egyptian army of some 12,000 men, supported by a considerable fleet. Most wars have been decided less by the quality of the troops than by the generalship of commanders. With his army of *fellahin*, the son of Mehemet Ali soon proved more than a match for the descendants of Epaminondas and Lysander. The leadership of Frankish officers, the assistance of valiant volunteers from all parts of Christendom, failed to stem the progress of the Moslems. By the time Stratford had taken leave of the Tsar (April 1825), and set his face once more towards England, it had become highly probable that there would be no Greek question and no Greek people to discuss.

Ibrahim, it was rumoured in Russia, was considering a plan to exterminate all the males in the Grecian peninsula, to carry off the women and children, and to repeople the country with Arabs and Egyptians. George Canning might proclaim his contempt for the Greeks as a rascally lot and declare he had no intention of going to war on behalf of Epaminondas and Co., but he knew that the English, despite their affected contempt for quixotism, had a healthy abhorrence for wholesale massacre. Nothing had been achieved at the conference. At any moment Alexander, conscious of the reproachful gaze of his subjects, might remember that he was the Orthodox Tsar and draw the sword in defence of the Cross.

But the Greeks themselves despaired of him. They looked towards Britain. On September 29, 1825, they sent a deputation to London to solicit the protection of the English. This action was disavowed by the French and American Philhellene societies. Canning not only rejected the demand, but warned the delegation that if anything more were heard of it he would publish a formal declaration of neutrality. He turned now to the man who thirteen years before had forced a peace on Turkey. It was hard on Stratford to have to go back to "that hole," as he strangely called the city on the Bosphorus. This time, however, he had no reason to fear loneliness. On September 3 he was married to Miss Alexander at St James's Church, Piccadilly. Absence or his tenacity had made the girl's heart grow fonder.

We may suppose that her friends congratulated her on her tardy surrender when on October 10 her husband was gazetted ambassador extraordinary and minister plenipotentiary to the Porte. "We do not offer our mediation at present," so ran his instructions, dated two days later, "because we know it would be refused, but if asked by either party we shall offer it to the other. . . . We cannot hesitate to recommend to the Divan the pacification of Greece." It was probably at Stratford's own suggestion that the Turks were to be warned that the sympathies of all Christendom were with the Greeks. "The inhabitants of both the Americas are, to a man, in their hearts favourers of the Greek cause." The gift of an aigrette, worth sixteen hundred guineas, to the Sultan, and presents totalling £3000 in value to his high officers of State, would render the ambassador's advice, it was hoped, less distasteful. Mr Henry Parish was attached to the embassy as man-of-all-work at a salary of £250 per annum, and Messrs Buchanan and Scarlett were to go as unpaid *attachés*. His Excellency was asked to consider these gentlemen members of his own family.

The Cannings picked them up at Naples, where they all embarked on Admiral Neale's flagship, the *Revenge*, for Corfu. At that port (then and for many years after under British protection) the party was detained by an outbreak of scarlet fever. Young Mrs Canning was among the sufferers. Happily all recovered, and at the beginning of the year 1826 the eastward voyage was resumed.

It was fateful and abounding in ill omens. Stratford, who had in 1812 opened up communications with a Power with which we were nominally at war, took the bold course of establishing relations with the rebel subjects of the Power to which he was accredited. The necessary invitation was sent, it is thought, through Captain Hamilton to the Grecian provisional Government at its precarious headquarters on the rock of Hydra. On January 9 the *Revenge* cast anchor in the narrow channel between "the grand little island" and the mainland of Argolis. Before noon, records the envoy,

> we were boarded by two of the Greek leaders, then at open war with the Ottoman Government. These patriotic gentlemen were Prince Alexander Maurokordatos and Zographos, both of distinguished position among the insurgents and thoroughly acquainted with the state of public affairs and the prevailing current of public opinion in Greece. I could only receive them privately, with such reserves as my official character and due respect for a friendly Power imposed. Sad was the picture presented by Greece at that period. Resources all but exhausted—counsels more than distracted—hopes daily declining within—only barren sympathies without—discouragement approaching to despair—and hatred of the Turks unsoftened, nay inextinguishable, like the Greek fire of old.

The Greeks, Stratford was able to inform his Government as a result of this interview, were anxious for British mediation, and would accept something short of independence, a concession which they had never made before. This abatement of their claims may have been precipitated by the news of the premature death of Tsar Alexander when he was on the point, as was widely believed, of declaring war against the Ottomans—news, says Stratford, which reached him on the very day of the conference at Hydra, and probably by the mouths of the delegates. Maurokordatos and Zographos managed to get ashore in the teeth of a terrific hurricane. The sails of the *Revenge* were torn to shreds, and her consort sent to the bottom.

Surviving the storm, the ambassador's ship touched at Psara. They found it an island of the dead. The Turks had been at work. "Heavens!" exclaimed Stratford, "how I longed to be the instrument of repairing such calamities by carrying my mission of peace and deliverance to a successful issue!"

Fierce, cold winds forbade the passage of the Hellespont. Stratford, in a hurry to find how the change of rulers in Russia had affected the Porte, took horse and, attended by a secretary, rode through Thrace to Constantinople. Near Rodosto he was thrown from the saddle, but received no injury. Entering the Sultan's capital, he was startled by the hooting of a great horned owl from the ivy of an ancient tower.

> So close was the sound to my ear [he writes] and so dismal its tone that it seemed to indicate a fresh series of mischances on shore. To confirm this melancholy impression, I had scarcely alighted at the ambassador's residence in Pera when Mr Turner, the principal secretary, greeted me with a most unexpected and unwelcome admonition: "I am sorry," he said, "to inform your excellency that you have a traitor in the embassy."

This last ominous intimation referred to a dragoman who was betraying all that was said in the embassy to Baron Miltitz, the Prussian ambassador. Knowing that the Baron had been the intimate friend of his predecessor, Lord Strangford, the new ambassador decided to keep on his guard, but not to dismiss the traitor for the present. But all these horrid portents—fever, shipwreck, adverse winds, the fall from his horse at Rodosto, the hooting of the owl, the discovery of treachery within the embassy —proved illusive. By the middle of March Canning's wife and the rest of his staff arrived at Istanbul without further mishap, and the period of Stratford's sojourn was destined to be the most glorious, if not the best known, chapter in his whole career.

News was awaiting him from London. At Petersburg Lord Strangford had taken it on himself to advise a collective remonstrance from the Powers to the Turkish Government. By so doing he had nearly cut the ground from beneath Stratford's feet and incurred the historic rebuke from George Canning, "The instructions I have now to give your Excellency are comprised in a few short words—to be quiet."

The attitude of the new Tsar, Nicholas, was at the moment incalculable. There were grounds for assuming that he was less disposed even than his brother "to talk Greek." The Duke of Wellington had been sent to propose a joint Anglo-Russian intervention if the mediation of Britain alone did not succeed. Meanwhile Stratford was to tell the Sultan that England would not tolerate the depopulation of the Peloponnesos or the creation of a new Barbary state in the Mediterranean. The ambassador's hand was strengthened at this time by the endorsement of the terms agreed to at Hydra by the Grecian National Assembly at Epidauros (April 12, 1826), from which Demetrios Ypsilanti alone dissented. The Greeks invoked the mediation of England, and would accept independence subject to the suzerainty of the Sultan.

That with the Turks everything might be done by kindness appeared still to be the ineradicable belief at Downing Street. The man on the spot knew better. The Divan was encouraged by the death of Alexander, by the continued intrigues of Austria and Prussia, and, above all, by the military prowess of their formidable vassal. "The Greeks," wrote Stratford, "were pretty well run to earth, and the burthen of the war was thrown almost entirely on Egypt." That Turkey in these circumstances would make concessions to her revolted subjects was hardly to be expected. It was only with great difficulty that our envoy obtained an audience of Saida Effendi, the Ottoman Foreign Secretary. The conversation, like all others between the parties, was conducted through the medium of the dragomans or interpreters. Stratford dwelt on the naval might of his country. We controlled the seas, we could intercept the Turkish and Egyptian fleets, but we also could serve Turkey, stop Russia, and pacify Greece.

> The Reis Effendi listened in silence and remained a long time without uttering a syllable. Stratford insisted.
> "I can do no more than listen, to make my report," at length said the Reis Effendi. "My instructions permit no more."
> "But may I at least hear the opinion of Saida Effendi?"
> "It is this. The Porte will not suffer any outside interference in its domestic affairs. The Greeks are our rayahs. No one has the right to come between us and them. The Porte is at peace

with all foreign Powers. We decline to believe that peace can be violated."

"This language," said the Turk to the French dragoman, "may be new to Mr Canning. He must get accustomed to it."[1]

This language was bold to use of Mr Stratford Canning, as the Turk should by now have known. His hand was itching to strike, but his orders hardly permitted him to threaten. He exclaimed aloud, one imagines, on reading a letter from the Duke of Wellington at Petersburg. The Porte might rely upon it that Nicholas would never intervene except as a friend to Turkey in the cause of the Greeks. Mr Canning was advised to show this letter to the Sublime Porte, together with a lecture from the Tsar which accompanied it.

To the Duke the preservation of harmonious relations between two legitimate sovereigns no doubt seemed worth purchasing by the total extinction of the people to which Europe owes her culture. Stratford Canning was no such fool. However dutifully he might appear to conduct himself towards his own Government, he desired above all things to put a stop to the devastation of the Peloponnesos and to see Hellas rise from the dust of ages. He did not show the Duke's letter to the Reis Effendi. To have done so would have been to throw away the last arrow in his quiver. The Turks must be forced to yield, as he had previously advised, by the menace of war. Nor was he at all convinced of the pacific intentions of the new Tsar. The event quickly proved him right. Russia presented an ultimatum to the Porte, dealing, it is true, only with the Danubian principalities and the Serbs, but well calculated, in the expressive modern phrase, to 'put the wind up' the Sultan and his advisers. "You are now authorized to say," wrote cousin George from London, "that Russia joins with us as to the question of the Morea [the Peloponnesos], and to insinuate that we may join with the Russians hereafter if the Turks will not come to some understanding about the Greeks."

[1] Driault, *Histoire diplomatique de la Grèce*, vol. i, p. 310.

The English statesman had seen in the abated pretensions of the Hellenes put forward at Hydra a basis of settlement which might be acceptable to Russia. In the protocol of St Petersburg, signed by Wellington and Nesselrode on April 4, 1826, it was agreed that the two Powers should act in concert should England's mediation fail. The boundaries of the country called Greece were not defined. "But for your conference with the Greeks," wrote Canning to his cousin, "there would have been no protocol."

Stratford himself was not so pleased with the protocol. He did not think that Turkey's attitude would be altered by the friendly representations of Russia with her sword not only sheathed, but, as a result of Wellington's diplomacy, rammed down into the scabbard. "Surely," he said, "it is best for the Turks to suppose that coercion is intended." The Reis Effendi was resolute in denying the right of England or of any other Power to intervene in the internal affairs of the Empire. "Mr Canning will obtain nothing from us," he informed the dragoman of the French embassy. "He can return to the charge as often as he pleases. We know that he will try every door before he abandons his project." It was useless, at any rate, to knock at the door of the Austrian and Prussian embassies. Metternich was furious at the new Tsar's abandonment of the Holy Alliance, and of this the Turks were well aware. Baron Miltitz frequented the house of Stratford's interpreter, not solely, as our ambassador suspected, for the sake of his attractive wife. There was rejoicing at the German courts when Missolonghi fell after an heroic defence. Desperately Stratford suggested that Mehemet Ali might be induced to offer his mediation to his nominal suzerain by a promise of the pashalic of Syria.

Still, all through the year the valiant Greeks held out. Stratford alone among diplomatists and statesmen was zealous in their cause. Of the temper of the nation with which he was contending he had a striking illustration in June. Sultan Mahmud was resolved to be master in his own palace as well as in his distant dominions. He made an end of the Janissaries, the formidable corps which had so long terrorized the Seraglio. Everywhere in the lane-like streets of Istanbul one stumbled over the bodies of the slaughtered soldiery. The Sea of Marmora was mottled with corpses. Not a day passed but our intrepid representative was called on by the Porte to deliver up the officer and soldiers of the doomed regiment who had served him as his official guard. On one pretext or another Stratford Canning detained them from one day to the next till he was at length able to obtain from the Sultan's Government a promise that the men's lives should be spared. They were sent into banishment. Many years later the ambassador was rewarded by a visit from the officer, who came from a distance to offer him a bunch of dried grapes and a flagon of sweet water. This, says his Excellency, was only one of many instances of good feeling on the part of a Turk towards a Christian.

The destruction of the Janissaries and the organization of a new force, trained on European lines, lessened the pressure on the Greeks. They had to thank their deadliest enemy, the Sultan, rather than their tepid friends, Russia and Britain, for their survival. Ribeaupierre, the long-expected ambassador from the Tsar, at last appeared in Pera in February 1827. Mrs Canning had reason to rejoice at this accession to her very restricted social circle, and her husband at finding a diplomatic ally; but though on June 9 the Porte categorically refused to receive any further representations on behalf of the Greeks, neither of the Powers which had signed the protocol was in haste to recognize that the *casus fœderis* therein provided for had in fact arisen. Possibly George Canning, having called a New World into existence on the other-side of the Atlantic to redress the balance of the Old, thought that the loss of the most ancient civilized nation would not disturb that equilibrium. "I am in a dreadful state of anxiety about the unfortunate Greeks," wrote Stratford.

"Assistance will come too late and in too feeble a shape, I fear."

Always fearing that Russia might suddenly take command of the situation, George Canning went over to Paris in the summer and discovered a new ally in the old King Charles X. The descendant of St Louis deeply resented the hanging of a Christian patriarch from the lintel of his own cathedral by Paynim hands. "If you will send a fleet to the Mediterranean," he said, "the fleet of France will co-operate with you." But even when a treaty was signed between Britain, France, and Russia on July 6, 1827, there was still talk of mediation, and only in a secret article did the Powers reserve the right to exercise force:

> If within one month, the Porte did not accept the armistice, or if the Greeks refused to execute it, the said High Powers intend to exert all the means which prudence may suggest for the purpose of obtaining the immediate effects of the Armistice, by preventing as far as possible all collision between the contending parties, without, however, taking any part in the hostilities between them.

Stratford did not expect more of this convention than of the protocol of which it was the development. Without taking part in hostilities, the Powers would find it difficult to interpose between a Turkish army and the insurgents. However, on August 3 the dragomans of the three allied embassies were sent to demand the consent of the Porte to the conditions of the treaty. Angrily the new Reis Effendi asked what exactly was meant by the expression "means which prudence may suggest." "We are not here to offer commentaries, but to communicate the ambassadors' demands," was the bold reply. "If you asked me," added Desgranges, the French interpreter, "what boat I intended to take to-morrow on the Bosphorus I should say that would depend on circumstances." The Reis Effendi refused to take the note. Chabert, Stratford's man, laid it on the sofa. There it remained. Next day the dragomans came back for an answer. This was short and to the point. "The Sublime Porte refuses to discuss the question of Greece. This is positive, absolute and definite."[1]

The Turkish Foreign Secretary, it should be said, was no longer Saida Effendi. His successor, Pertev, on one occasion, Stratford tells us, used his scissors for our discomfiture.

> He cut off a piece of thick Turkish paper, and drawing a long horizontal line upon it, divided the line into two parts, and then subdivided each part in the same manner. On one side of the centre, possible concessions were described in two degrees; on the other was a positive and active *non-possumus*. These several distinctions were thrown away upon us. We could only reject the open side as being wholly inadequate, and made a stand against that which was declared to be irrevocably closed.

The Greeks professed their readiness to accept an armistice, but Ibrahim Pasha harried the country with fire and sword. In the spring Vice-Admiral Sir Edward Codrington had taken command of the British force in Greek waters. He was joined on September 21 by a French squadron under Rear-Admiral de Rigny, and on October 13 by a Russian squadron commanded by Rear-Admiral Count Heiden. Codrington, in supreme command, found his orders embarrassingly vague. What George Canning himself intended will never be known with certainty, for he died on August 8, and it was to his cousin at Istanbul that the puzzled Admiral applied for enlightenment. Stratford's reply is important. He had talked the matter over with his French and Russian colleagues.

> On the subject of collision, we agree that, although the measures to be executed by you are not adopted in a hostile spirit, and although it is clearly the intention of the allied Governments to avoid if possible anything that may bring on a war, yet the prevention of supplies [to the Egyptian army] is ultimately to be enforced, if necessary and when all other means are exhausted, by cannon shot.

---

[1] Driault, *op. cit.*, vol. i, p. 377.

In dealing with an officer of Codrington's temper the introduction of the words "cannon shot" Stratford, in his old age, thought injudicious. But by what other means could the operations of the Moslem fleet have been checked? If Stratford Canning had not thus interpreted his dead cousin's treaty Hellas might have met the fate of Abyssinia.

One Sunday towards the end of October his Excellency was on his way to a conference with his colleagues when a soiled scrap of paper was thrust into his hands. It proved to be a message sent from Smyrna by Captain Cotton, the commander of an English ship. While becalmed off the island of Cytherea, at the southern extremity of Greece, he had heard a violent and continuous cannonade, interrupted by several terrific explosions, from the north-west. He had no doubt that a general action had taken place and that several vessels had been blown up. Stratford showed this note to his fellow ambassadors. Guilleminot, the Frenchman, changed colour.

> "Trois têtes dans un bonnet—n'est-ce-pas?" he said. I could have added, "Et dans un panier, peut-être—qui sait?" [writes Stratford]. But I confined myself to a word of assent, and as we could only wait for further information, it was useless for the Russian and myself to keep our French colleague from his soup.

The news, though he did not know it, had also reached the Porte. Captain Cotton had heard the cannonade of Navarino. On October 20, 1827, Codrington, at the head of the allied fleet, had signally defeated the Turkish and Egyptian squadrons and assured the independence of Greece. Mehemet Ali preserved a countenance of Spartan immobility in face of the destruction of the fleet of which he was so proud. His lord, the Sultan, was otherwise moulded. He sat stunned by the disaster, rallying only to utter bloodcurdling threats against the Christian dogs. His astrologer foretold blood, earthquakes, and famine. Fifty years before the three envoys would have been locked up in the Seven Towers. Stratford half-expected that they would be the victims of the Sultan's wrath. He asked Codrington to send a frigate to fetch his wife away, but she refused to stir from the post of danger. The Turks set a cordon of troops round each embassy, but they curbed their rage. When a detailed account of the action reached Constantinople it appeared clear to the ambassadors that the Moslems had fired first, and to the Porte that a powerful portion of their navy remained seaworthy. Furiously the Reis Effendi summoned the dragomans before him. Canning sent another than the interpreter who had betrayed him to the Prussian. The man soon returned with the Turks' demands—the Powers must indemnify the Sultan for the damage inflicted on his fleet and discontinue their agitation on behalf of the rebels. The language of the Porte was not that of men who admit defeat, but of those who indignantly demand redress for a wanton outrage. From the ambassadors there could be but one sort of reply—they were inflexibly determined to enforce the treaty with a view to the pacification of Greece, and the right of the Porte to any indemnity could not be entertained till it was proved beyond all doubt that the allied fleets had been the aggressors.

In this dire hour the Reis Effendi resorted to that policy dear to the Turks, which was pursued with such consummate skill by Abd-ul-Hamid three-quarters of a century later. On November 11 he invited Guilleminot to talk with him, and hinted that his master might be induced to listen to the representations of two Powers, but not of three. The ambassador of France loyally rejected the bait and communicated the proposal to his colleagues. When, therefore, Stratford was sent for by Pertev four days later he was prepared for a similar overture. "I told him," he writes,[1] "in the name of my Government that the time had passed for any mediation by a single Power or for a direct negotiation between the Porte and the Greeks." He was, however, mistaken

[1] F.O. Stratford Canning Papers, 352. Public Record Office.

in presuming that the resistance was weakening. The Sultan would not grant an armistice to his insurgent subjects. They must lay down their arms and trust to his clemency. "The Sultan was the father of his people." Beyond all doubt the Turks had been advised by the Austrian internuncio, Ottenfels, of the change in the disposition of the English Cabinet which had ensued on the death of George Canning. It is hardly more doubtful that our ambassador, also conscious of this, decided to force the hands of the men at home who were trying to undo his cousin's work. He and his colleagues demanded their passports. These were refused. We are not at war with any of the Powers, objected the Reis Effendi, and if the ambassadors choose to leave their stations without producing the orders of their Governments we cannot officially recognize their departure. Ribeaupierre, notwithstanding, sailed for Odessa. Stratford, followed on the same day by Guilleminot, and accompanied by the staff of the embassy, left Constantinople on December 8. It was by no means sure that he would be suffered to escape. Where the Dardanelles are commanded by two castles the British vessel was boarded by a customs officer. The ambassador ordered the man to be entertained with coffee, and meanwhile rowed ashore to pay his respects to the pasha commanding the garrison. He was received with the courtesy usually extended to British travellers of apparent opulence, and refrained from disclosing his official character till he could see through the windows that his ship had drifted beyond the range of the castle guns. Possibly the hospitable Turk had received no instructions from Constantinople to detain him or realized that it was too late to carry them out. At all events, he manifested no surprise on hearing who his visitor was and offered no hindrance to his departure. Canning arrived safely at Corfu, and thence made his way as fast as he could to London, leaving his wife to follow by easy stages.

Before he had set foot again on his native shore the

PRINCE METTERNICH
From an engraving after a painting by Sir Thomas Lawrence

armed intervention of Russia, which it had been the settled policy of his cousin to avert, had become a fact. Goaded by the partial destruction of his fleet, Sultan Mahmud had published an indiscreet manifesto which amounted almost to the proclamation of a holy war against the infidel. As such, at least, it was accepted by the Tsar. The Russian armies crossed the Pruth. Though he was cordially welcomed by George IV and by Lord Dudley, the Foreign Secretary, Stratford was soon made unpleasantly aware that the Duke of Wellington, now the head of the Government, wanted to drop the Greek Question. The ambassador, as he himself puts it, "faced the lion in his den." He argued that, since Russia was now at war with Turkey, England and France were bound to dispatch an expedition to Greece, in order to put a stop to hostilities there and to throw their weight into the scales against their ally. Wellington entirely disagreed. He had always disapproved of the Treaty of London. He took Metternich's view of the Grecian Question, and had made up his mind to do as little for the Greeks as he possibly could, consistently with the literal interpretation of the treaty. In the King's Speech Codrington's victory, as is well known, was referred to as an untoward event. The Admiral himself was recalled, though not ostensibly for his part in that business. The Turks, exclaimed Stratford, will certainly take his supersession to be a formal disavowal of the policy which had culminated at Navarino. "We cannot too strongly impress on your Excellency," wrote Lord Aberdeen, Dudley's successor, at a later date, "that we are not at war with Turkey." But Russia was; and now France invited Britain to join with her in an armed expedition to the Peloponnesos. Wellington at once refused his co-operation, so the French King acted alone and dispatched a force of 12,000 men under Marshal Maison to impose the armistice on the belligerents in the peninsula.

Wellington and Aberdeen realized that they must do

something or leave the settlement of Greece entirely to the allies whom they so profoundly distrusted. Kapodistrias, Stratford's old colleague in Switzerland, had lately been elected President of the Hellenic Republic. In Whitehall he was regarded as merely a warming-pan for Russia. News travelled slowly in those days, and it was desirable to have a man on the spot. On July 2, 1828, Stratford Canning was informed by Lord Aberdeen that his Majesty had been pleased to entrust to him, in conjunction with the plenipotentiaries of his allies, the negotiations which were still necessary to carry into execution the Treaty of London of July 6, 1827. He was to return to the Levant, but not to Constantinople. He was to confer with the Greek Government and take Greek representations into consideration. In the protocol which he and his fellow-ambassadors would prepare the frontier of the new state should be clearly defined and easily defensible. Four frontiers, continues Lord Aberdeen, have been proposed: one drawn from the Gulf of Volo to the mouth of the Aspropotamos, a second from Thermopylæ to the Gulf of Corinth, a third to include Attica and Megara along the crest of Mount Parnes, and a fourth across the isthmus, limiting Greece to the peninsula. Whichever boundary-line was chosen, a large proportion of the islands and all the Cyclades were to be included; but the large island of Euboia, being mainly inhabited by Turks, was to be left entirely outside the scope of the negotiations. Ottoman suzerainty was taken to be a condition of the mediation.

Wellington and his Foreign Secretary were seldom conspicuous for sagacity in the management of public affairs. Still, one thinks that men of even less intelligence might have perceived the danger of entrusting this mission to the cousin and disciple of George Canning. Reading these first instructions, the ambassador himself no doubt conceived it practicable for him to interpret them in a sense not wholly unfavourable to the Greeks; and he may have decided that his duty to humanity at large would justify him in exceeding them. Leaving his "dear E." behind him, he started once more for the East. His letters penned *en route*, and mostly on shipboard, give a graphic account of his meeting with his old friend General Church, now commanding the Greek army; with Marshal Maison, whom he found with his Frenchmen occupying a part of the Southern Peloponnesos; and with Ibrahim Pasha, short, ruddy, blue-eyed, and good-humoured, who was awaiting transportation with his Egyptians back to Alexandria.

The Ottoman Government, pressed by Russia on the side of the Danube and anxious to conciliate the western Powers, consented to a cessation of hostilities in the peninsula, as from September 19. Their troops were still in possession of Athens and other strategic points in continental Greece. Being at war with Russia, the Porte would not send a representative to a conference at which the enemy Power's ambassador was present. The three ambassadors met at Poros, an island in the Gulf of Aigina; and there, or rather on H.M.S. *Dryad*, the deliberations began about the middle of September.

They lasted till the beginning of December. Much time was consumed by extracting information about the population, resources, and financial prospects of the Greek nation from Kapodistrias. "The failure of our endeavours," writes Stratford, "would have been no disappointment" to the Russophil president. The resurgent people were turning towards France. The actual British Cabinet's bias in favour of the Moslem Power was no secret. The Most Christian King, at any rate, could not find it in his conscience to sustain a Mohammedan empire because, as Castlereagh had said, it was exempt from the revolutionary danger. Stratford with difficulty restrained Maison from acting upon Kapodistrias's invitation to turn the Turks out of Attica. But the castle of Morea, a stronghold commanding the Strait of Lepanto, yielded to French arms. In August the Greek president had sent a force under Baron de

Rheineck to raise the Cretans. The Turks called on Mehemet Ali for help, since the island was not covered by the armistice. There were rumours of massacres. Upon the orders of the three ambassadors the British fleet re-established the blockade, which had been lifted by Aberdeen, and prevented the landing of the Egyptian troops.

Confinement on shipboard wearied Mr Canning. He listened sympathetically to the French view that if Greece were too small she would become subject to England—in fact, an eighth Ionian island—and that if she were too large she might one day ally herself with some powerful state and menace the equilibrium of the Mediterranean. This view marched so well with our ambassador's heartfelt desire to help Greece that one morning he rose from his cot after a sleepless night, and without dressing wrote out the draft of a convention for the settlement of the country on the lines hinted at by Guilleminot. The frontier was drawn from the Gulf of Volo to the Gulf of Arta—farther north, therefore, than any of the boundaries specified by Aberdeen. Greece, subject to the suzerainty of the Sultan, was to be an hereditary monarchy under a Christian prince. The tribute to Turkey was to be reduced to 1,500,000 piastres a year. Euboia and the Cyclades were included in the new state, and the addition of Crete was recommended to the benevolent consideration of the three contracting Powers. This, thought Canning, was as much as a London conference would approve or the Porte accept. The protocol came to form the basis of the independence of the Greek nation. Stratford Canning should, therefore, be remembered with Byron, Codrington, Church, and Cochrane as one of those high-minded Britons who, despite the frowns of their petty and mean-spirited Governments, pushed back the stagnant flood of Turanian conquest.

The plenipotentiaries were in haste to depart. Ribeaupierre could not restrain his tears at the thought of a further separation from his wife. "So you see," wrote

Stratford to his dear "E.," ".that I am not the only good husband in the world." Having forwarded the protocol, together with a mighty package of papers supporting it, to London, the ambassadors sailed in the middle of December for Naples, there to await instructions. Mrs Canning came to join her husband. Probably he needed her sympathy. To his arguments in favour of one or other of the more northern boundaries being assigned to Greece, Aberdeen had replied on November 18 by expressing the desire of the Government to see the new state limited to the Peloponnesos and the islands. No idea of the inclusion of Crete and Euboia could be entertained. His Britannic Majesty, insisted his lordship, had from the first desired only the pacification of Greece. He did not intend to make conquests at the expense of his ancient ally Turkey. The insurrection (it was strangely alleged) was practically confined to the peninsula, and to that part of the Grecian world the stipulations of the Treaty of London could therefore only be said to apply.

Stratford's intervention on behalf of the Cretans brought down on him a direct censure (dated December 20). "His majesty can never approve of such a departure from positive instructions, upon grounds inadequate at best, but which in your excellency's case could have had no real existence at all." By forbidding the introduction of reinforcements for the Ottoman garrison the ambassadors had made themselves allies of the insurgents. In an unfortunate passage Lord Aberdeen spoke of the apparent complacency with which his Excellency calculated the number of British or French troops required to effect the evacuation of the island. Hardly less severe was the Foreign Secretary's condemnation of the protocol, the substance of which had been communicated to him by a dispatch from Stratford dated November 26. "Notwithstanding the account you give of General Guilleminot's opinions, the limits of Greece proposed by the French Government, so far as we can learn from the Prince de Polignac, are not very different from our own proposition."[1] Another conference was sitting in London to receive the ambassadors' report. The Cabinet found the result of the deliberations at Poros highly embarrassing and scarcely consistent with his lordship's instructions to Mr Canning or with what he knew to be their views.

Lord Aberdeen forgot that in the official instructions dated July 2 Canning had been directed to take Greek representations into consideration and to provide the new state with an easily defensible frontier. His later letters had been inspired by news of the progress of the Russian armies, and in any case could have reached the ambassador too late to decide him on an attitude of opposition to his colleagues. Moreover, the protocol embodied the recommendations of the three allied Powers, not the separate proposals of England or any one of them. Having pointed this out, his Excellency took strong exception to the form and substance of his chief's comments to his action in regard to Crete.

> I should really think myself unworthy, I will not say of my present situation, high as it is in confidence and dignity, but of any place whatever in the trust of my sovereign, if I were to shrink from the responsibility of modifying or suspending any part of my instructions when happening to be in possession of information unknown at the time to H.M.'s ministers and calculated to affect materially their views. . . . Your lordship, when taunting me with "complacency" in calculating the number of troops necessary to effect the evacuation of Candia by the Turks, appears to impute to me a sentiment which I am scarcely more capable of applying to that contingency than to any speculations founded on the number of victims in the late massacre at Canea, however I may have erred as to the degree of importance which I attached to that deplorable occurrence.

The retort was merited. Lord Aberdeen, of course, could not be expected to admit this, and he called on the

[1] Brit. Mus., Add. MSS. 43090 (private letter from Aberdeen to Stratford Canning).

ambassador to submit another dispatch from which the sarcastic passage was excised. This Stratford at last consented to do, upon condition that the offensive phrase in the minister's letter was also expunged from the official records. The words "apparent complacency" were accordingly very neatly erased from the copy of his lordship's dispatch preserved in the Public Record Office, although a blank space titillates the curiosity of the uninformed.

Stratford defended himself lustily and said "Recall me," but he liked as little as other proud men the stigma of disgrace. Another letter came from the Foreign Secretary:

> I know of no person, whom I should see with so much pleasure engaged in bringing the whole of this Greek question to a termination. But it is indispensable that we should clearly understand each other before we engage in what may be considered almost a new work. . . . It is the intention of your Government to use every exertion to limit the Greek state to the Morea [the Peloponnesos] and the isles which have been placed under the guarantee of the three Powers. We may possibly be beaten in this attempt; but whatever may be the private opinion of the minister acting for us, it is clear that we must be able to rely upon his utmost endeavours to carry our intention into effect.

Steadying his temper, Canning replied that if all the three Powers could agree on the desired boundaries no opposition need be expected from him. If, however, Britain alone favoured the narrower limits every one would know that the British representative was putting forward a view contrary to his known and expressed opinions. He did not like to leave the ship while it was labouring. But, so far from an agreement being arrived at between the three Governments, Russia and France declared their adhesion to the Protocol of Poros. Therefore, wrote Aberdeen,

> it would be too much to expect of you that you should labour with zeal to destroy at Constantinople what you had constructed

with so much pains at Poros. . . . I can therefore entertain no doubt that you would not feel yourself disposed to attempt such a duty as would be imposed on you at Constantinople. I have therefore considered your letter as a conditional resignation of your present situation.

The Earl's brother, Sir Robert Gordon, had been appointed to conduct the negotiations with the Porte and was leaving at once for Naples. When Stratford Canning had read half this letter, and realized he was recalled, he flung it on the floor and stamped on it. Presently he picked it up and read it to the end. "Thank God," he exclaimed, "they haven't dared to ask me to do the dirty work they have given that fellow Gordon!"

Some months later, when his wrath had cooled, he learned from the unfriendly Duke that the acceptance of his "conditional resignation" had been far from inevitable. The British envoy's instructions were to support the Poros protocol, and only in the face of its rejection by the Porte was the alternative British project to be put forward. Stratford's hands would thus have been untied. He had been treated unfairly, and he knew it. Seizing on a vague hint of reward, he wrote on April 11 to Aberdeen,[1] pointing out that, unless he received some signal mark of his Majesty's favour, it would be universally supposed that he had been disgraced and that his diplomatic career had ended in failure. He was promised the red riband of the Bath, but he had to wait for it till the end of 1829. Considering the terms of his letter of April 11 and the urgency of the frequent reminders he addressed to the Cabinet in the course of the year, one can but smile on hearing that he told his wife he found his new dignity a great bore and was so tired of being addressed as Sir Stratford by the servants that he had a good mind to go back to Windsor and ask the King to unknight him. It does not appear that much pressure was needed to dissuade him from this step.

[1] Brit. Mus., Add. MSS. 43090.

The ultimate triumph of his policy may have gratified him much more. The Porte, relying no doubt on Sir Robert Gordon's support, did indeed reject his protocol, but it was embodied in the Treaty of Adrianople dictated to Turkey by the Russians. It now appeared probable that Greece would become dependent on the great Orthodox Power, the culmination which Canning had steadily striven to avoid. In desperation Wellington now went farther than the Philhellenic ambassador. He agreed to the abandonment of the Turkish suzerainty and to the erection of Greece into an independent monarchy under a king to be chosen from one of the lesser European dynasties. Stratford had talked with Leopold of Saxe-Coburg at Naples, and it may have been his depressing account of the country which determined that astute prince finally to refuse the offer of the new throne. It was at last accepted by Otho of Bavaria—a strange choice, since he was too young to govern and belonged to the Roman Church.

Wellington's Cabinet fell, as it deserved to fall, on November 15, 1830. Unfortunately, it bequeathed to the Foreign Office a spite against Greece which has broken out again and again down to our own day. Having granted her the Ionian Islands, Britain has opposed her natural expansion inch by inch, year after year. By her own good sword Hellas wrested Macedonia and Crete from the Moslems; her failure to hold Smyrna was largely due to the lukewarmness of our support. Palmerston, who succeeded Aberdeen in November 1830 as Foreign Secretary and professed to be a disciple of George Canning, nineteen years later subjected the young kingdom to profound humiliation in order to enforce the fraudulent claims of a Gibraltar Jew.

That was hardly to be foreseen when, in the autumn of 1831, he sent Stratford back to his old station to settle the eternal boundary dispute in favour, if possible, of the Greeks. In the meantime the tyrannical Kapodistrias had been assassinated, and his brother held the presidency till the king should be chosen. Sir Stratford on landing at Nauplia saw skirmishing going on between the different factions in the Plain of Argos. He warned the Government to keep better order and addressed strong representations to the ambassadors' conference still sitting in London. Still, the country was safe enough to permit his visiting Athens. Constantinople was reached on January 28, 1832. The dispute with the Ottoman Government narrowed down to the definition of the Arta-Volo boundary, though Nejib, the Reis Effendi, artlessly called the attention of Canning and his colleagues to the advantages of the Gulf of Lepanto as a frontier. It was evident that the Turks were resolved to protract the negotiation indefinitely. On May 17 Mehemet Ali and his son Ibrahim, who had invaded Syria, were proclaimed rebels against the Sultan. One boisterous night Sir Stratford, who liked doing things dramatically, was rowed up the Golden Horn to the house of a wealthy Greek, Stephanaki Vogorides Bey. As a result of this nocturnal visit it was conveyed to his Imperial Majesty that the support of Britain against his terrible vassal might be purchased by the inexpensive method of speeding up the boundary negotiations. The like representations were made to the Grand Vizier by an agent sent to the army headquarters in Asia Minor. The upshot of these manœuvres was the sudden appearance at the conference on May 26 of the commander of the imperial bodyguard with an appeal from his Majesty to the plenipotentiaries to dispatch the matter at issue as quickly as possible in conformity with the wishes of the parties. Even so, the opposition of the Reis Effendi could only be overcome by leaving the towns of Volo and Arta to Turkey and drawing the frontier line half-way across the two gulfs. So the boundary remained until the year 1881, when Thessaly was annexed to Greece.

Now that the English diplomatist, with so little encouragement from his court, had helped to give the Hellenic people a fresh start in life, he turned his mind

to the problem of preserving the Ottoman Empire.
Three days after an interview with Mahmud he had urged
Palmerston by letter to afford the Turks naval assistance
against Egypt. From Paris, on his way home, he sent
in a memorandum on the Turkish Question. The empire
had reached, in his opinion, in its decline that point at
which it must either revive and commence a fresh era
of prosperity or fall into a state of complete dissolution.
"To Gt. Britain, the fate of this empire can never be
indifferent." It would necessarily affect the interests of
her trade and her intercourse with India, apart from the
disturbance to the balance of power in Europe. Britain
was under the necessity of rescuing Turkey from a war
which threatened to lay her at the feet of a Power already
too great for the security of Europe. He spoke of
Russia. Palmerston read the memorandum, and upon
Stratford's arrival clapped him on the back. "You are
the man," he said, but he was too busy with Belgium
to act upon the advice. The Egyptians drew nearer and
nearer to the Bosphorus, and, finding no help from
London or Paris, the Sultan in desperation accepted it
from the Tsar. In February 1833 a Russian army
forbade the further advance of Ibrahim Pasha. Russian
ships of war rode in the Bosphorus. By the Treaty of
Unkiar Iskelesi, signed on June 8, 1833, the two empires
entered into an offensive and defensive alliance for a
term of eight years. In case of war the Porte would close
the Dardanelles against the enemies of Russia. The
British Government protested at Petersburg and Constantinople. But the renewed truculence of Mehemet Ali
gave an excuse for British intervention in 1840. The
Treaty of Unkiar Iskelesi had expired and was not
renewed.

III

The prospect of Whitehall was dearer to the returned
envoy than the view from an embassy window. He got
into Parliament first for Old Sarum, which he knew to

be the rottenest borough in England, then for Stockbridge, finally for King's Lynn.

At forty-two, after a life spent mainly abroad, he should have known that only by a protracted and intensive study of domestic affairs could he usefully serve his country in the House of Commons. Opportunities of observing the life of the poor in his own country, of acquainting himself with the economics of trade, industry, and agriculture, he had had very few. Says his biographer, Lane-Poole:

> His opinions, indeed, were respected, and his counsel sought, especially on Eastern questions. . . . As a speaker . . . he had to contend with a nervousness which generally kept him silent. No man possessed more completely the power of impressive speech when a message had to be conveyed to a sovereign or a statesman; none knew better how to combine grace of diction with accuracy, lucidity, and completeness of expression.

But most of these messages, it should be remembered, were delivered through the mouths of interpreters and had been carefully committed to paper beforehand. In Washington Canning left no special reputation for eloquence. That he made no mark in the House of Commons was no surprise to his powerful political friends. In 1839 Sir Robert Peel, by obstinately refusing him an appointment at home, fairly drove him back to the sphere to which his personality and his talents unmistakably assigned him.

To the interval belongs that episode which is generally believed to have warped his diplomatic outlook and brought British and Russian soldiers face to face in the Crimea.

Sir Stratford's seat of Stockbridge was demolished by the Reform Bill. It was then that Palmerston decided to accredit him to the court of Petersburg. As our chief concern with Russia lay in her relations with Turkey, no better selection of an ambassador could have been made. For that reason, as appears on the whole most probable, the Emperor Nicholas informed the British

Government that Sir Stratford was not acceptable to him. The famous Princess Lieven, wife of the Russian ambassador to the court of St James's, and probably the most powerful woman in London, gave an account of this business to the diarist Greville (February 16, 1833). When Earl Grey took office she was told by Nesselrode to see that Lord Heytesbury remained at the Petersburg embassy.

> She asked Palmerston and Lord Grey, and they both promised her he should stay. Some time after, he asked to be recalled. She wrote word to Nesselrode, and told him that either Adair or Canning would succeed him. He replied, "Don't let it be Canning; he is a most impracticable man, *soupçonneux, pointillant, défiant*"; that he had been personally uncivil to the Emperor when he was Grand-duke; in short, the plain truth was, they would not receive him. She told this to Palmerston, and he engaged that Canning should not be sent. Nothing more was done till some time ago, when to her astonishment, Palmerston told her he was going to send Canning to St Petersburg. She remonstrated, urged all the objections of her court, his own engagement, but in vain; the discussions between them grew bitter; Palmerston would not give way, and Canning was one day to her horror gazetted. As might have been expected, Nesselrode positively refused to receive him.

In the meantime, Bligh, our *chargé d'affaires* at Petersburg, had been instructed to sound Count Nesselrode as to the real ground of his objections. The minister was obliged to admit that the Tsar had no recollection of any uncivility offered him by Canning. The two, in fact, had met only once, and that in Paris in 1814 at a *fête* given by Prince Schwarzenberg. "The Emperor," added Bligh, "had expressed himself very warmly on the subject, but had never alluded to the supposed affront."

Palmerston described the Emperor's bald refusal as "a piece of intolerable arrogance and as an interference with the right of the King of England to choose his own servants which we can never consent to." Lady Cowper told Greville that the fault was Princess Lieven's. She had told Nesselrode she was able to prevent the appointment, and Palmerston thought that both she and her court wanted to be taken down a peg. He took them down several pegs by simply abstaining from accrediting any ambassador to the Russian court. By way of retaliation Nicholas withdrew his ambassadors, the two embassies being managed by *chargés d'affaires*. "It remains to be seen whether the Lievens will not have to make a back somersault over the Baltic," Canning had said; and in May 1834 the Princess took a sad farewell of the capital where she had queened it twenty years. Seven years later Sir Stratford, meeting the formidable lady in Paris, was unkind enough to express his regret that his exclusion from Russia should have resulted in the premature loss of her society to England.

While still officially ambassador to the Emperor of All the Russias, Canning was employed in 1832 on a mission to Madrid. In those spacious days Britain had her fingers in many pies. A liberal and chivalrous policy impelled us to support the girl Queen of Portugal, Maria da Gloria, against her absolutist uncle, Dom Miguel. Since Ferdinand of Spain had rescinded the Salic Law in the interest of his daughter, Isabel, it was hoped that he would take the same side in the quarrel. Our envoy found "your Spaniard as hard a negotiator as your Turk." Before long he realized that tyrants held together, and that Ferdinand's zeal for the feminine right of succession did not extend to the neighbouring kingdom. The Cannings found Madrid a dull place. Sir Stratford witnessed a bull-fight. "It is a disgusting sight," he wrote; "the horses are cruelly used, and the men are not killed half often enough. My only consolation was in seeing a picador carried several yards round the ring on the horns of the bull."

This outburst of indignation is notable and helps to explain Stratford's persistent hankering after political employment. He hated cruelty and injustice; he wanted to do positive good; and for the expression of an active humanity diplomacy, it must be admitted, affords little scope. (Within very recent years our representative at Caracas was withdrawn at the request of the Venezuelan Government for protesting against its cruel massacre of dogs.) He was right in declining to continue at Madrid as ambassador. He had no liking for Spain or Spaniards. Less comprehensible is his rejection of the Governorship of Canada, an office which should have suited well his love of domination and arbitrary beneficence. An explanation may perhaps be found in the declining health of his only son, who was to remain an invalid all his life. He had claims on Peel, who took office again in 1841, but was disappointed of a place in the Government. From Aberdeen, once more at the Foreign Office, Stratford Canning could not expect very much. At the age of fifty-four he found himself sent for the fourth time to Constantinople, tempted, not impossibly, by the *rôle* assigned to him of benevolent adviser to the Porte. He was called on now to do something more serious and useful than checkmating the wiles of Russian and French rivals. His instructions were to impart stability to the Sultan's Government by promoting judicious and well-considered reforms. He was to advise a reorganization of the army and the civil administration, the development of the empire's natural resources, the improvement of the fiscal system, and, above all (so he at least would have said), to secure the better treatment of the Christian subjects of the Padishah; he was to compose the differences between the Porte and the people of the Lebanon, the Greeks, and the Pasha of Egypt—and all this, he was warned, without meddling in the domestic affairs of the empire!

Mahmud the Reformer was dead, and it fell to his young successor, Abdu-l-Mejid, to follow in the furrow he had merely traced. On his previous visit in 1832 Canning had noticed that the Turks were laying aside their turbans and gowns for fezes and frock-coats, and that the Padishah and his ministers were learning to stand on their legs. By the *hat*, or charter, of Gülhanè, promulgated by Reshid Pasha, all the Sultan's subjects were to be considered equal before the law. That they were not so considered in fact would be taken as a matter of course by anyone acquainted with the mechanism of an Oriental despotism. A reaction had already set in. Warmly welcomed by the Christian peoples of Turkey, the British ambassador was looked on coldly by the Sultan's ministers. Riza Pasha, the Grand Chamberlain, had the young sovereign's ear, and took care to remind him that it was largely by the machinations of Canning that the Greeks had escaped from the Ottoman yoke. If the advice of the Frank was followed the Osmanli would cease to be masters in their own country. "It would be a great mistake," wrote Sir Stratford to Lord Aberdeen, "to suppose that the Porte is the best judge of its own interests." Governments, he might have added, like ordinary individuals, are generally swayed by passion, custom, and prejudice. If England wanted to stand well with the Turks it would be better not to meddle at all, but to let things drift, probably towards a general insurrection of the rayahs. On the other hand, the decaying state might not impossibly be saved by an active and friendly interference, to be supported by the Powers generally lest the Turks should play their old game of setting one against the other.

A passive course was impossible to Stratford Canning. As he grew older he grew less tolerant of injustice, keener on the righting of wrongs. Knowing his power over the Turks, he could not refrain from exercising it in the interests of humanity. In August 1843 a young Armenian, who 'had turned Turk,' and then reverted to the faith of his fathers, was publicly put to death in Constantinople as a renegade. This was in accordance with what all Moslems regarded as a fundamental law of Islam. Turks acquainted with our western ways might have argued they had as much right to execute those who forswore the creed of the Prophet as we had to hang children for rick-burning. By a seeming paradox, moreover, religious liberty existed and had existed for centuries in the Ottoman dominions to a far greater extent than in any Christian state. Every man was free to profess and practise the law of his ancestors, and proselytism was not encouraged.[1] But if anyone should voluntarily abandon Islam he was held to have insulted the Prophet and the religion of the masters.

Such arguments had no weight with Stratford Canning. Nor, strange to say, with Lord Aberdeen, usually so fearful of 'meddling' in the internal affairs of another state. One suspects that the influence of the young Queen, Victoria, was beginning to tell on her Cabinet. Bourqueney, the ambassador of the essentially 'Liberal' Government of Louis-Philippe, was also instructed to protest against this ancient restraint upon that most sacred of Liberal principles, religious liberty. Canning demanded of the Porte that those who reverted from Islam should no longer be punished by the law. "It would not succeed," Frederick Pisani, the dragoman to the British embassy, remarked when the note was placed in his hand. "Mr Pisani, it shall succeed," said the ambassador, terrible in his resolution. It ultimately succeeded, even when Stratford's French colleague had withdrawn his support in despair. Success was due not so much to the ambassador's urgency as to the erudition of Charles Alison, his Oriental secretary. "It is written in the Koran," was the invariable answer of the Sultan's ministers. "It is not written in the Koran," rejoined the English scholar. He proved that the law was derived only from the Sunna, or book of traditions. Finding that the Devil could quote Scripture, the Porte was shaken, but protested that the tradition was equally binding and irrevocable. To quiet Stratford the Sultan gave him a verbal promise that the law should not be put in force.

[1] Kinglake, in *Eothen*, written in 1843, tells how a girl who abjured Christianity in order to marry a Turkish bey was compelled by the Ottoman authorities to return to the Christian fold.

This was not enough. The ambassador drafted a note: her Britannic Majesty's Government observed with satisfaction that the Sublime Porte, in taking effective measures to prevent the execution of any convert from Christianity who should return from Islam to his original faith, would further declare that Christianity was not to be insulted in the Ottoman dominions nor anyone professing it to be treated and punished as a criminal. This note, of course, went very much farther than the Sultan's promise, and, suspecting its nature, Rifa't Pasha, the Foreign Secretary, refused to receive it. Encountering Stratford as they were proceeding to the Sultan's audience, he put his hands behind his back. "Then the great *elchi*, advancing in his wrath, literally thrust the paper upon him." The audience set the seal to the whole, and a far-reaching revolution in Islam was thus peacefully accomplished. Abdu-l-Mejid declared he was pleased to be the first sultan to make such a concession. "And I hope to be the first Christian ambassador to be allowed to kiss your majesty's hand," was Stratford's courtly rejoinder. "No, no!" said the Sultan, and he shook the infidel's hand warmly.

Here was some positive good done by the great diplomatist—conscience freed, and more human lives saved than it would be possible to calculate. He next secured the abolition of judicial torture among the Turks —a practice, to do them justice, to which they had never been much addicted. Kinglake, his fervent admirer, tells us that he intervened successfully on behalf of two excellent Persian princes, refugees from their own country, for whose extradition the Shah had clamoured. Peculiarly gratifying to Queen Victoria was the recognition of the Protestant religion, also procured at the instance of her ambassador. At the time he was inclined to regard it as a diplomatic success. Russia persistently claimed to be the protector of the Orthodox subjects of the Sultan. France posed as the protector of the Roman Catholics; Britain, as the defender of the other Christian sect, might have played a similar *rôle* but for the fact that Protestantism never made any headway on the ground which had been covered by the old Byzantine Empire. The British consuls throughout Turkey, however, had orders from the embassy to take the Christians generally under their protection. This they did so energetically that Aberdeen felt constrained to issue a circular, directing them not to interfere in the internal administration of the country. Canning read the circular, as one imagines, with a frown. When he sent it out he attached to every copy a private note assuring the consul to whom it was addressed that the admonition could not possibly apply to him.

In those days he could more safely reckon on the countenance of the Ottoman Government than on his chief's. The reactionaries at Istanbul were turned out in October 1845, and his trusted friend Reshid once more took the helm. About this time Henry Layard, the eminent traveller and archæologist, drifted to Constantinople. After a curt and dubious reception by some underling of the embassy he was warmly welcomed by Stratford, and his unequalled knowledge of the Near East secured for the benefit of his own country. Russia and Britain had jointly undertaken the delimitation of the boundary between Turkey and Persia. Upon Layard's expert advice Canning awarded the town of Mohammerah, at the mouth of the Shatt-el-Arab, to the Osmanli. Aberdeen overruled him and concurred with the Russians in giving the town to the Shah. In Layard's presence the ambassador gave way to a furious outburst of anger against the Foreign Secretary. He was hostile to him personally, he shouted, and under the thumb of Russia. The Tsar, he added, was determined to thwart his policy on every possible occasion. In a dispute over the hereditary Governorship of Serbia Aberdeen, again to our representative's outspoken indignation, lent a negative support to the Russian candidate.[1]

[1] Sir Henry Layard, *Autobiography*, vol. ii, p. 70.

By some Stratford Canning will be most gratefully remembered for defraying at his own expense the cost of Layard's work at Nineveh. The spoils of the excavation were presented by him to the British Museum, where also repose the treasures of Halicarnassus, discovered in a Turkish fort at Budrun.

To the eminent archæologist we owe a close view of the man to whom his countrymen learned to apply in a personal sense the description of the Great Elchi. In Turkish, we are informed, the words describe any full-fledged ambassador, as distinguished from a mere minister plenipotentiary. But great Canning certainly was in the estimation of the people among whom he dwelt. In Layard's opinion he abused his power over them. He terrorized the ministers of the Sultan. If some demand was refused he would knit his brows, rise to his feet, and pour out a torrent of invective—the harsher-sounding because not understood—upon the unfortunate pasha cowering in a corner of the divan. The Turks would resort to any trick or evasion to avoid an interview with him. Unfortunately, seeing the success which attended his methods, other foreign representatives set themselves to copy them, so that the Turkish statesmen came to lose all sense of self-respect and dignity. The hectoring tone which Sir Stratford had before long to condemn in Russian envoys to the Porte they had in fact imitated from him.

> The terror which Sir Stratford Canning inspired among the Turkish ministers and pashas was amusing to witness. The only one amongst them who ventured to stand up against him and to brave his frown was Ahmad Vefyk Effendi. He consequently soon fell under the ambassadorial displeasure. I remember, on one occasion when he dined at the embassy, a discussion arising between him and the ambassador as to the imprisonment by the Turkish police at Galata of some British subject, a rascally Ionian or Maltese, who had no doubt been seized *flagrante delicto*, when committing some crime richly deserving punishment. The Effendi attempted to justify the conduct of the

Turkish authorities. Sir Stratford maintained they had violated the capitulations.... The dispute waxed warm, and the expression of the ambassador announced an approaching storm. Suddenly striking the table with his fist, he exclaimed, "And supposing I went down to Galata myself with a *kavass*, to effect the release of the prisoner, what would your authorities venture to do?" "Why," replied the Effendi with his imperturbable calm, "they would probably put you and your *kavass* in prison to join him—and they would only be doing their duty!" It would be difficult to describe the burst of anger to which this somewhat audacious answer gave rise. Although Sir Stratford could not but admire the singular abilities of this remarkable man, he looked upon him as much too independent in his opinions, and as unmanageable, and consequently as a dangerous man should he attain to high rank and to power.[1]

The ambassador did not reserve his frowns for the ministers of the Sultan. By all accounts he was an ill man to live with. An indefatigable worker, finding, as far as I can discover, little pleasure in life outside his job, he became the sternest of taskmasters. The *attaché* summoned to his presence was always careful during the interview to keep his hand on the door-knob. A young gentleman newly arrived from England was kept six weeks copying dispatches before he was allowed to get more than a glimpse of the strange capital in which he found himself. Drummond-Hay after a continuous spell of thirty hours at the desk went to bed and warned his servant that if he disturbed him he would shoot him. Canning sent for him, was told of the order, and waited for his reappearance. "Damn your eyes! How dare you lock yourself up in your room?" he shouted. Young Hay looked the terrible *elchi* straight in the face and said, "Damn your Excellency's eyes!" "You return to England at once," said his chief. But Lady Canning intervened. The stern brow relaxed. The youth was forgiven, but it was a pity, Sir Stratford told him, that he had such a bad temper!

[1] Sir Henry Layard, *op. cit.*, vol. ii, p. 85.

Besides Drummond-Hay many men who achieved diplomatic distinction graduated in the hard school at Pera. There was Robert Curzon, afterwards Lord Zouche, who much preferred wandering about the bazaars of old Istanbul to copying dispatches. One wonders how he escaped from the embassy with his life. Percy Smythe, afterwards Lord Strangford, Lord Stanley of Alderley, Odo Russell, and Henry Wellesley, who became Earl Cowley and ambassador to Napoleon III, were among those who survived this rude schooling. The last-named, it was credibly rumoured, was sent out by the Foreign Office to spy on Canning, and, not unnaturally, received as courteous a welcome as would be extended by a defaulting tenant to a sheriff's officer. A biographer speaks of these budding diplomatists as subalterns who had to be disciplined, but the unfortunate young men were not protected, like subalterns, by the Queen's Regulations.

They had to endure something worse than their chief's vile temper. Sir Stratford wrote verses, and these he insisted on reading aloud to his staff. Distrustful at last of their applause, his Excellency one day invited Layard's opinion of a poem about an engine in a tunnel, which he represented as the work of his children's governess. The Orientalist described the verses as turgid doggerel, and said the lady should be urged to give up all attempts at poetical composition. Canning had then the grace to admit he was the author and to profess amusement at the trap which he had set for himself. Layard he was obliged to treat with respect. Another of his subordinates not easy to browbeat was his Oriental secretary, Charles Alison. This man liked the Turks and had little sympathy with his chief's passion for reforming them. But he had his own methods of dealing with them, not less effective than the ambassador's. While in conference with him an Ottoman dignitary interrupted his discourse in order to perform his devotions, in the course of which he audibly called down curses on the Christians and spat right and left over his shoulders as he mentioned them. Alison listened unmoved, and in his turn craved leave to utter a prayer which he said was enjoined on men of his faith at that hour. The next moment he was on his knees, beseeching God in fluent Turkish to confound the Moslem dogs. The Turk listened, boiling with indignation, but had perforce to admit that the secretary was no less bound than a true believer by the law of his religion.

IV

In the autumn of 1846 Stratford went home on leave. The timid, unsympathetic Scot, Lord Aberdeen, was out of office and had been succeeded at the Foreign Office by the *elchi's* staunch friend and supporter, Palmerston. In 1847 there was trouble in Switzerland. The Catholic cantons formed a league, or Sonderbund, in opposition to the Liberal and anti-clerical policy of the Federal Government. Austria and Prussia meditated intervention on behalf of the dissidents. Palmerston inclined towards the authorities of Bern. Here at hand he had a man whom he could trust and who had had a share, of which now he was not probably very proud, in drawing up the federal pact. Canning was dispatched to Switzerland with offers of friendly mediation. When he reached Bern, however, there was no room for mediation. The Liberals had acted swiftly and decisively. The Sonderbund was crushed.

In the spring the ambassador returned at a leisurely pace to his station across a Europe seething with revolt. His Excellency was specially commissioned by the Foreign Secretary to look in at the capitals on his route. His welcome does not appear to have been over-cordial at either the courts or the embassies which he visited. He broke his journey at Athens to arbitrate between the young Bavarian King Otho and his people, who clamoured for a constitution. His task was not made easier by Sir Edmund Lyons, the British minister on the spot. This sailor-diplomatist appears to have adopted the methods which Canning had found successful at Istanbul, with very different results. To advertise his lofty impartiality Sir Stratford would not allow his wife to enter the city in his colleague's carriage because a seat in it was occupied by General Sir Richard Church—an old friend, indeed, but also the head of a particular faction. This act was interpreted, not unnaturally, by Lyons as a personal slight, when Canning went farther and refused his offer of hospitality on the ground that his party was too large. England's high-handed attitude tended for a moment to rally national sentiment round the unpopular King. Having read his Majesty a lecture, quite in the style to which Lyons had accustomed him, the ambassador to the Porte sailed, probably with some sensations of relief, for Constantinople.

In his absence the Old Turks had crept back to the Sultan's side. They were soon sent packing, and the trustworthy Reshid restored to power. The duel with Russia was at once resumed. The Hungarians had broken away from Austria, and the battle thunder rolled across the Carpathians. It stirred the Wallachians into revolt against the Hospodar appointed by Russia. "Whatever I may be in London or Germany," wrote Canning to Palmerston, "I always told you that I was a Radical in Turkey." He counselled the Sultan to investigate the cause of his remote vassals' dissatisfaction and to turn a deaf ear to the Tsar's proposal for a joint occupation of the principality by Russian and Turkish troops. A rumour got abroad that there was a movement to form a great Slavonic state in the Danubian provinces. The Turks lost their heads and moved a force of troops into Wallachia. Thereupon a Russian army of 4000 men promptly invaded the principality. The ambassador backed the Sultan's appeal to England for her countenance and support; but Palmerston held his hand. Presently came General Grabbe to reassure the Porte on behalf of his Russian Majesty and to explain the situation to the implacable Canning. The General maintained the view that no other Power had a right to come between Russia and Turkey where the Danubian provinces were concerned. Britain and France he styled *les ingérents*. In the end he had his way. Most of his demands were conceded by Abdu-l-Mejid. The Hospodar was to be nominated for a term of seven years, the assemblies of the boyards, or magnates, were to be suppressed, and a joint occupation to be admitted as a temporary measure.

Consent was extracted from the Ottoman Government in the teeth of Stratford's opposition. But the timid Moslems looked in vain over his shoulder for the mastheads of a British fleet. Even when the Russians used the country nominally in their mere occupation, as a base from which to attack the hard-pressed Magyars in the rear, Palmerston would not interfere. He attached great importance, he told Canning, to the maintenance of the Austrian Empire, and would deeply regret anything that would cripple her. We did not mean, he said, to meddle with the matter of the Russian use of the principalities in the way of protest or any other means.

For a moment the angry ambassador held his peace. The short-lived success of the Hungarians, over which he and Reshid had unofficially rejoiced, finished with the surrender of Vilagos. The leaders, Kossuth, Bem, Dembinski, and some fourscore others, took refuge in Ottoman territory and reached Vidin. The Porte was bombarded from the two Imperial embassies with demands for their extradition. Canning and the new ambassador from the French Revolutionary Government counselled unfaltering resistance. A note, revised and edited by the Englishman, was sent to the irate Powers to inform them that the Sultan could not honourably surrender political refugees.

This was an attitude that Alexander I might have admired. His brother's rejoinder was to send Prince

Michael Radziwill to Constantinople with what sounded like an ultimatum. The fugitives must be given up; the escape of any one of them would be taken as a declaration of war by Turkey. Canning was at once sent for. He bade the Turks stand fast. "Stand fast," urged his French colleague, General Aupick. It was to be presumed, said both these envoys, that their Governments would support Turkey should war result from the rejection of the Russian demands. There was no time to consult Palmerston. The thought of the unfortunate and highly distinguished exiles, "Zamoyski, among others," whose fate hung on the lips of the Sultan, steeled Sir Stratford's resolution. "If you yield," he warned the Porte, "you will alienate your most cordial supporters." Thus encouraged, the Sheikh-ul-Islam, the highest religious authority in the empire, declared that the surrender of the fugitives would be a violation of the right of asylum contained in the law of Mohammed. The Porte returned no categorical refusal; but on September 17, 1849, the flags over the Russian and Austrian embassies were hauled down, and the Tsar's emissary left Constantinople.

It was a ticklish moment for Stratford Canning. He has recorded his reflections. Long before a reply could be received from London the Russian Black Sea fleet might issue from Sebastopol and bombard Constantinople. If his Government disavowed his assurances he would not only be ruined himself, but would have brought about the ruin of the state to which he was accredited. With such feelings as Sir Edward Grey awaited the decision of Parliament that fateful hour in August 1914, our ambassador waited six weeks for Palmerston's reply. On October 18 Lieutenant Robins, who had left London on the 2nd of the month, drew rein before the British embassy in Pera and handed his Excellency a dispatch from the Foreign Secretary. One imagines Stratford's long-drawn sigh of relief as his eye picked out the decisive phrases on the paper. "The

Cabinet has this day decided . . . an affirmative answer
. . . moral and material support for Turkey. . . ." So
that was all right! "The French and British squadrons
would proceed at once to the Dardanelles. . . . The
Government here has resolved to support the Sultan at
all events." Friendly and courteous representations were
to be made at Petersburg and Vienna.

Palmerston had been well served by his messengers.
The dispatch had been sent in triplicate. Robins was
followed by Captain Townley. Leaving London on
October 11, he reached Constantinople on the 26th,
having ridden the 820 miles between Belgrade and the
Bosphorus in five days eleven hours. Here, surely, was
a finer theme for Stratford's anæmic muse than the
passage of a locomotive through a tunnel! Nicholas and
Francis Joseph must also have been well served by their
couriers, and the "friendly and courteous representations"
been persuasively worded, for on November 7, only
twelve days after Townley's arrival, Canning was able
to report that the ambassadors of Austria and Russia
had withdrawn the demand for extradition, in view, as
Count Titov the Russian strangely explained, of the
state of public feeling in England. It may have been
less galling to the Tsar to make this admission than to
acknowledge that he owed his defeat to the man whom he
had snubbed.

The Magyars had saved their skins, and Kossuth
expressed his gratitude becomingly to his preserver;
but the Austrians prevailed on the Porte to keep him
and his fellows under a supervision which differed
little from close confinement. Palmerston and Canning
fought hard for their enlargement. It was, however,
only by a strong personal appeal to Abdu-l-Mejid that
the ambassador procured the final release of the patriot
leaders on September 1, 1851. Thus ended the epilogue
to a revolt begun by the insurgent Magyars' denying
equal rights of citizenship to the Slavs whom they held
in subjection. England and Turkey may be thought to

have emerged with more credit from the affair. Eighty years ago England's was a chivalrous spirit. That nation, too, which repudiated President Wilson must read with astonishment of the action of their grandfathers. In 1853 one Martin Koszta, a Hungarian refugee who had not completed the process of his naturalization as a United States citizen, was seized at Smyrna and confined aboard an Austrian brig. Upon his captors' refusal to give him up Captain Ingraham, commanding the U.S. ship *St Louis*, anchored within half a cable's length of the brig and cleared the decks for action. The Austrian was supported by other vessels, but fighting was only averted by the interposition of the consular body, to whom Koszta was handed over, as a prelude to his ultimate release. Ingraham's action was enthusiastically endorsed by his Government and his countrymen. Austria, it seems to us, had good reason to congratulate herself on her issue from the business. A conflict with the United States would have resulted, beyond all doubt, in the disappearance of her flag from the seas.

Canning had worsted the Tsar in the last encounter, yet he began to lose heart. Turkey, he thought, could not continue to resist these repeated assaults on her independence. He advocated a defensive alliance with Britain. His country was not ready for this. Prince Albert, for one, was opposed to the "reimposition of the ignorant, barbarian, and despotic yoke of the Mussulman over the most fertile and favoured portion of Europe." "The Porte," he wrote, "can either sink or swim—he [*sic*] cannot float." And the Great Elchi himself despaired of the Turks. In 1851 he admitted that "the great game of improvement is up for the present, and though I shall do my best to promote the adoption of separate measures, it is impossible for me to conceal that the main object of my stay here is all but gone."

Even Reshid, he perceived, was succumbing to the all-pervading apathy and corruption of Turkish government. When he went on leave again in June 1852, it was with little hope of returning and with the sad conviction that as many tares as he had uprooted would spring up the instant his back was turned.

He was smarting, moreover, under a double personal disappointment. In the previous year Lord Stanley, afterwards Earl of Derby, then in opposition, had promised him the Foreign Office when he should be called on to form a Government. That event came to pass in 1852, but Canning was passed over in favour of the third Earl of Malmesbury, somewhat to that nobleman's surprise. The excuse given was that the vacancy had to be filled immediately and that Sir Stratford was on the other side of Europe. It was rumoured, however, as a more probable explanation that the autocratic Powers would have taken Canning's appointment in ill part. The same plea of urgency was advanced when Cowley, who had so lately served under the great diplomatist as a junior, was promoted to the Paris embassy. To that appointment Sir Stratford justly considered himself entitled as the crown of his long career. A peerage was offered him instead. He accepted it on the explicit understanding that it was a reward for past services, "not as a substitute for effective office or as an honourable consignment to the shelf." In the sixty-sixth year of his age, he took his seat in the House of Lords as Viscount Stratford de Redcliffe. He was too proud of his name to lose his identity under some territorial description. "Redcliffe" was tacked on to it in memory of an ancestor who, upon the close of the Wars of the Roses, had taken Orders and helped to rebuild the noble church of St Mary Redcliffe at Bristol.

V

While the new Viscount was keeping his Christmas in his own country there was great jubilation among those subjects of the Sultan who owed allegiance to Rome. As far back as the sixteenth century the King of France had taken the Latin Christians of the Levant under his protection, and as lately as 1740 the Porte, in gratitude for France's help against Austria, had entrusted them with the keys of the Churches of the Holy Sepulchre at Jerusalem and of the Nativity at Bethlehem. To the succeeding generations of Frenchmen these far-away Christian communities were not the objects of any great solicitude. The Latins were pushed aside by the more numerous Orthodox Christians and their privileges usurped. Wishful to secure the support of the strong clerical party in France, Louis Napoleon now directed his ambassador at Constantinople to press for the execution of the Capitulations of 1740. This step at once called forth remonstrances from the Tsar, the patron of the Orthodox. To the Sultan it mattered little which sect of infidels mounted guard over the shrines common to both; indeed, both to the Porte and the British ambassador the spectacle of the French and Russians at loggerheads was not wholly disagreeable. There appeared small likelihood of this 'churchwardens' quarrel,' as some one styled it, ever developing into a first-class political issue. Stratford before he quitted Constantinople was able to report that the claims of the conflicting sects were satisfactorily adjusted. The Orthodox were to retain the guardianship of the great church at Jerusalem; to the Latins, on the other hand, was assigned the custody of the sanctuaries at Bethlehem, with which went the privilege of placing a silver star at Christmastide over the reputed site of the Saviour's birth.

It will have been noted by this time that finality in diplomacy is usually a long way off. Representations are followed by notes, and notes by protocols, and these require the enactment of treaties, which again require ratification. The compromise devised by the Ottoman Government might or might not be imposed on its Christian subjects, but it was very far from satisfactory to the Tsar. Perhaps it would be truer to say that he found here a bone of contention far too valuable to bury.

While the Latins were exulting over the restoration of their privileges in Palestine, his Imperial Majesty was speaking his mind very freely on the subject of Turkey to our ambassador, Sir Hamilton Seymour. "We have on our hands a very sick man," he observed, and he suggested that the time was ripe for the Powers to come to an agreement about the division of his estate.

Nicholas may well have flattered himself that he had chosen his moment well. Stratford Canning, that lion in his path, had quitted Istanbul, as it was supposed, for ever. Aberdeen, whose feeble hands once more grasped the reins of government in Britain, was well affected to Russia and profoundly suspicious of the new *régime* in France. Since France had elected to put herself in opposition to Russia, it appeared hardly possible that Britain would range herself on the same side. Unluckily, however, for the Tsar, and as some think for Europe, his first tentative proposals for the liquidation of the Turkish Empire came before Lord John Russell, during his temporary occupation of the Foreign Office.

> [Lord John] regarded himself as a mere *locum tenens* . . .; he was in no mood to face large problems of foreign policy or make critical decisions concerning them. Moreover, he was on uneasy terms with Aberdeen, whose place as Premier he was eager to assume. Hence, we may well believe that the dispatches of Seymour from Petrograd received from neither Russell nor Aberdeen the anxious consideration they deserved.[1]

The Whig statesman coldly replied that the dissolution of Turkey appeared to him still far off, and that it might be only hastened by the remedial measures proposed. England, in fact, took alarm. Nicholas had shown his hand too plainly. Even his chief's well-known sympathy with Russia could not prevent Lord Clarendon, on whom the office of Foreign Secretary had now devolved, from calling on the tried champion of Turkey to return to his ancient post. While at Petersburg Prince Menshikov, one of the most trusted lieutenants of his Emperor, was

[1] *The Cambridge History of British Foreign Policy*, vol. ii, p. 344.

preparing to start for Constantinople on a special mission, Lord Stratford de Redcliffe was drawing up his own instructions. He was to counsel prudence to the Porte and forbearance to France and Russia. He was "to moderate the dictatorial if not menacing attitude they had assumed." He was left a free hand as to the dispute over the Holy Places. He was to keep the Porte in the path of reform. In the event of imminent danger to the existence of the Ottoman Government he had powers to bid the admiral at Malta hold himself in readiness, but he was not to summon him to approach the Dardanelles without reference to his Government. On his outward journey he was to sound the views of the courts of Paris and Vienna.

It is important to note that at this moment, as Lane-Poole points out, Stratford was far from anticipating a catastrophe. Nearly forty years had passed since Waterloo, and Englishmen were rather inclined to look on war as an obsolete method of settling our disputes with foreign Powers. "I question whether Russia even is ready to bring on a crisis, provided she be satisfied, which is by no means impossible, with respect to the Holy Places in Palestine. But as to any real change in the Porte's system of administration. . . ." Our envoy, in his letter to Lady Stratford, continues in a lugubrious strain, evidently believing that his mission was to save Turkey from herself and not from the threatening Muscovite.

Accompanied by Layard, Alison, and the trusty dragoman Pisani, his Excellency started for Paris. On March 10, 1853, he dined with Louis Napoleon and his lovely bride. To the Englishman, keen and vital despite his sixty-six years, the Emperor did not appear to take a lively interest in anything. He threw the blame of engaging in the Holy Places dispute upon the clerical party, and declared he desired nothing better than to finish the affair. When the ambassador recommended a strict adherence to the actual arrangements "he acquiesced like one who knew little of the subject." It was Persigny, as perhaps his visitor did not then know, who was jockeying him to take up the quarrel with Russia. As to the regeneration of Turkey the sad listless man was not hopeful. Stratford decided that the maintenance of his dynasty was the mainspring of his policy, and thought that his co-operation must for that reason be accepted with a shade of caution. Englishmen have proved themselves very bad judges of character at different stages of their history. Stratford, like most of his countrymen, half suspected the honesty of the most magnanimous and farseeing prince of modern times.

To doubt the word of Nicholas, on the other hand, Lord Clarendon thought would be unjustifiable. This view he expressed in a letter to Stratford, communicating the ominous intelligence that Colonel Rose, our *chargé d'affaires* at Constantinople, had summoned the squadron at Malta to Turkish waters. To the enormous relief of the Foreign Secretary, Dundas, the admiral in command, had refused to move without orders from home.

> The French Government [went on Clarendon] have come to a precipitate decision in ordering their fleet to sail, but it will not go further than Salamis. Why it goes at all, they are rather puzzled to say. . . . I am sure under the grave circumstances, you will not lose an unnecessary moment in getting to Constantinople.

Stratford had already started for Vienna on March 17. For considerable stages of his long journey he availed himself of the newly opened railways. His lordship disliked this method of conveyance.

> Railways are really good for nothing [he wrote to his wife] except to go blindfold from place to place with superior velocity, and here the latter advantage is not always to be had. [The train hurried them past towns and villages and churches] as a set of outcasts having nothing to do with religion and home. Hurry, noise, jostling, confusion of tongues and persons, the dirty accommodation, the ignorance of all that one passes through, have all to find their compensation in the single advantage of speed.

ENVOYS EXTRAORDINARY

At the Hofburg his Excellency found the young Emperor Francis Joseph and his minister Count Buol in general sympathy with the conservative and defensive policy of London. They knew of no cause for alarm or of any other motive for Prince Menshikov's errand than the settlement of the ecclesiastical dispute. So far reassured, Lord Stratford pursued his uncomfortable journey to Trieste, where he took ship. On April 5, 1853, he descried the familiar cupolas and minarets of Constantinople rising above the pale Thracian shore. That the harassed Osmanli hailed him as their saviour we can easily believe; but to describe his landing as "the angry return of a king whose realm has been suffered to fall into danger"[1] is to discredit our ambassador's pacific intentions and to help to fasten on him the responsibility of the war which was to come.

At different points on his route he had been kept advised of the progress of events at the Turkish capital. Menshikov had arrived with a formidable retinue, which he excused by the plea that he came to ask the hand of the Sultan's daughter in marriage. His matrimonial scheme appears to have been quickly forgotten, and to the Turks it seemed that he came prepared more for a battle than a betrothal. He had made preposterous demands, so the Grand Vizier informed Colonel Rose; but, out of fear of the Russian, the Turks could be persuaded only with difficulty to communicate these to Stratford. The ambassador read them and looked grave. Over and beyond the restoration of the privileges of the Orthodox Church in the Holy Land, the Tsar required the rights and immunities of his co-religionists to be guaranteed by Turkey in a treaty, in return for which he would bind himself to come to the assistance of the Porte, if called upon, with 400,000 men. Very cleverly the Ottoman Divan refused to discuss these ulterior proposals until the original dispute had been finally adjusted.

[1] Kinglake.

This answer Stratford approved. The ostensible purpose of the Russian mission was to settle that question, and to that question he determined to limit the discussion. De la Cour, his French colleague, eyed him suspiciously. The proud Englishman, as he saw it, wanted to play the part of mediator between France and Russia and was prepared to acknowledge a Russian protectorate over the Holy Land.[1] Unaware or heedless of this suspicion, Stratford approached Menshikov in a conciliatory spirit. Fearing that the ambassadors might come to blows, the Turks placed guards outside their place of meeting. But Stratford, on this as on other occasions, showed that he could control his temper if he chose. With the Tsar's solicitude for his fellow-Christians his lordship displayed much tactful sympathy. Menshikov was, indeed, led on to hint at his further demands, but very firmly, though gently, the Englishman insisted on the difference between a guarantee resting on an act of the Sultan and one resting on a convention with an alien Power.

> We both avoided [he says] entering into a discussion which might have proved irritating on this question; and I was glad to learn from Prince Menshikov that there was no danger of any hostile aggression as the result of its failure, but at most an estrangement between the two Powers and perhaps an interruption of diplomatic intercourse.

It is clear that our ambassador had no thought of provoking a war. He was working strenuously in the cause of peace. Writing to his wife, he complains, "My brain is half on fire, and my fingers worn down to the quick. I get up at five; I work the livelong day, and I fall asleep before I reach my bed."

Not less earnestly than Nicholas he desired the security of the Christians of Turkey. On April 13 he was able to inform Rifa't Pasha, the Ottoman Foreign Secretary, that he had brought the ambassadors of France and

[1] Bapst, *Origines de la Guerre de Crimée*, passim.

Russia into complete accord as regarded the sanctuaries. The Porte was urged to promulgate the necessary decrees without delay. "The Holy Places question is virtually settled," he wrote on April 23. "If the Sultan would at the same time confer some substantial benefits on his Moslem subjects, there would be little left to desire." While rejecting Menshikov's note as objectionable since it derogated from the Sultan's sovereignty, the Porte might leave a door open to negotiation.

This is not the language of a firebrand. Stratford was content with having cut the ground from beneath his adversary's feet. All that the Tsar asked for on behalf of the Orthodox Ottoman subjects the Sultan was prepared to grant them. Menshikov said he was ready to yield on the worst features of his very ugly treaty. Stratford, like his chiefs in London, seems to have reposed undue confidence in the Muscovites. Menshikov slowly awakened to a sense of defeat. He had been manœuvred into abandoning the main purpose of his mission. Sharply he took the Turkish ministers to task for having betrayed the negotiations to the Englishman. On May 5 he presented what was in fact an ultimatum. He insisted that the guarantees conceded by the Sultan to his subjects should be confirmed by a treaty. The Porte was given five days in which to reply.

The Turks turned to Stratford. He took counsel with de la Cour. The two ambassadors remonstrated with the Russian. At a conference held at night at the Grand Vizier's villa on the Bosphorus Stratford reiterated his advice. Concede all that is asked for to the Christians, so long as it is done by the Sultan's authority. As he rose to go the Grand Vizier, hearing, perhaps, the wash of the waters, asked if Turkey could rely on the support of British ships. To have said yes would have been to precipitate hostilities. Sternly the ambassador deprecated any allusion to warlike demonstrations. Yet, later, it struck him that the Turks might need some definite encouragement. He attended the Sultan's *levée*. As he took his leave he informed Abdu-l-Mejid that he had been given power to hold the fleet in readiness should danger be imminent.

To the Russian envoy, sulking in his villa at Buyukdere, it seemed also that the time had come for bolder measures. Stratford's old ally, Reshid, was itching to return to power. He employed one of his creatures, a Greek named Aristarkhi Bey, to worm himself into the confidence of Menshikov and to insinuate that he might prove more pliant than the Sultan's actual advisers. The Prince fell into the trap. Forcing himself into the Imperial presence on May 13 he insisted upon the dismissal of the Grand Vizier and the formation of a new council of ministry. The feeble autocrat, distracted by the death of his beloved mother, gave way. The department of foreign affairs was again confided to Reshid. He asked for five or six days in which to consider the Russian proposals. Menshikov waited hopefully. Convinced of Reshid's goodwill, he was willing now to accept a note, instead of a treaty, accompanied by the promise of a site for the erection of a Russian church and hospice at Jerusalem. He added, however, that any act guaranteeing the spiritual rights of the Orthodox community but diminishing their temporal advantages would be considered an act unfriendly to Russia and to her religion. This was vague but ill-natured. The ambassadors of Britain, France, Austria, and Prussia were by now persuaded that nothing less than the recognition of Russia's right to interfere in the affairs of Turkey was aimed at. Upon their advice the Ottoman Government refused to sign the note. On May 21 Prince Menshikov, realizing he had been duped and uttering dire threats, sailed for Odessa. On the following day the Imperial escutcheon was removed from over the door of the Russian embassy.

> In settling the Jerusalem question, I have been of some use [wrote Stratford to his wife on May 29]. I would have settled the other, but it could not be. The Russians were determined to have the whole, and it was necessary to prevent them. . . .

All now depends upon the Cabinet at home. Shilly-shally will spoil all. "Oh, for one glance of Chatham's eye!"

For another nine months the ambassador was doomed to watch a policy which, as directed by Lord Aberdeen, might certainly be described as shilly-shally. But for Palmerston and Lord John Russell, Nicholas would probably have had his way and established a protectorate over millions of the Sultan's subjects. As it was, the feeble Prime Minister was forced by the more bellicose members of his Cabinet to approve the action of Turkey. The fleet was ordered to Besika Bay, near the mouth of the Dardanelles, and Stratford was empowered to call upon it in case of need. On the same day (May 31) Nesselrode, the Tsar's minister, sent a dispatch to the Porte, intimating that, unless Menshikov's note was accepted without qualification within eight days, Russia would occupy the Danubian principalities "by force but without war." On July 7 it became known at Istanbul that the invasion had begun. The timid Sultan's first act was to dismiss Mustafa, his Grand Vizier, and Reshid Pasha. Stratford "went bang to the Padishah and put them in again." He then sat down to await the action of the Powers.

Prussia was bound to Russia. Austria owed her existence to the Tsar, but could not view the occupation of Wallachia and Moldavia with indifference. Napoleon III hated war and would have been glad of an excuse to escape from the imbroglio with some enhancement of prestige. No one wanted to force the Tsar into war. There ensued what Alison wittily called the story of the *Mille et Une Notes*—if not a thousand and one, at least eleven different schemes were elaborated in the chancelleries of Europe by means of which the Tsar's face might be saved, the Russians cleared out of the principalities, and the independence of the Ottoman Empire secured. On July 22 Reshid, with the co-operation of Stratford as one suspects, drew up a note embodying Turkey's final concessions. It included the four firmans, or decrees, by which the privileges and immunities of the Greek Christians had already been affirmed, and it guaranteed to them all the benefits which might at any time be enjoyed by the Sultan's Christian subjects. The evacuation of the principalities was demanded. This ultimatum was approved by the representatives of Great Britain, France, Austria, and Turkey, assembled at the British embassy, and dispatched to Vienna.

It was delivered just a day too late. The telegraph did not extend as far as the Bosphorus, but unluckily it did unite the other European capitals. The Powers had already agreed on the words to be put into the Sultan's mouth. He was to acknowledge the active solicitude of the Russian Emperor for the Greek Christians within the Ottoman dominions, at the same time declaring that the Sultans had never failed to consecrate by solemn acts their ancient and constant benevolence towards their Christian subjects; he announced further that he would remain true to the letter and spirit of the Treaties of Kuchuk Kainarji and Adrianople, and would secure to the Orthodox all the advantages granted to other Christian communities within his empire. This note was telegraphed from Vienna to Petersburg for the Tsar's acceptance. "What!" exclaimed Lady Stratford de Redcliffe, on being informed of this by Lord Clarendon in London, "without the Turks knowing your proposition?" "Oh, yes," replied the Foreign Secretary; "we are to decide for them, you know."

Of this decision Stratford himself was apprised on August 9. He received from Lord Westmorland, his colleague at Vienna, a copy of the note with Lord Clarendon's instructions to secure its confirmation by the Porte unless some other arrangement had been made. Knowing that by this time the Turks' own ultimatum must be in Count Buol's hands, he bided his time while the French and Austrian ambassadors pressed the note on the attention of Reshid Pasha. The Prussian representative lent it only a tepid support, admitting his preference for the draft prepared in Constantinople. "I prefer," wrote Stratford, with a tinge of sarcasm, to his chief on August 11, "not to forgo the advantage of acting upon your lordship's deliberate instructions." Two days later those deliberate instructions were brought by ship. The Turkish note, having arrived subsequently to the dispatch of the Vienna note to Petersburg, was considered *non avenue*, and the Tsar had signified his acceptance of the latter. It was for Lord Stratford to recommend its adoption by the Porte.

It was the situation of 1828 over again. This time, however, Stratford obeyed. In his official capacity he urged upon Reshid the acceptance of a note which appeared to differ little in its terms from his own, which had the earnest backing of the British Government, and which was regarded as satisfactory by Russia. This much he said, but none knew better than the Pasha that his words belied his own opinion. We can well believe, as Aberdeen told the Queen and as de la Cour reported to his court, that he spoke of the behaviour of his Government as infamous, that he talked of resigning and vowed he would let the world know his name was Canning. In fairness to the angry diplomatist, it can, however, hardly be supposed that the Porte was indifferent to the slight put upon them. The difference in terms between their own note and that framed for them at Vienna was vital. The one affirmed and the other repudiated the right of an alien Power to interfere in the internal affairs of the Ottoman Empire. On August 20 the Sultan's council declared that the note could be accepted only with certain amendments, designed to assert his Majesty's sovereignty. Stratford says he scrupulously abstained from expressing his own views while the matter was being debated, but he told Clarendon that he deemed the amendments necessary unless the Tsar was to be given a full right of intervention with twelve millions of Turkish subjects.

The reservations of the Porte might appear the merest quibbles to *The Times* and to many people in England, but their significance was clear enough to Nicholas. On September 7 he declined to admit any modification of the note already agreed to by him. In an official analysis of the correspondence the Russian Foreign Office ingenuously admitted that its propositions had been put with a certain vagueness since it was always in the power of Russia to interpret them in accordance with her own views. The acceptance of the Vienna note, according to the same authority, would have meant the triumph of Russia over the maritime Powers, the exhaustion of Turkey, and (which was dearest of all to Nicholas) a complete check to the personal influence of the ambassador, "which, in his patriotism, he identified with that of his Government." The Great Elchi's opinion of the famous Vienna note was thus confirmed out of the mouth of his adversary.

Meanwhile the Turks were mobilizing. While gentlemen in London, Paris, and Vienna were writing polite notes for the Sultan to sign, the Russians were installing themselves in his provinces and appropriating his revenues. Stratford saw the Bosphorus about Therapia swarming with ships of war, and the opposite heights crowned with the green tents of the Egyptian auxiliaries. He wrote to his wife, "Do not think your ancient is a chimæra breathing fire and flame. He is neither for peace nor for war. He is for the Question—its settlement on firm grounds. The extreme desire for peace, if care be not taken, may bring on the danger of war."

If Lord Aberdeen's policy was here glanced at, the same view was expressed a few weeks later by one not at all favourable to Stratford or to his strongest supporter in the Cabinet. Queen Victoria is quoted [1] as writing:

> Lord Palmerston's mode of proceeding always had that advantage that it threatened steps that it was hoped would not

---

[1] *The Cambridge History of British Foreign Policy*, vol. ii, p. 357.

become necessary; whilst those hitherto taken, started on the principle of not needlessly offending Russia by threats, oblige us to take the very steps which we refused to threaten.

Alarmed by reports transmitted by the French ambassador of rioting at Constantinople and threats to the foreign population, Lord Clarendon told Stratford to call up the fleet from Besika Bay. Very coolly his Excellency replied that he had not deemed it necessary to send for more than two steamers and that he reserved the right to act according to his own discretion conceded him in his earlier instructions. It may be true, as he went on to state, that he wished to save her Majesty's Government from any embarrassments likely to accrue from a premature passage of the Straits by our squadron; it is equally probable that his Excellency was pleased to do things in his own way and his own time and to let the officious people in London know who was in charge of the situation. The Queen, Prince Albert, and Aberdeen all knew that Lord Stratford was too strong for them. Whether but for Palmerston they would have dared recall him is doubtful. Meanwhile the chancelleries were strewn with 'notes,' varying only by a comma from each other. Too many cooks spoil the broth, commented Stratford, calmly confident that he could have settled the whole business if it had been left to him. The peace of Europe was lost through the multitude of peacemakers. The Moslems clamoured for war. The Padishah more than the foreigners stood in danger of his usually submissive subjects. Bowing to their opinion, he addressed on October 1 an ultimatum to Prince Gorchakov, the Russian commander-in-chief in Wallachia, summoning him to evacuate Turkish territory within fifteen days. The paper was delivered by Reshid's son to the Russian general on October 10, and the term should thus have expired on the 24th. It was on October 22 that the fleets of Britain and France entered the Dardanelles.

> I would have preferred [wrote Stratford to the Prime Minister] an additional delay of a few days; but the instructions of my

French colleague were so peremptory that by longer postponing my decision I should have incurred the risk of separating from him.

The delay, according to a French writer (Bapst), was due to the Englishman's desire to achieve peace by his own exertions where the concert of Europe had failed. That was not an ignoble ambition. Stratford wrung from Reshid the promise not to open fire before November 1. In the interval he and his three fellow-ambassadors submitted yet another note to the patient Porte. It included the Turkish amendments, also a guarantee by the four Powers that Russia would make no further demands and that Turkey would faithfully observe her undertakings. This note, which was not exactly flattering to the two principals to the dispute, was eyed askance by the Divan. It was approved in London and Paris, and rejected by Vienna on the ground that a state of war already existed between Russia and Turkey. "To address such a note to Petersburg at the present time," said Count Buol, "would be to expose ourselves to a rude rebuff and to deprive Austria of her *rôle* of mediator." Omar Pasha, one of the able commanders whom Turkey has often produced, had crossed the Danube and defeated Gorchakov at Oltenita. On November 2, 1853, the Russian Tsar published his declaration of war against Turkey.

The principals had crossed swords, but their seconds by no means despaired of a reconciliation. The Turks were doing well in the field, but Stratford reminded them that the tide of battle might flow the other way. He pressed them to announce their willingness to negotiate. In the first days of December came the news that a Russian squadron had entered the port of Sinope, on the northern coast of Asia Minor, and destroyed eleven Ottoman warships. Yet Stratford de Redcliffe, still regarded in some quarters as a firebrand, went on counselling peace. There was fresh rioting among the exasperated Mussulmans. Reshid, denounced as a peace-monger, left the city. Stratford had the fire-hose turned on the rioters, invited all the pretty ladies of the foreign community to accept the hospitality of his embassy, then "trotted off on foot to the Padishah" and got him to take vigorous, though not brutal, measures to restore order. Reshid was reinstated, to the discomfiture of the war-at-any-price faction, and, accepting the disaster at Sinope almost as another untoward event, announced that Turkey was ready to negotiate.

So also was Russia. Strange to say, the olive-branches were brushed aside, not by Stratford or the Mussulman fanatics, but by the men in London and Paris. Foul weather alone had prevented the two fleets from entering the Black Sea in order to protect the coasts of Asia Minor. The two Governments were therefore as little disposed to forgive the attack on the Turkish fleet as a policeman is to forgive a burglar who enters a house when his back is turned. To the angry astonishment of the Russians, as the fog lifted on the morning of January 6, 1854, a frigate flying the Union Jack was observed to enter the innermost harbour of Sebastopol. It carried the insolent message that the British and French admirals had assumed command of the Black Sea and that the Tsar's ships must not leave port. Nicholas recalled his ambassadors from London and Paris. The two western Powers issued their declarations of war at the end of March. The Austrians and Prussians folded their arms and looked on.

VI

One regrets that Lord Stratford de Redcliffe did not at this moment intone his *nunc dimittis*. His most devoted apologists cannot deny that the last chapter of his Constantinople diary makes the least agreeable reading. The position of an ambassador from one ally to another becomes almost inevitably subsidiary when the guns begin to talk. The diplomatist sees himself obliged to stand aside while the soldiers get on with the war which he has been unable to avert. Stratford was the last man to realize this or to admit that his importance was in any way lessened by the actual outbreak of hostilities. Nor was this immediately recognized by his Government at home. The war was being waged on Turkey's behalf, and it was expected not only that her Majesty's ambassador would see that the Turks gave the fullest assistance to their allies, but that he should remedy the shortsightedness and blunders of those officially responsible for the conduct of the campaign. Stratford Canning throughout the whole of his adult life had been engaged in diplomacy. It was unfair as well as stupid to expect him at the age of sixty-eight to supply the deficiencies of ordnance officers, commissaries, and surgeons-general. Before very long he found himself, in reality to his own intense satisfaction, Lord High-Everything-Else in the rear of the British army at Constantinople. Generals of a certain type would have brushed him aside and put him in his place; but Lord Raglan, that pleasant gentlewoman, as Kinglake styles him, was pleased to leave him as much work as possible. It would have been better if the General Staff had taken the attitude of the Duke of Cambridge's valet, who on being told that the fussy old gentleman he had been so rude to was no other than her Majesty's ambassador curtly replied, "Well, I never said he wasn't!"

There can be no doubt that Stratford exerted himself to the utmost of his powers (which were great) to purchase stores, provide barracks, and install hospitals, but so doing he trod on everybody's corns and became the scapegoat for everybody's failures. Like Lord Raglan, he had some difficulty in remembering that the French were the allies of Britain. It vexed him that by far the major portion of the expeditionary force should be contributed by France. He fell foul of the successive French ambassadors, Baraguay d'Hilliers and Benedetti. He was generally right, as when he defeated an 'intrigue' to remove the capable Omar Pasha and to place the whole

Turkish army under the command of Saint-Arnaud. But he was too much inclined to talk of our allies' 'intrigues,' just as in more recent times the British Press spoke of any people at war with us as 'rebels.'

For this Stratford would readily have been forgiven by the British public. Far more damaging to what little popularity he had ever enjoyed were the attacks of Florence Nightingale. Britain had not been at war with a first-class Power since Waterloo. Humane sentiment in the intervening years had developed, at least in England, enormously. For the first time in history, upon the outbreak of hostilities, the care of the sick and wounded became of paramount importance. Exactly what ought to be done only a very few people knew. Like many haughty and irascible Englishmen, Stratford was tender-hearted. "I have thought of little else than the hospitals during the last five or six days," he says in a letter to Raglan. The Tsar Nicholas on his dying bed spoke of his old adversary gratefully for his solicitude for the wounded Russian prisoners. Lady Stratford and her daughters journeyed from England to minister to the sick. But when the capable, domineering Florence came out, with her forty nurses, she dismissed his lordship as a heartless and ill-tempered old man and his wife as a busybody and a hindrance, for whose visits to the hospitals she could see no reason except that she might say one thing while her husband did another. By this time, now that the siege of Sebastopol was being vigorously pressed, Stratford had become intolerant of any outside interference. In vain he appealed to the Army Medical Department for exact lists of what they wanted. The War Office should attend to these things, instead of leaving everything to private enterprise. When it did do so he made the irretrievable mistake of suggesting that a fund raised by *The Times* for the relief of the wounded, now that its object had been anticipated by the Government, might be employed in building an Anglican church at Constantinople. Such a proposal, even in that church-going age, shocked the public conscience. But when the War Office sent out a fresh batch of nurses whom Miss Nightingale had not asked for, and of whom she contemptuously refused to make use, adding that of course these unoccupied women would go to the devil, the petulant old man obtained the loan of a cavalry barracks from the Sultan, and with the new staff established another hospital under his wife's control. Oddly enough, before the stout Florence's schemes had received official approval Stratford had suggested that the soldiers' wives (who in those days accompanied the regiment almost to the front) might be entrusted with the care of the sick. The proposal was turned down by the medical authority as savouring somewhat of impropriety.

The ambassador paid two visits to the Crimea and conducted himself with the coolness characteristic of Englishmen of his kind. On his return to his station he was at once informed by one of his *attachés* that the wicked French had prevailed on the Sultan to appoint Mohammed Ali, his Majesty's exiled brother-in-law, to the command of the Ottoman fleet. This Ali, it may be remembered, was the man who had murdered his concubine, for which crime Stratford had procured his disgrace. His lordship presented himself before the Grand Turk and read him such a remonstrance as perhaps no sovereign had listened to since John Knox bullied Mary Stuart. Even the patience of the meek Abdu-l-Mejid was exhausted. "Then curled his very beard with ire," as Byron said of one of his pashas. His Majesty called for one of his secretaries, and the terrible *elchi* paused in the recital of his indictment. "It was clear that matters could not be pressed to extremes without the risk of throwing the Sultan completely into the arms of France, and the ambassador succeeded in pacifying him at the cost of sacrificing the rest of the memorandum."[1]

In truth Stratford drove over-hard, and was himself

[1] Stanley Lane-Poole.

over-driven. On August 13, 1854, Colonel Fenwick Williams arrived at Constantinople as military commissioner to the Turkish army operating on the frontiers of Armenia and Georgia. Soon after reaching Erzerum he began to bombard the embassy with requisitions, remonstrances, and demands of every kind. The Turkish Army of the East was insufficiently equipped with arms, ammunition, stores. In the colloquial phrase, Stratford was snowed under by Colonel Williams's dispatches. He left it to his secretaries to make summaries of them, and submitted each specific demand and recommendation to the Porte, generally through the medium of Pisani. On December 17 his Excellency was startled to receive from Lord Clarendon a severe rebuke for not having answered a number of the commissioner's letters. Stratford, of course, answered as sharply. A reply had been sent, he insisted, whenever one had been required. This defence brought down a more general complaint from the Foreign Office. It was evident that his Excellency never paid attention to anything in the nature of an instruction. Meanwhile Williams threw himself into the fortress of Kars, and was presently besieged by a greatly superior force of Russians under the command of Muraviev. In the summer urgent appeals for help reached the allied Governments. On July 13, 1855, the British Government rejected the Turkish plan of creating a powerful diversion in the Russian rear by way of Georgia. Stratford, now keenly alive to the danger, protested. The French cared little for what happened on that remote frontier, and neither of the Powers would suffer the force in the Crimea to be seriously weakened in order to relieve Kars. The fortress fell, after a magnificent defence, on November 22. A day's march away abundant stores had been collected. These, it is said, could not be transported farther because the Turks could not or would not pay the carriers. But after the war the blame for the surrender was thrown on the unpopular ambassador. His inattention to Williams's letters in the early autumn of 1854 was supposed to have caused the disaster eighteen months later. Furiously attacked in the Commons by a Member named Whiteside, the absent diplomatist was championed by Palmerston. If, said that spirited politician, the Government had recalled Lord Stratford de Redcliffe simply because he omitted to answer every communication from Colonel Williams it might indeed have been credited with energy, but certainly not with much foresight. Kars fell because Omar's expedition started too late to its relief.

But Nicholas was dead, Sebastopol had fallen, and Austria threatened to join the allies. France was weary of the war, and on January 16, 1856, the new Tsar, Alexander, announced his readiness to negotiate. Stratford raged. Britain was now well equipped for a second campaign. He wanted to see Russia *pollarded*. On March 30 the Peace of Paris was concluded. "I would rather have cut off my hand than have signed it," declared the disappointed diplomatist. He had hoped to see Poland resurrected at least within limited boundaries, the Crimea restored to Turkey as a tributary state, and the Ottoman Empire buttressed round by a chain of semi-independent principalities. There remained his confidence in Turkey's powers of regeneration. At his instance Abdu-l-Mejid published a new and revised edition of liberties called the Hat-i-Humayun. This new constitution was formally recognized in the ninth article of the treaty, the Powers at the same time renouncing any claim to interfere collectively or severally with the internal affairs of the empire. The Great Elchi had devoted most of his political life to contesting the claim of Russia to intervene between the Sultan and his subjects; for this Britain had drawn the sword; yet he saw in the Powers' refusal to guarantee the new constitution the frustration of all his efforts. So long as he had the ear of the Porte—so long, it would be nearer the truth to say, as he could take it by the ear—the Christians would be safe. Now that the old sheepdog must retire he dolefully lamented the absence of other protectors for his flock.

The last chapter of his diplomatic career shows him tenacious as ever of the Sultan's sovereignty, as jealous of France as he had ever been of Russia, and more arrogant, more contemptuous than before of his chiefs in England. "He is the sixth of the Great Powers," cried his latest rival, Thouvenel, Napoleon's ambassador to the Porte. "He is not an ambassador but a sovereign," said a friend, the Austrian internuncio, Prokesch-Osten. Upon the conclusion of the Treaty of Paris the old man quickly recovered his supremacy. In his zeal for the consolidation of nationalities Napoleon III directed his pensive, far-seeing eyes upon the Danubian principalities. To the project of merging Moldavia and Wallachia into one state Austria was naturally opposed. "A fine example for Serbia!" exclaimed Prokesch-Osten. Stratford, ever jealous of the Sultan's interests, took the same view. By the statesmen in Paris it was settled that the populations of the provinces should be consulted as to their future organization, subject always to the suzerainty of the Padishah. Electoral colleges, or divans, were to be constituted, and a commission composed of delegates of the Powers was to oversee the elections. Britain's commissioner was Sir Henry Bulwer, a man of more pleasing manner but not less haughty than Stratford. His arrival at Pera had been preceded by the rumour that he was to take over the embassy. Prepossessed against him Lord Stratford de Redcliffe, in defiance of his Government's instructions, shut him out of the room where the ambassadors were discussing with the Sultan's ministers the regulation for the Danubian elections. When the two Englishmen came face to face

> Sir Henry Bulwer expressed himself warmly against the manner in which he had been treated by the English ambassador. . . . Lord Stratford, stung to the quick by Sir Henry's remarks, forgot himself as usual, and retorted in a manner not justified by the circumstance, and which provoked an altercation in the open

sitting between these two personages which had better not be described. . . . Reshid Pasha intervened, it is said, to stop the dispute.[1]

Throughout this Rumanian business his lordship displayed an anything but edifying disregard of instructions. In Wallachia the Kaimakam, or interim Governor, was Alexander Ghika, a partisan of union. But at Iasi, Vogorides, a kinsman presumably of Stratford's friend of 1832, was exerting himself to secure a majority pledged to the contrary policy. His tactics were revealed to the French embassy by a letter which his wife or sister betrayed to the French consul. Thouvenel, backed by the envoys of Russia and Sardinia, called on the Porte to annul the Kaimakam's illegal acts. It was this moment which the British ambassador chose to celebrate the anniversary of Waterloo by a banquet. He and his Austrian colleague told the Turks to stand firm. Thouvenel demanded a fortnight's postponement of the elections. While their representatives were at daggers drawn the sovereigns of Britain and France were preparing for a friendly conference at Osborne. Unfortunately for Stratford, the telegraph was now in operation between London and Pera. Clarendon signified his acquiescence in Thouvenel's demand. Stratford found an excuse for disobeying; he went on disobeying; on August 4 Clarendon reprimanded him and bade him do as he was told. On the following day the representatives of France, Russia, Prussia, and Sardinia broke off their relations with the Porte for its refusal to inquire into the conduct of Vogorides and to cancel the election if it should prove to have been illegally conducted. Stratford rubbed his hands with glee.

The rulers of Britain and France, however, had no intention of being dragged into war over the Rumanian question or by the obstinacy of their ambassadors. Clarendon spoke of Stratford as that old maniac who was always doing the right thing in the wrong way.

[1] *The Times*, January 29, 1857, p. 10.

Thouvenel, that "6 ft. 3 of Frenchman," was recalled. But his rival continued to flout his Government up till the last minute. On August 11 he received a telegram from London, directing him to support the requirements of the four Powers. "Not being ordered to act at once," his Excellency postponed obedience on the ground that his Austrian colleague had not received similar instructions. On the 13th Clarendon reiterated his commands. The old man cried out, "He would lay me as a sacrifice at the feet of the French Emperor!" Not till the 22nd could he bring himself to carry out his orders and advise the Porte to annul the elections. For the second time in a month he was reprimanded by his chief. The new elections were held, and the voting clearly manifested the people's desire for union—a wish which was not fulfilled till 1862.[1]

Stratford had struck his last blow for Turkey. He was now seventy-one years of age. Going on leave at the end of 1857, he is said to have expected to continue at his embassy. It seems, however, more probable, in view of his serious acts of insubordination, that he seized on Lord Palmerston's fall from office in the following year as an opportunity to escape dismissal by offering his resignation. Almost immediately he regretted the step. He must go back to Pera to wind up affairs. Lord Derby, the new Prime Minister, glad to do him honour, consented. Only after his departure from London did the old man learn that Bulwer had already been appointed to succeed him at the embassy.

The Turks, who appear to be more capable of gratitude than most nations,[2] received him with cordiality and courtesy. But Reshid was dead, and the Sultan Abdu-l-Mejid like soon to follow him. Holding his head high

---

[1] For an exhaustive account of Stratford's part in the negotiations affecting Rumania see W. G. East, *The Union of Moldavia and Wallachia* (Cambridge, 1929).

[2] This was Pierre Loti's opinion, and is warranted by history and the experience of individuals.

as ever, the aged diplomatist for the last time turned his back on the strange capital to which he had first come as a youth of twenty-two. He had given Turkey a new lease of life as a political entity, but he knew that his hopes of saving her from herself were vain.

He settled down at Frant Court, in that country to which his thoughts had so often turned longingly from his palace in Pera. To the last day of his wonderful life his brain was active, his pen ever busy. It was too late for him to take any share in the government of Britain. Never an orator, he rose at times to speak in the House of Lords upon foreign affairs. His experience commanded respect, but it was the experience of a world which was passing away. The Treaty of Vienna, to which he clung, sounded to the public as out-of-date as the Treaty of Utrecht. He had little sympathy with the idea of Italian unity. He condemned the cession of the Ionian Islands to the nation which he had helped to liberate. He foresaw no advantage to Britain in the digging of the Suez Canal. But though statesmen were no longer swayed by his counsels they were not ungrateful for past services. In 1869 Gladstone procured for him the Order of the Garter.

His only son, a lifelong invalid, died in 1878. Two years later, on August 14, 1880, Lord Stratford de Redcliffe himself died peacefully at Frant in the ninety-fourth year of his age. The Eastern problem, to the settlement of which he had devoted so many years, remained at the moment of his passing unsolved. No finer tribute to his statesmanship could have been paid than that contained in a leader in *The Times*, appearing on August 17, three days after his death. England was sending a new ambassador to Constantinople in not very different circumstances from those with which he had had to contend. Turkey had to be saved from her enemies without and within.

If these objects are to be accomplished, it must be by the exercise of similar qualities to those which Lord Stratford displayed. That which is still needed is the straightforward, but resolute attitude, which was characteristic of Lord Stratford, and a complete absence of condescension to the intrigues of Turkish diplomacy. The line of conduct for an English ambassador at Constantinople is, in short, clearly marked out in the history of Lord Stratford's career.

That remained true for many years after Lord Stratford's death. "Who wert the voice of England in the East," Tennyson apostrophizes him. Much that we like to think of as essential to an English character—boldness, honesty, love of liberty—he did express. But for the greater part of his life, and when he spoke most loudly on the side of freedom and humanity, the voice was Stratford Canning's very own.

SIR HENRY LYTTON BULWER
(1801-72)

Lord Stratford's successor at the Constantinople embassy was entitled to more respect than the aged diplomatist had shown him when the Danubian elections were under discussion. Sir Henry Lytton Bulwer, son of General Bulwer and brother of the novelist Edward Bulwer Lytton, was as old as the century. Educated at Harrow and Cambridge, which university he left without taking a degree, he could look back at the time of the Crimean War on nearly thirty years passed in the diplomatic service. For this he seemed designated even more clearly than Stratford. In the handsome Englishman of languid, graceful manners, dispensing his inherited wealth freely, foreigners delightedly recognized the typical *milord*. At the age of twenty-six he was seen at Paris to win between £6000 and £7000 at the tables in a single night without betraying his satisfaction by the faintest gleam in his eyes or the merest beginnings of a smile. With the same apparent indifference he would lose 500 louis on a single rubber of whist at Prince Wittgenstein's. Languor was the young diplomatist's pose. Having beguiled a foreign minister into supposing that he had hardly paid attention to what had been said, Bulwer would in drawling tones announce an opinion or decision which went to the very root of the matter. He is stated by a journalist, Charles Kent, who remains our authority for his earlier life, to have been the model of George Sand's Mauprat; a statement which those who have read or intend to read the novel of that name may be interested to confirm or to deny.

Like all the choice spirits of his time, Henry, then aged

twenty-three, espoused the cause of Greece. He had gone to the trouble of buying himself a commission in the Guards, but in the 1820's a military career offered as little inducement to an ambitious young Englishman as it does in the 1930's. Part of the time which should have been spent in the barrackyard Mr Bulwer spent in the Peloponnesos, where as agent of a Philhellene committee he was charged to hand over £80,000 to the Grecian leader Maurokordatos. In 1827 we find him attached to the embassy at Berlin, whence he was transferred to Vienna. Having resigned his commission, he was appointed to the legation at The Hague, at the head of which was Sir Charles Bagot. Apparently wind of the young man's talent had reached Downing Street, for in the same year he was given a secret mission by Lord Aberdeen to examine and report upon the growing discontent in the Belgian provinces of the Netherlands. The first rift in the fabric woven fifteen years before at Vienna was becoming apparent. The union of Holland and Belgium under one crown has been compared to those marriages, arranged by sensible go-betweens, which have everything to recommend them except that the parties hate each other. A few weeks after the expulsion of Charles X from France a serious riot broke out in Brussels. The arms of the house of Orange were torn down.

> The insurrection [writes Bulwer] broke out at Ghent, when I was in the Grand' Place, and the commissionnaire of the hotel was shot by my side. I proceeded to Brussels, where the Dutch troops under Prince Frederick were on the heights, with their commander, evidently undetermined; barricades were erected throughout the town and the most respectable of the middle classes were in arms. I turned into the country: the roads were covered with peasants marching under the guidance of the priests to support the insurrection—fast becoming a revolution. The insurgents took possession of Ath as I was passing through that fortress. The troops nowhere could be depended upon; for one of the clever devices of the King of the Netherlands had been to mix Belgians with Dutch in every regiment, so that the colonel

HENRY BULWER, AFTERWARDS LORD DALLING
From a pencil sketch by Count d'Orsay

never knew in a crisis whether his orders would be obeyed or controverted. My opinion therefore as to the immediate result of the conflict then going on was pretty well formed, when after many adventures, I acquired by an accident a full and complete knowledge, not only of all that was actually doing by the Belgian party throughout Belgium at that moment, but of all that was to be done during the next few days. I was informed of the officers who were gained, the regiments that would revolt, the fortresses on which the Belgian flag would be hoisted on a certain day. And as my information came to me in no way that imposed secrecy, I returned home and communicated it. But my reports were not —and this was very natural—in conformity with Sir Charles Bagot's, who was in Holland; and they were received coldly and with no small degree of disbelief.

I had hardly, however, been in the country a week, when I was summoned up to town by the Minister of Foreign Affairs. The events that had taken place since my return were so precisely in conformity with my predictions, that the merit of my reports, which as I have said, owed a great portion of their exactitude to accident, were exaggerated. Lord Aberdeen complimented me, and desired me to go back at once to Brussels, to reside there and regularly communicate events and my opinion on them.[1]

The young diplomatist now occupied a seat in Parliament as an advanced Liberal. He reported strongly in favour of Belgian independence. His views were endorsed by Palmerston, who took over the Foreign Office in November 1830. From this time dates the warm friendship and loyal co-operation between the great statesman and Henry Bulwer. Belgium was recognized as an independent state, Leopold of Saxe-Coburg was placed on its throne, and on November 27, 1835, Bulwer returned to Brussels as Secretary of Legation. As *chargé d'affaires* in the following year he was mainly concerned in negotiating a treaty of commerce with the new kingdom. He succeeded so well that Palmerston, with a similar end in view, sent him in August 1837 as secretary of the embassy to Constantinople. Here he met Stratford's friend and collaborator, Reshid Pasha.

[1] Sir Henry Bulwer, *The Life of Lord Palmerston* (1871), vol. ii, p. 3.

He describes him as essentially a civilian, who had grown up in the bureaux of the Porte, throughly conversant with all its forms and ways; of audacious imagination but physically timid. Unable to get much help from his superior, Lord Ponsonby, or from his French colleagues, Bulwer picked up what information he could about our trade with Turkey and the vexations to which it was subject. Some verses he had written in a lady's album gained the new secretary the reputation of being a poet; Pera talked of his romantic tendencies and of the eccentricity of Englishmen in general; no one was surprised that the lackadaisical young aristocrat should make a retreat in a Persian tent in a beautiful valley beside the Bosphorus. As it happened, the Minister of Commerce also had his summer villa in the same happy hollow; and so one day it came about that these two lovers of nature signed the draft of a treaty of commerce, which Palmerston declared to be a model of its kind.

The secretary of the French Embassy, who had refused to place his expert knowledge of commercial affairs at the disposal of the poetical Englishman, was surprised and annoyed.

"Est-il possible, mon cher, que vous nous avez joué ce tour-là ?"

"Quel tour ? Seulement nous avons trouvé possible ce que vous avez cru impossible."

"Mais que faire ?"

"Nothing more easy, my dear fellow; here is a copy of our treaty; have another copy made and sign it to-day, and then let the journal at Smyrna [a journal said to be in the French pay] say that this happy result was entirely brought about by Admiral Roussin's influence and your great knowledge of commercial affairs." [1]

The French Secretary took this advice, Lord Ponsonby got a step in the peerage, and Bulwer was promised the secretaryship at Petersburg.

---

[1] So given, half in French, half in English, in the original, Sir Henry Bulwer, *op. cit.*, vol. ii, p. 263.

Instead, however, he was sent to Paris. France, as it seemed to Palmerston, was playing a crooked game. Mehemet Ali was in arms against the Sultan. The dismemberment of the Ottoman Empire was threatened. France, which had at first appeared willing to co-operate with the other Powers in maintaining the *status quo*, hung back and displayed unmistakable sympathy with the rebellious vassal. Her attitude was undefined when Lord Granville, our ambassador at Paris, was compelled by illness to go on leave. Bulwer remained minister *ad interim*. France, he told Palmerston, was simply endeavouring to amuse us by an apparent acquiescence in our views, while she meant to adhere to her own, which were quite different. The Foreign Secretary concurred.

> Nothing [wrote Palmerston from Windsor (September 24, 1839)] can be more miserable than the shifts and changes of the French Government; and it is evident that they have wishes and objects at bottom which they are ashamed of confessing. Their great and only aim is to do as much as possible for Mehemet Ali, without caring a pin for the Sultan, or having the least regard for their declarations and pledges.

Adolphe Thiers, the successor of Marshal Soult as head of affairs in France, wanted to bring about an arrangement between Cairo and Istanbul which would strip all the Powers except France of their pretensions to be the Turk's protectors. Bulwer, again left in charge at the beginning of July 1840, warned his chief that the little Frenchman was a warm friend but a dangerous enemy. Now, a warning was always accepted by Palmerston as a challenge. "I highly approve your conciliatory language," he wrote, "mixed as it has been with proper firmness; but it would never do to let Thiers bully us."

How near the two countries came to war in the autumn of 1840 is revealed by Bulwer's interesting account.

> I had ridden down to see him [Thiers] at a beautiful château he then occupied at Auteuil (Sept. 18); I found him walking up

ENVOYS EXTRAORDINARY

and down in a long room or gallery, and I joined him in his perambulations. After a turn or two, he stopped and said, "I have dispatches from Walewski. He has terminated his negotiations with the Pasha"; and he then stated to me the conditions, in some abatement of his original demands, which the Pasha, through Walewski's mediation, was willing to accept. "Well," he continued, "France thinks these conditions just and reasonable. If your Government will act with us in persuading the Sultan and the other Powers to accept them, there is once more a *cordiale entente* between us. If not, after the concessions we have obtained from Mehemet Ali, we are bound to support him." With these words he fixed his eyes upon my countenance, and added gravely, "Vous comprenez, mon cher, la gravité de ce que je viens de dire." "Perfectly," I said, with an intentional air of imperturbability. "You wish me to understand that if we accept the arrangement made through Walewski, you and we are the best friends in the world; if not, you mean to declare for the Pasha and go to war with us in his favour." We resumed our perambulations. "You know what I have been saying to you," Thiers resumed, "is said by me as M. Thiers, not as president of the council. I have to consult my colleagues, the King also. But I wished you to understand clearly the tendency of my own personal opinions."

"I am much obliged to you," I replied, "for this distinction; but the fact is, you are president of the council, and you think your opinions will prevail. My position is a very difficult one. If I say more or less than you mean, I may do incalculable mischief; so, if you please, I will ride back to Paris, and recount in a dispatch our conversation, and you shall read it and correct it just as you think proper." [1]

Within a few hours, then, the French statesman was confronted by an accurate report of the conversation, attached to which were certain observations addressed by Bulwer to Lord Palmerston. His lordship, said the *chargé d'affaires*, need not have the slightest apprehension of M. Thiers's views being adopted by King Louis-Philippe; on the contrary, if he offered his resignation the King would certainly accept it without a moment's hesitation.

[1] Bulwer, *op. cit.*

Thiers looked very hard at this dispatch. "My dear Bulwer," he protested, "how could you make such a mistake? You are ruining a promising career. The King is much more disposed to war than I am. But do not let us compromise the future more than we can help. Don't send this dispatch. Let Lord Palmerston know *generally* what you think of our conversation."

And, rightly deeming that the greatest victory of the diplomatist is peace, Bulwer put the dispatch he had written on one side. He had had, he reported, a long conversation with M. Thiers, which it was difficult to repeat without giving it the wrong shade of meaning. He felt convinced that the French minister was anxious for peace,

> that with this view he had done all in his power to persuade Mehemet Ali to be reasonable in his conditions; that he thought the present conditions reasonable; and that if they were accepted, there was an end of the impending struggle. But if they were refused, he for his own part, without giving any pledge to the Pasha, still felt in a certain degree pledged to him; and that it would be difficult if not impossible to form any Government which would remain a perfectly passive and disinterested spectator of the measures to be pursued. Consequently, that without any act of decided hostility, or any positive declaration of war, such a state of things would ensue as would, ere long, disturb the peace of the world.

This brilliant example of the art of watering down not improbably saved France and Britain from war. When one reads Palmerston's reply to Bulwer's dispatch one can have little doubt what effect the unmodified version would have had:

> If Thiers should again hold out to you the language of menace, however vaguely and indistinctly shadowed out, pray retort upon him and convey to him in the most friendly and unoffensive manner possible, that if France throws down the gauntlet, we shall not refuse to pick it up; and that if she begins a war, she will to a certainty lose her ships, colonies, and commerce before she sees the end of it; that her army of Algiers will

cease to give her anxiety, and that Mehemet Ali will just be chucked into the Nile.

Tempers on both sides of the Channel were badly frayed. It was by no means the last time that the two western Powers were prepared to fight over the sharing out of the Ottoman's ill-gotten empire. Palmerston's threats were matched by French mutterings about the British fleet. Bulwer mixed very freely in Parisian society. Without being ostentatiously busy, as he discreetly puts it, he could take steps to obtain all useful information. One day he was told that an attempt would be made to burn our ships. He passed on the information to his chief. On September 27 a fire broke out at Devonport and caused the destruction of two men-of-war, the *Talavera* and the *Imogene*. "You remember that report you received as to an intended burning of our ships?" said Lord Granville to the secretary. "I disbelieved it at the time, but I have good reason to know that there was much more in the scheme than I supposed." The ambassador then mentioned a name which Bulwer withholds. He adds that he thought the business was connected with stock-jobbing, and only indirectly with politics.

The Levantine matter was at last taken out of the hands of the politicians by Admiral Napier. He took the fortress of Acre from Mehemet Ali's son, Ibrahim, and, sailing to Alexandria, forced the Pasha to evacuate Syria on condition of retaining Egypt as an hereditary government. The dispute was finally settled by the Five-Power Treaty of 1841, to which France was a party. By that time Bulwer had left the Paris embassy; and in September of the same year Palmerston went out of office.

II

Writing thirty years later than the events about to be recorded, Bulwer observed:

It must have been by a singular fatality that after having

rescued their country with skill and dignity from the Egyptian difficulty . . . Louis-Philippe and his minister [Guizot], who we really believed desired to maintain friendly relations with Great Britain, entered on a policy in the Spanish peninsula which could not fail, a little sooner or a little later, to produce serious disagreement with our Government, and to shock the moral sense of all Europe by its cold-blooded immorality and injustice.

Before leaving Paris Bulwer had ventured the prediction that the French would, in the words of the Chinese, endeavour to recover 'face' by dabbling in the turbid waters of Spanish politics. At that time Isabel II, an ugly, voluptuous girl in her early teens, sat uneasily on the throne of Philip II. Fairly to appreciate the part played by the two great western Powers we must remember that it was thanks to their influence, and in some measure to their arms, that the girl had been enabled to keep her throne in the teeth of the opposition of her father's brother, the first Don Carlos. In those days England was not afraid to throw her sword into the balance on the side of right. For our support, and that of Louis-Philippe, the astute Queen Mother had made pretensions of Liberal and constitutional ideas. We backed the young Queen against her absolutist and clerically disposed uncle, and incidentally compelled both combatants to accept the Convention of Logroño, by which they bound themselves to spare the lives of prisoners taken in war. Such a measure of humanity is apparently deemed outside the interests or the power of Great Britain at the time of writing (1936).

The young Isabel having been seated on her father's throne, the question of her marriage began to occupy the minds of statesmen. Ever since Charles II, the last Habsburg monarch of Spain, had bequeathed his crown to Philip, the grandson of Louis XIV of France, and that prince had renounced for himself and his successors all rights of succession to his ancestors' throne, English statesmen had lived in dread that the promise might be broken and the two great countries united under one sovereign. Now, Louis-Philippe, as Bulwer had rightly observed, was not warlike; he had, as he often boasted, a head for affairs, and, vaunting his *bourgeois* instincts, was apt, after the fashion of Austria, to promote the interests of his house and his realm rather by judicious marriages than by the sword. Unfortunately, a new family had by the middle of the nineteenth century entered for the matrimonial stakes with marked success. Unknown before Waterloo outside the limits of a tiny duchy, the house of Saxe-Coburg-Gotha had entwined itself with some of the leading dynasties of Europe. Leopold, the widower of George IV's daughter, Charlotte, had established himself on the throne of Belgium and married one of the Citizen King's daughters; his nephew Albert had as lately as 1840 married Queen Victoria; another nephew, Ferdinand, had married Maria da Gloria, the young Queen of Portugal—a princess almost as ill-favoured as her Catholic Majesty. It looked as if the rue which encircled the escutcheon of the enterprising Coburgs would presently spread itself over half the royal arms of Europe.

The surprising success of the ducal house must have aroused Louis-Philippe's fears. At any moment the cunning Leopold of Belgium might produce another cousin or nephew, like a rabbit from a conjuror's hat, for the acceptance of the youthful Isabel. The Queen Mother, having been expelled from Spain in 1840, had taken up her abode at Malmaison, the Empress Josephine's ancient retreat, close to Paris. With her was her second husband, the ex-guardsman, Muñoz, now Duke of Rianzares—a man as shrewd as herself. She kept up a secret correspondence with her daughter and busied herself with fomenting opposition to Espartero, the general who had taken her place as regent. Her Majesty had, of course, abundant opportunities of discussing her daughter's marriage with her uncle, the King of the French. To these discussions Bulwer, that lackadaisical *chargé d'affaires*, while listlessly staking his money at the gaming-tables and strolling in and out of Paris *salons* kept his ears carefully attuned.

Presently there were friendly conferences at Eu, on the Normandy coast, between the British and French royal families. The Citizen King could not make too much of our "dear little queen," Victoria. She was accompanied by Lord Aberdeen; but Louis-Philippe was accompanied by Guizot, for whom his lordship was no match. The French minister, taking him aside, broached the question of that other dear little queen at Madrid. Of course, France held by the Treaty of Utrecht, and no one dreamed of France and Spain ever being united under one crown; but it would be a most happy domestic arrangement and one most agreeable to the French Government if Isabel could be persuaded to marry one or other of her Bourbon kinsmen, not in the line of succession to the throne of France.

"But what possible right have we to limit the young lady's choice!" exclaimed the excellent Scot. The objection no doubt sounded absurd to a Frenchman. In his country every girl was expected to marry the man chosen for her by her lawful guardian. Aberdeen was as wax in the hands of Guizot. Disclaiming any interest in a Coburg suitor, he said her Britannic Majesty's Government would see no objection to the French scheme. Guizot talked pleasantly about a certain nonentity, the Count of Trapani, a Neapolitan prince—an unpleasant suggestion since he was the young Queen's uncle. He was, however, to be preferred to a son of Don Carlos, who had been proposed as a candidate, in order to consolidate the reactionary forces of Spain against Espartero.

The attitude of our neighbours appeared thus far reasonably disinterested. The Dowager Queen was careful to keep her hands untied. Two months after the conference at Eu she told Bulwer, hearing that he was going to Madrid, that, failing the Duc d'Aumale, one of Louis-Philippe's younger sons, she must have Leopold of Coburg as a son-in-law. This frank statement, as will be seen, had a profound influence on our envoy's subsequent policy. Gazetted ambassador to her Catholic Majesty on November 14, 1843, he took up his appointment two or three months after the expulsion of Espartero and the accession of the formidable General Narvaez to the regency. Cristina returned to Spain in the following March, and was received with filial enthusiasm by the girl-Queen. Bulwer's instructions were to co-operate with his French colleague, Bresson, in support of a moderate and impartial policy.

> Whether [reflected our ambassador] a moderate and impartial policy was possible in a country distracted by passions and parties, is a doubtful matter; but at all events, M. de Bresson made it pretty clear that it was not one he was likely to adopt by saying with a haughty sincerity, on the first occasion on which I proposed a joint action, "Voici, mon cher! Toutes ces théories sont belles et bonnes; mais le parti anglais a été dernièrement au pouvoir. . . . Maintenant, le parti français est au pouvoir, et je suis ambassadeur de France. Eh bien! je ferai de mon mieux pour maintenir ce parti au pouvoir et d'agir d'accord avec lui. Allez donc votre chemin, comme j'irai le mien; nous serons toujours de bons amis, car je ne crois pas que vous plairez à votre gouvernement si vous faites une révolution pour mettre M. Olozaga dans la place de M. Martinez de la Rosa; et vous savez aussi bien que moi que rien ne se fait dans ce pays-ci que par des révolutions."[1]

Unhappily Bulwer knew this to be true. Olozaga stood for those Liberal principles which were shared by Palmerston, but certainly not by the cautious Scot now

[1] "Listen, my dear fellow! All these theories are all very well. But the English party has been lately in power. . . . Now it is the French party, and I happen to be the ambassador of France. Very well, I shall do my utmost to maintain that party in power and to work with it. You go your own way, as I shall go mine. We shall not quarrel because I do not fancy you will please your Government by making a revolution to put M. Olozaga in the seat of M. Martinez de la Rosa; and you know as well as I do that nothing can be done in this country without a revolution."

at Downing Street. Bulwer (so he says) stood aside therefore, letting "French vanity and Castilian pride knock against each other." Meanwhile he busied himself by bringing about a satisfactory settlement of a dispute between Spain and Morocco. This service was rewarded by his admission to the Privy Council. On his way to London to be sworn in, in the summer of 1845, he called on Guizot at his apartment overlooking the Bois de Boulogne. Whether Queen Isabel married a Bourbon or not, said the French statesman, both the King of the French and Queen Cristina were anxious for family reasons—or, in plain English, in order to keep a fortune in the family —that her sister, the Infanta Fernanda, should marry Louis-Philippe's fifth son, the Duc de Montpensier. There was no risk of disturbing the accepted rule of succession. It was not desired that this marriage should take place till the young Queen was herself married and had produced an heir to the throne of Spain. When our ambassador apprised his chief of this proposal his lordship expressed himself by one of those *hums*, accompanied by a thoughtful, half-satirical smile, which showed he was not altogether pleased. In another conference at Eu, notwithstanding, in the following autumn he raised no objection to the scheme, subject to the important proviso that the Infanta should not marry the French prince till her royal sister had *children*.

On his return to his station Bulwer found that the French were not letting the grass grow under their feet. Guizot admits that he assumed power under a pledge to conclude the match with the Neapolitan Count of Trapani within three months, so that all might be clear for the Infanta's marriage. But even Narvaez, a man of blood and iron, was compelled to recoil before the tempest of indignation which the idea of a marriage between their sovereign and a mere Neapolitan excited among Spaniards generally. For the time being the would-be dictator retired into the background. "A new ministry under Senor Isturiz was formed to deal diplomatically with the disposal of the young Queen's hand." Guizot spoke feelingly about this unexpected obstacle to his project.

No one, it will have been noticed, cared at all about the girl-Queen's inclinations; but her mother at least knew that it was by no means safe to ignore her violent and precocious passion. Here, it is suggested, lies the explanation of Cristina's feverish haste to get the girl married. However closely she may be guarded, a queen may be relied on to find some minion, male or female, ready to promote an intrigue. Cristina and her guardsman husband eyed the lusty girl anxiously, and scanned the horizon for a substitute for the despised Trapani. Now, although the Roman Catholic princesses of Europe (and the Protestant princesses too) appear to have passed the greater part of their time in bearing children, these children for the most part died young; a fact submitted to moralists of the old school without comment. In the year 1846 her Catholic Majesty could count only two male cousins of Spanish birth. These were the sons of her father's brother by the Infanta Luisa Carlota; and Cristina hated that princess (her own sister) with a hatred transmissible to her sons. The younger of the two, Don Enrique, was a good-looking fellow, who made a parade of his Liberal sentiments. Years after, having married a commoner, he was stripped of his royal quality, became a Mason, was killed in a duel by the Duc de Montpensier, and was described by his fellow-Liberals as "a Bourbon, the only honest man of his race." His elder, Don Francisco de Asis, was of a different stamp. No one troubled about his opinions, not because, as Bulwer hints, "he was already in the hands of the mysterious agents of the order of Jesuits [*sic*]," but because his personality was sufficiently indicated by the nickname conferred on him —"Fanny."

The Queen Mother of Spain preferred to break with her rich uncle at Paris rather than bestow her daughter— and with her the crown matrimonial of Spain—on either of these detrimental young men. What followed had best be told in our envoy's own words.

M. Donoso Cortes, the young queen's private secretary, and a gentleman on whom (it would appear from Mr Guizot) Count Bresson implicitly relied, was the first person to speak to me of her [Queen Cristina's] resolve to break loose from the thraldom in which France traditionally assumed to hold the Spanish nation. He expatiated with an eloquence for which he was remarkable on the dictatorial manner of the man who believed him to be his instrument; on the paternal avidity of his master; on the unhappy position of the poor young queen; on the natural feelings of her mother; on the part which England ought to play under such circumstances. By degrees he introduced the subject of Prince Leopold of Saxe-Coburg, whom Queen Christina had once met somewhere; said that the choice was neither French nor English, since the young prince was allied to both the French and English courts; adding that he was charged by the two queens to speak with me with respect to him. I was guarded with Donoso Cortes, who occupied no responsible post; and who did not disguise that he was intimate with the person of whom he most complained. In M. Isturiz, however, a man of the strictest personal honour, and whom I had always found courageous and sincere, I had greater faith; and he soon held to me similar language. Finally, came the Duke of Rianzares, Queen Christina's husband, who said that Spain was not strong enough to stand up against Louis-Philippe; but that if England would promise her support, the young queen would not passively submit to have her destiny subjected to foreign dictation, and to be treated with supercilious indifference. What was I to say? The language of our Government was ambiguous; it had no objection to a Bourbon prince; it had no candidate of its own to propose; it recognized no right in the King of the French to impose one, and had declared that if he attempted to prevent by force any marriage which the Queen of Spain and the Spanish nation determined on, such a course would, it believed, be resisted not merely by Spain but by Europe. This implied that England would support Spain in an independent choice, but it did not clearly say so, and I knew that Lord Aberdeen would not like me to say so. On the other hand, to leave it to be understood that the Spanish Government had no resource but to submit to the hard fate that the pride and family interest of a neighbouring potentate prepared for her, would expose me equally to censure. The affair was more complicated by Queen Christina's selection of a Coburg prince—such a selection would be a matter of indifference to the English Government and people; but it was not indifferent to the family of the English sovereign.

The minister of the King of the Belgians did not disguise the interest which his master took in a Coburg alliance. The Portuguese minister, who had recently been staying at Coburg and had passed through England on his way to Madrid, told me much—no doubt, with exaggeration—as to the wishes of our own Court. Such confidences, I allow, were not wholly without effect on me: but what had more effect was pity for the young princess about to be so heartlessly sacrificed; resentment to the haughty heartlessness with which this sacrifice was demanded; interest for the fate of the Spanish nation itself and dislike for the somewhat pitiful manner in which we resisted in words what we seemed willing to submit to in fact.

Unless at this time Bulwer foresaw that the young Queen was to be paired off with the ridiculous "Fanny," it is not clear why pity for her should have moved him to countenance among suitors she had never seen one more than another. Her youthful Majesty is not represented as being in love with the Coburg prince. Bulwer had, of course, other motives:

> I also entertained a belief which has made me not unfrequently pass—most unjustly—for an enemy of France, that her ruin as well as the ruin of our good understanding with her lay in the road of those attempts she was constantly making to obtain a preponderating influence in European affairs, and that the policy of every good Englishman and of every wise Frenchman was to resist them. I was, therefore, I confess, altogether opposed to the Bourbon pretensions; but I was in one of those positions in which success is almost impossible, because decided action is not allowed.

Had I been able to guide the conduct of the Spanish court, I should have tied its tongue and confined its endeavours to getting Prince Leopold to visit Madrid, when a marriage taking place suddenly, with the approval of the Cortes and amid the acclama-

ISABEL II, QUEEN OF SPAIN, AS A GIRL (1842)
From an engraving after a painting by D. Vicente Lopez

tions of the army, would have been irrevocable. A scheme of this kind suited the Spanish character, and I could easily have got it adopted. But the general spirit of my instructions, although they did not command me to oppose a marriage without the Bourbon pale, prevented me from promoting one. I could listen but not advise. Consequently, when Queen Christina informed me she had determined on addressing herself to the head of the Coburg family and showed me confidentially the letter she had written, and which she would not communicate to Louis-Philippe till it was answered, I did not think myself called upon to express an opinion on the course she had adopted. I did, however, explain that a Coburg marriage would not be considered in England, an English one, that no support could be expected from us on that ground, but (I allow myself to have stated) it appeared to me that a marriage so reasonable and unobjectionable could not be consistently opposed by the King of the French if the Duke of Saxe-Coburg, the young prince and the queen, with the approval of the Cortes, were bent upon it. The obstinacy of one side, I said, would give way to the obstinacy of the other.

In this, the queen-mother agreed: she regretted exceedingly, the Duke of Rianzares told me, any difference with her uncle; stating she was disposed to make any reasonable concession to him; but adding that what he insisted upon was unreasonable, and that she would oppose it if she could do so with any chance of success. . . . If on account of the queen's espousals, the King of the French withdrew his demand for the hand of the Infanta, then she should consider herself free to dispose of it in the manner most accordant with the interests of the family and those of the Spanish nation. Her language and her conduct throughout the whole of this stage of the proceedings were frank and consistent and did not deserve the suspicions of duplicity . . . entertained concerning them by some of our statesmen.

The career of her Majesty Maria Cristina, it should perhaps be observed, in some degree warranted suspicions of duplicity. It was probably remembered that for many years she had kept her second marriage with Muñoz a secret, or, rather, flatly denied it, even when it was manifest she had borne him children, in order that she might retain the regency, and with it an enormous salary, in her own hands. In the art of rigging the stock markets she and her second husband proved themselves adepts; and their extensive interests in slave-holding at a later stage stood very much in the way of applying the law of Spain in Cuba. Knowing with whom he was dealing, the simple-minded Scottish nobleman who directed Britain's foreign policy appears to have thought a trap was being laid for him, since upon reading Bulwer's confidential dispatch communicating the conversation with the Duke of Riánzares he straightway disclosed its contents to the French Government and reprimanded Bulwer severely for having acted without consulting Bresson.

If, says the ambassador, he had disclosed the conversation to Bresson, the very person of whom the Queen Mother complained, his conduct would have been rather that of a French spy than of an English gentleman. He hints that the same analogy applies to Lord Aberdeen's unexpected action. Bulwer at once tendered his resignation, and he had only time to receive his lordship's firm but courteous rejection of it when, in July 1846, Lord Palmerston resumed control of the foreign department.

For her overtures to the British the Queen Mother was severely scolded by her uncle in Paris. That she looked with indignation on the ambassador who, she thought, had betrayed her confidence may be taken for granted. She was quickly brought to heel by Bresson. Isabel had to be married at once, and since Trapani was out of the running there remained only the absurd "Fanny," otherwise known as the Duke of Cadiz. That the prince was impotent his French Excellency was prepared to disprove. (Probably he got some woman to swear that her child or children were the Prince's.) Even now Cristina hesitated to sacrifice her daughter, when she received from Paris the summary of a dispatch dated July 19, 1846, addressed to Bulwer by Palmerston and communicated, with an ineptitude only equal to

Aberdeen's, by his lordship to Jarnac, Louis-Philippe's representative in London. The choice of suitors, said our Foreign Secretary, lay between Coburg and Don Enrique (the republican nephew). The British Government was not disposed to use its influence in favour of one of these more than of the other. What was to be urged was a reconciliation between Cristina and the Progresista party. There was to be an amnesty on the one hand and a pledge never to molest or oppose her Majesty's private interests on the other. Bulwer was to get in touch with the Liberal leaders, and the Reign of Terror men must be got rid of. Palmerston had told Guizot that he regarded Montpensier's marriage with the Infanta as nearly as objectionable as with the Queen herself. This amazing dispatch, which ignores the understanding of Eu, concludes:

> I should hope that such a marriage may be prevented, but the best thing that could happen would be that the disinclination to it should have its origin in Spain, and that we should not have to make objections to an arrangement proposed by Cristina for her daughter. If Coburg married the queen, Don Enrique might marry the Infanta or *vice versa*. But I mention all these things rather that you may know our views and opinions than in order that you should at present take any steps upon them.

Bulwer may be imagined tearing his hair on the receipt of this dispatch. If we did not mean to oppose Louis-Philippe's schemes our policy was clearly to make friends of both the French and Spanish Governments. If we were determined to counteract those schemes, contrary to the pledges given by Lord Aberdeen, we ought not to make an enemy of the Queen Mother by asking her to quarrel with her own partisans and admit her avowed political opponents to power. But Palmerston was deaf to these representations. He told Bulwer that obedience was an agent's best title to the confidence of his chief; and Lord Clarendon wrote to Isturiz, the Spanish Prime Minister, to insist that Don Enrique was the only proper candidate for the Queen's hand.

Says our ambassador:

> Isturiz brought this letter to me and said: "Are your ministers mad? They wish for the independence of Spain—so do we; and we are in power, and instead of uniting with us, they say in reality, whatever they may say in words, that their only conditions of an alliance are our surrender to our opponents. Supposing I was willing to make this sacrifice, would the court do so? would my political friends do so? would the officers in command of the forces do so?"

Bulwer argued as well as he could against this reasoning. But his orders were positive, and he recommended the Queen Mother to favour her republican nephew as a suitor for the hand of her daughter. Her Majesty, it is hardly necessary to say, was in no mood to listen to any proposals from Palmerston. Bresson had represented his dispatch as virtually a declaration of war against her Government. He urged that the royal sisters should be married on the same day. The machinations of England, he reminded his Government, had set them free from their previous engagement to the contrary. Louis-Philippe, to do him justice, wanted to keep his word till he realized how lightly Palmerston regarded the undertaking given by his predecessor in office. He would be justified, he told his Prime Minister, in giving back blow for blow, but he did not wish to bracket the Duke of Cadiz and Montpensier, as this would savour too much of simultaneousness.

The two bridegrooms could hardly be restrained in their eagerness to take their places at the altar. But poor little Isabel knew her cousin and despised him; nor were there wanting in that curious royal household women to whisper in her ear that he could not make her a husband. She preferred Enrique. Her mother could not manage her, and left her to the tender mercies of her stepfather. His Grace of Rianzares soon brought the girl to reason. On August 28 the Queen of Spain announced her intention of marrying her cousin, Don Francisco de Asis, Duke of Cadiz, and that she had given her consent to the marriage of her sister to the Duc de Montpensier.

> Thus at midnight [wrote Bulwer (September 2)] was consummated this important act, consigning a young queen of sixteen, for the rest of her life, to a husband by whom it was said, but a month ago, that she was not likely to have children, and marrying her Royal sister, in better health and with fairer prospects, to the son of the monarch of that powerful state, which has so long domineered over this country.
>
> What M. de Talleyrand said in one case (Napoleon's enticement of the Spanish Bourbons to Valençay) may be applied to the other, "Ce n'est pas prendre une couronne, c'est l'escamoter."

Very soon he had to report that the double marriage was fixed for the end of October. Palmerston anticipated a public demonstration against the matches at Madrid, and warned Bulwer not to encourage openly any insurrectionary movement. The caution, perhaps, was not superfluous. Bulwer relates:

> On the morning that the French princes entered Madrid, a young man of respectable appearance presented himself, bringing me a letter from a tradesman I employed, which said he had something particular to communicate to me.
>
> He then told me that he and seven other young men had got an apartment in the street (I forget its name) where there are arcades, and by which the Princes had to pass to the Palace; that they were in connexion with others who would form a crowd near the house, and that as the Princes stopped opposite their window they would shoot them. What he wished was that in case of accident or pursuit, they might find refuge at the Embassy. I let the young man proceed quietly, then asked his name and address, which he gave me, but hesitated as to naming his friends. I then told him I should not betray him, but that I should warn the police to pay particular attention to the house he named, and that if I had the slightest reason to apprehend that he had not abandoned his plan, I should have him at once arrested and tried for his life. The young man seemed very much surprised; but finally retired somewhat awkwardly, saying that as I did not approve of the attempt, it would not be made.

The Queen and her sister were married, in fact, considerably in advance of the time stated—on October 10, 1846. If Louis-Philippe ever indulged the hope that his son's children would reign over Spain it was disappointed. Her Majesty Queen Isabel II, as we all know, bore a son. Whatever scandal may have to say about his birth, he was undoubtedly a Bourbon on his mother's side. And twenty years before her Majesty was sent packing across the French frontier the house of Bourbon had ceased to reign in France.

Palmerston observed of the Coburg candidate:

> I know what his father is, I know what his second brother is, and I know what his sister, the Duchess of Nemours, is. If all these high and distinguished persons were to put together all the energy and ability which they severally possess, it would fall far short of the quantity necessary to endow a great prince. They are all of them, except the King of Portugal, below par.

At a distance of ninety years it must be allowed that the English statesman gravely underestimated the abilities of the house of Coburg. Queen Victoria's husband, the first King of the Belgians, and the first Tsar of Bulgaria were certainly above par. Had not Lord Aberdeen—by an excess of honesty, it may be—betrayed Bulwer's scheme to Guizot, had Prince Leopold instead married the young Isabel out of hand, the throne would not in all probability have lost the respect of Spaniards and, freed from vicious Bourbon traditions, might have endured to this day.

The "Spanish Marriages" was a dirty business, from which no one but the Scottish lord emerged with entirely clean hands. Bulwer had little to blush for; still, it may be read between the lines that he wanted to thwart the policy of the French, and was not therefore acting with the perfect loyalty enjoined upon him by his superiors. Palmerston by backing Leopold of Coburg undoubtedly violated the spirit, if not the terms, of the undertaking entered into by his predeccessor. As to Guizot and his master, their plan of forcing an impotent husband on a sixteen-year-old girl was base from the start. As to our charges of bad faith:

> Guizot had asserted that though at Eu in 1845 he had agreed that Montpensier should not marry till the Queen was married and had children, yet he was free from that engagement through the declaration subsequently made to Lord Aberdeen—viz., that if any danger of a Coburg marriage arose, the French Government would consider itself absolved from that engagement. But as Lord Aberdeen never assented to that reservation, it comes to nothing. The most that can be said to justify Guizot is that he had asserted at Eu that the Queen must marry a Bourbon; that the British Government had not opposed this view, and that Palmerston's injudicious mention of the Prince of Coburg . . . made the French minister think that the British Foreign Secretary was stealing a march on him. So he resolved to take a leading part in the race and be well ahead.[1]

III

The two marriage knots having been tied, England was probably expected by the victorious French minister to renounce further interest in Spain, or at any rate in the affairs of the Spanish court. Palmerston, however, always appears to have taken the view that the business of a Foreign Secretary is to look after the affairs of foreign countries. In common, moreover, with many of his countrymen in the spacious days of Queen Victoria, he conceived it to be a duty to exert the undoubted might of Britain in the cause of right and justice wherever these might be threatened. Nowadays the view is held that our obligations to humanity end at our own frontiers—it may be our business if our neighbour's house is on fire, but as sensible men we turn a deaf ear to cries for help proceeding from his windows. Nor do we appear to have that confidence in our strong right arm which built up the British Empire, and among other things

---

[1] R. B. Mowat, in *The Cambridge History of British Foreign Policy*, vol. ii, p. 197.

wiped the slave-ship from the seas. Palmerston, who threatened to chuck Mehemet Ali into the Nile, in his inmost heart certainly believed in the power of England to chuck any and all of her opponents into any convenient expanse of water. Of course, after the manner of Englishmen, he was the first to disclaim any chivalrous or quixotic motives. Utterances such as the following have probably encouraged the popular and entirely unhistorical theory that all England's actions have selfishness as their mainspring and that all wars are waged for 'economic' motives:

> The British Government know that foreign influence can best be exerted over the court of a despotic monarchy, and that such influence becomes far weaker, if not entirely paralysed, when it has to act upon the constitutional representatives of a free people. The British Government therefore saw that in aiding the Spanish people to establish a constitutional form of government, they would assist in securing the political independence of Spain; and they have no doubts that the maintenance of that independence would be conducive to important British interests.

This sounds very practical; but his lordship, I fancy, would have been at some pains to show why a Spanish democracy should be more favourable to England than to France. In America, at any rate, "the constitutional representatives of a free people" manifested surprisingly little sympathy for important British interests. Lord Palmerston, despite his curious approval of the *coup d'état*, liked political liberty for its own sake. This was one motive for continuing to interfere in the internal affairs of Spain; another, unquestionably, was his very natural desire to 'get his own back' upon the Power which had tricked him.

With Bulwer's insistence that an English party should be formed in Spain (October 6, 1846) the Foreign Secretary cordially agreed. He approved his efforts to unite parties for national purposes against French influence. The miserable King Consort and his father,

"Francisco papa," were to be won over. An alliance was to be brought about between the governing or Moderado party and the Progresistas. The man on the spot did not attach much weight to the support of the latter. Its chief, Espartero, was in exile, and Palmerston himself felt by no means sure of Olozaga, another of the leaders. While in typically English fashion his lordship was hoping to achieve his purpose by party manœuvres the game was decided by influences which Bulwer describes as romantic. The young Queen had wasted no time in taking a lover. He was General Serrano. Having been ordered by the ministry, "who undertook the somewhat difficult task of duenna," to quit Madrid, he turned out the ministry instead, and formed another composed of his personal friends. The King Consort retired in dudgeon to the hunting-seat of El Pardo, outside the capital, and Queen Cristina, shocked by her daughter's depravity, retired once more to Paris. The redoubtable Narvaez, unused to these backstairs revolutions, followed her.

"I found myself," says Bulwer, "in one of the most disagreeable situations in which a British minister could be placed." He means that he had to pay court to the Queen's almost openly acknowledged lover; for Serrano professed Progresista opinions, and also had considerable support among the opposite faction. Palmerston, it need not be said, rose superior to the narrow prejudices of Victoria's court and saw no objection to the handsome general as an ally.

> Looking at the young queen's conduct as the natural result of the alliance she had been more or less compelled to make, [he] regarded her rather with interest and pity than with blame or reproach, and was for taking advantage of the attachment she had formed for the purpose of dissolving her own marriage, which, it was said, had never been consummated, for setting aside the Montpensier succession, and bringing his favourite Progresistas into power.

Here again the English statesman showed his ignorance

of the people he was dealing with. As Bulwer points out, the Spaniards are a decorous people. They were deeply shocked by the idea of a divorce. Murder, many of them thought, was a venial offence beside 'immorality'; and "some very respectable and respected men discussed very gravely the propriety of putting the King Consort quietly out of the way by a cup of coffee." The decencies of family life must be maintained.

Serrano turned a willing ear to the proposals of the British envoy. To remain in power he was prepared to come to terms with the Liberal party. He saw no objection to a law excluding the possible issue of Montpensier from the throne—indeed, it has been cruelly suspected that he had a dynastic interest in the succession. But, according to Bulwer, all was spoilt by the veteran Progresista leader, Espartero, who, having been invited by the Queen's favourite to return to Spain, declined to call upon him, on the ground that it was no farther from the general's house to his than from his to the general's, and who would not call on the British minister because his house was not closed to the Moderados.

> In short [says Bulwer bitterly], he managed so well that there was a smart reaction, and General Narvaez was summoned from Paris to protect from the Progresistas the men who had been inclined to place them in power. A palace intrigue hastened the catastrophe, and by one of those abrupt jerks which makes exiles ministers and ministers exiles, Serrano got thrown into the captain-generalship of Madrid, the queen-mother brought back from Paris, and Narvaez at the head of the Moderado party, with his heel on the young queen, installed *nemine contradicente* in unrestrained authority. In another country [continues the ambassador] the fact that both our Government and its agent had been doing their utmost to overturn their policy and keep them out of office would have created an awkward position with the Moderados; but it had been so long admitted in Spain that foreign Governments took part with parties that I found no difficulty, as I was on good terms personally with most of its members, in getting on with the new Government, which was the more easily satisfied that it felt itself perfectly secure.

That comfortable assurance was seriously disturbed by the news of the revolution in February 1848. The King of the French, from whom so much was hoped and feared in the Peninsula, was ejected from the throne and driven to seek an asylum in the land of Palmerston. Soon it became evident that the revolution was spreading like a forest fire across old Europe. This was a situation which Narvaez could be trusted to handle. He prorogued the Cortes, in defiance of a promise given when he took office. An abortive insurrection in Madrid gave him an excuse to suspend the constitutional guarantees. Olozaga and other prominent Progresistas were seized and dispatched without trial to the Philippine Islands. Bulwer found his embassy invaded by a number of persons who stood in fear of arrest. Most of them succeeded presently in effecting their escape from Madrid.

Our ambassador had already decided to refuse Narvaez's tempting bid for his support, on the ground that his government was a system of unsparing despotism, boldly avowed and installed. The masterful general, strange to say, still tolerated the expression of opinion in the Press, and Bulwer, it may be taken as certain, subsidized a journal called *El Clamor Público*, strongly opposed to the new *régime*. The faint growl of the revolution was already heard in Downing Street when Palmerston on March 16 took up the pen and, flatly disobeying his Prime Minister, Russell, wrote the following dispatch to his man at Madrid:

> I have to instruct you to recommend earnestly to the Spanish Government and to the queen-mother, if you have an opportunity of doing so, the adoption of a legal and constitutional course of government in Spain. The recent fall of the King of the French, and of his whole family, and the expulsion of the ministers, ought to teach the Spanish Court and Government how great is the danger of an attempt to govern a country in a manner at variance with the feelings and opinions of the nation, and the catastrophe which has happened in France must serve to show that even a large and well-disciplined army becomes an ineffectual

defence for the crown, when the course pursued by the crown is at variance with the general sentiments of the country.

It would be wise then for the Queen of Spain in the present critical state of affairs to strengthen the executive Government by enlarging the basis upon which the administration is founded, and by calling to her councils some of those men who possess the confidence of the Liberal party.

This badly drafted dispatch must have given the ambassador furiously to think. There was less of impertinence in the British minister's unsolicited admonition to the court of Madrid than in most of the other letters of advice which he was sending out just then, so freely, to our embassies; for, as has been said, the Queen of Spain owed her throne to Britain and the defunct Government of France. Emboldened by this reflection, Bulwer sought out the Duke of Sotomayor, Narvaez's Foreign Secretary, and dropped a hint or two in the sense of Palmerston's letter. He waited. No attention having been paid to what he said, he addressed himself to the wily Cristina. He spoke of the dangers of the system under which she was living, staking the safety of her Government, as she was, on the doubtful fidelity of the troops. He urged the convoking of the Cortes. He produced no sort of impression on her Majesty, who told him she had nothing to do with politics. His remarks, instead of serving as a warning, were rather taken as an offence.[1]

Out of compassion, as he says, for the poor young Queen, Bulwer decided to make a last effort and to place on record the sentiments which a British minister in his situation ought to express. On April 7, therefore, he sent a note to Sotomayor, enclosing a copy of Palmerston's remarks. This was a blunder—he should undoubtedly have confined himself to verbal and personal representations. Urging the convocation of the Cortes and the restoration of civil liberties, Bulwer proceeded:

---

[1] For what follows see F.O. 72/741 (Public Record Office).

SIR HENRY LYTTON BULWER

> I cannot but express at the same time my earnest desire that her Catholic majesty's Government may deem it expedient to return to the ordinary forms of government established in Spain, without loss of time. . . . What especially distinguished the cause of Queen Isabel from that of her royal competitor [Don Carlos] was the promise of constitutional government inscribed on her Catholic majesty's banners. It was that circumstance which principally gained her Catholic majesty the sympathy and support of Great Britain and consequently your excellency cannot be surprised at the sentiments I here express even if the general state of Europe . . . made it not evident that the last security for the throne of a sovereign in these days is to be found in the rational liberty and enlightened justice which are dispensed under his authority.

From what follows it is plain that Bulwer took steps to point his advice by exciting public opinion at Madrid and, at the same time, to reveal himself as the friend of liberty. For the Duke of Sotomayor began his reply (dated April 10) by pointing out that the contents of Bulwer's note had already been published in *El Clamor Público*, "which, to judge from this fact, enjoys the advantage of being made acquainted with the diplomatic communications addressed by you to the Spanish Government before these arrive at their destination." The Duke continued that at the time Lord Palmerston wrote the Cortes was sitting, the Press was free—he was amazed at his lordship's recommending Spain to pursue a constitutional course, as if that followed had not been so.

> The last error committed by her Britannic majesty's minister in making this communication has been that of not understanding the peculiar character of Spain, where order and institutions only take root when foreigners take no active part in public affairs nor endeavour to support certain parties. . . . The cabinet cannot but view with the greatest surprise the unheard-of pretension of Lord Palmerston thus to mix himself up in the internal affairs of Spain.

What would Bulwer say if the Government of her

Catholic Majesty recommended measures for alleviating the condition of Ireland or to mitigate the restrictive *régime* deemed necessary for the maintenance of order in the British dominions? Or to ameliorate the lot of the unfortunate Asiatics under our sway? Or suggested that her Britannic Majesty should hand over the government to the illustrious Peel? "The Government of her Catholic majesty protests in the most energetic manner against the contents of Lord Palmerston's and Mr Bulwer's communications and returns the note, promising to do the same with any other such communications."

Spanish pride is not merely a legend. Bulwer and his chief had brought down upon England the most signal diplomatic rebuff. We are not used to having our notes returned, as nearly a hundred years later we returned a note from the Soviet Government.

Bulwer (who at this moment was gazetted a Knight Commander of the Bath) was flustered and angry. The communication of the note to the Liberal journal was a bad slip, and he lamely attempted to explain that it had come about surreptitiously. But on April 22 we find him admitting to Palmerston that he had in fact aimed at securing such influence with the Liberal party as might prevent it from becoming French or republican, without mixing himself in its intrigues or any projects of insurrection. To Sotomayor he protested that his advice "was solely and simply advice," but he could not refrain from reminding the Spaniard of the possible effect on the relations of the two countries of the rejection of the note.

Unfortunately, Sartorius, a powerful financier in close touch with the existing power, took a leaf out of the Englishman's own book by getting hold of the whole correspondence and publishing it in *Galignani's Messenger*, at a time when Sotomayor was writing to Bulwer proposing to suppress it altogether. The minister and the ambassador met to discuss the whole painful business. "It is rumoured," said the Duke, "that there is a revolu-

tionary committee of ten or twelve sitting in your house."
"There is but one person," said Sir Henry, "who took refuge at the embassy during my absence. Asylum has, however, been given to a number of persons when general arrests were taking place in Madrid. I ask you as one gentleman to another if you would not so have acted in regard to them?"

"Yes," said the Spaniard.

The discussion proceeded on friendly lines, but at its close Sotomayor announced his conviction that Narvaez was determined to break (*romper*). The General dominated the Court and the Cabinet. Bulwer speaks of him in exaggerated terms as a desperate man in a desperate position, and retells the story that when he lay on his deathbed and was asked to forgive his enemies he said he had none, for he had shot them all. There were certainly people in Spain who wanted to shoot her Britannic Majesty's minister.

> I myself thought the position untenable [continues Bulwer] and asked for leave of absence—this was refused me. I then received anonymous and threatening letters. On one occasion, these notices of assassination were not confined to writing. A respectable tradesman brought to me an upholsterer's workman. He said that while hid behind some curtains which he was putting up in the house of a member of the Government, this minister and a friend came into the room and he overheard a conversation in which my assassination was planned. I took down his deposition in the presence of Mr Otway, who was acting as secretary of Embassy, and the day after I had dispatched it home, called on the Minister of Foreign Affairs.
>
> I said, you say you hear absurd stories about my plotting insurrections. Now I have a story about your cabinet's plotting murder. Of course, I do not believe it, but I have sent it home.

To this Sotomayor retorted that he had certain proofs of Bulwer's having suborned officers and of his having used British ships of war, without the consent of his Government, to make the circuit of the coast and promote revolution. The Englishman complained of the libels against him published in the *Heraldo*. The Government, replied the Duke, cannot take proceedings—the Press is free. He advised his Excellency to seek a remedy in the civil courts.

The storm even now might have blown over but for the action of Lord Palmerston's enemies at home. The quarrel was no longer a secret. On May 6 a motion was brought forward in the House of Lords for the production of the correspondence between the Foreign Secretary, Bulwer, and the Spanish Government. Palmerston's passion for intermeddling in the domestic affairs of other nations was condemned by Lord Stanley. The Marquess of Lansdowne tried to shield the Cabinet by throwing the blame on Bulwer, who, he said, ought not to have disclosed the precise terms of the famous dispatch to Sotomayor. But when the papers were laid before the House, Lansdowne, to his chagrin and disgust, found they included a letter, dated April 20, in which his colleague expressed to the ambassador the entire approbation of her Majesty's Government.[1] It would have been most unjust to recall Bulwer, said Lord Aberdeen, for he had certainly acted according to the spirit of his instructions.

Lord Brougham concluded the debate by suggesting that amity among nations would be best promoted if such discussions were abstained from. His view was very soon justified. The report of the debate in their lordships' House reached Madrid. On May 17, 1848, Narvaez struck. Bulwer received a note informing him that public opinion had pronounced against Bulwer's person in every possible respect. His conduct had been reprobated in England, censured in the British Press, and condemned in Parliament. The Spanish Government could not defend it, if his own Government could not. Sir Henry Bulwer's life was in danger. He was required to quit Spain within forty-eight hours.

In the eyes of an Englishman, the humiliation is

[1] C. C. F. Greville, *Memoirs*, vol. vi, p. 178.

alleviated by the terms of our representative's acknowledgment of his dismissal:

> In regard to my personal safety, I place it under the safeguard of the Law of Nations, the good sense of the Spanish people, and *the power of my country which I feel resides in me, alone and in the midst of evilly excited men, as in the mighty armaments which under a sense of wrong, a word from the sovereign of Great Britain can ever call forth.*

There was nothing to do but go. Announcing his dismissal, Bulwer sat down and wrote to Palmerston, "I admire your character and your abilities. . . . They are five hundred times of more value to the country than mine. . . . Do not consider my interests. . . . My thoughts, my wishes are far more for you and the Government." Travelling without stopping to eat (the Northern of Spain railway, every sleeper of which was bedded in corruption, was not yet open) he not only passed on the road the messenger he had sent ahead of him, but arrived in London within a few hours after the news of his dismissal.

No such affront had ever been offered to a British ambassador in the course of history. Bulwer seems to have expected that his country would prove as swift as the Romans of old to avenge it. A squadron sent to Cadiz would have extracted an ample apology. So, at least, he thought. Palmerston, conscious that he had not his colleagues behind him, contented himself with refusing to see Mirasol, the special envoy sent by Narvaez to justify his step. Shortly after Isturiz, then Spanish ambassador in London, was given his passports. "I told you so," Queen Victoria said in effect, reflecting on the policy of the detested Palmerston. On May 22 she wrote to the Foreign Secretary:

> The sending away of Sir Henry Bulwer is a serious affair, which will add to our many embarrassments; the Queen, however, is not surprised at it from the tenour of the last accounts from Madrid and from the fact that for the last three years, Sir

Henry Bulwer has almost been sporting with political intrigues. He invariably boasted of at least being in the confidence of every conspiracy, "though he was taking care not to be personally mixed up in them," and after their various failures, generally harboured the chief actors in his house under the plea of humanity. At every crisis, he gave us to understand, he had to choose "between a revolution and a palace intrigue," and not long ago, he wrote to Lord Palmerston that if the monarchy with the Montpensier succession was disagreeable to us, he could get up a republic. Such principles are sure to be known in Spain, the more so when one considers the extreme vanity of Sir Henry Bulwer and his probable imprudence in the not very creditable company which he is said to keep. Lord Palmerston will remember that the Queen has often addressed herself to him and to Lord John, in fear of Sir H. getting into some scrape; and if our diplomatists are not kept in better order, the Queen may at any moment be exposed to similar insults as she has received now in the person of Sir H. Bulwer; for in whatever way one may wish to look at it, Sir Henry is still *her* minister.

Her Majesty concludes by regretting that such mismanagement should have occurred at a time when, owing to the establishment of a republic in France, England might have acquired a commanding position in Spain.

Her Majesty undoubtedly expressed the opinion of the propertied classes of the country. Bulwer was amazed to find that they cleaved to the champions of their material interests rather than to the upholder of their country's honour. Alarmed by the spread of revolutionary ideas, they sympathized with Narvaez as the strong man armed keeping his house in order. Two factions among them were discernible—those who wanted to make Bulwer a scapegoat and those who wished to get at Palmerston over his head. "I am afraid you should go and act the Knight Errant to screen Bulwer if he is attacked," wrote Lady Palmerston to her husband, "and really such a man does not deserve you should put yourself in any scrape for him."[1]

His lordship thought otherwise. When invited by

[1] Philip Guedalla, *Palmerston*, p. 286.

GENERAL NARVAEZ
From a contemporary engraving

Aberdeen to give an account of what had happened in Madrid to Sir Robert Peel, the Leader of the Opposition, Bulwer refused without his chief's permission. This was at once granted. Peel said he should condemn the attitude of the Spanish Government and take no part in an attack on the Foreign Secretary. The debate in the Commons was opened on June 6 by George Bankes. He would not allow that Bulwer had in any way exceeded his instructions. He held Lord Palmerston responsible for this unprecedented insult to our national dignity, and wished to know what steps he proposed to take to vindicate it. The Prime Minister, Lord John Russell, stressed the obligations of the Crown of Spain to Great Britain, and declared, probably to the amused surprise of many, that the Cabinet as a whole approved Lord Palmerston's action and assumed full responsibility for his policy. He blamed the motion as likely to weaken the hands of her Majesty's representative at Madrid. Disraeli was furious at the outrage offered to a British ambassador. Peel exonerated Bulwer, and, as he had promised, objected to the whole discussion. As to Palmerston, he stood up loyally for his man, though he said he had not intended his dispatch to be shown to the Spanish Government. Bankes at last withdrew his motion without calling for a division.

So, observed the diarist Greville, under date June 18, 1848, "Bulwer and Palmerston are triumphantly curvetting about, completely smashing their opponents in argument."

In this exultant mood Sir Henry in the following December celebrated his marriage with a niece of the Duke of Wellington. Palmerston even meditated sending him back to Madrid, in order to make Narvaez eat humble pie. This idea he abandoned—not out of deference, it may be guessed, to the objections of his sovereign. Diplomatic relations between England and Spain remained suspended for a few years. Meanwhile another field of usefulness was found for Bulwer. He was appointed minister to Washington on April 27, 1849.

IV

The relations between the two Anglo-Saxon countries, never very happy since the separation, had been embittered by the question of slavery. Britain was regarded especially in the southern states of the Union with grave suspicion and jealousy as the enemy of that iniquitous institution. When the great province of Texas broke away from Mexico her annexation was eagerly sought for by the slavers as a fresh market for their human livestock.

For this reason, and also because Britain had become dangerously dependent on the American Republic for the supply of raw cotton, Palmerston and the other farseeing statesmen of his time aimed at maintaining the new state's independence. Captain Charles Elliot, a member of that family for which every administration was able to find a job, after a bad failure to uphold the dignity of the flag against the Chinese, was sent to the other side of the world in 1841 with this end in view. His efforts were vain. Texas yielded to the seductions of Washington and was gained for slavery. Mexico took offence. War resulted. The Spanish-Americans were disastrously defeated by the North Americans. California and New Mexico became a part of the United States. By the treaty of 1845 the 49th parallel was accepted as the boundary between the British and American possessions on the Pacific coast. A long-standing difference was thus finally settled. But now, when the republic extended from ocean to ocean, the American people became vitally interested in the means of communication from one coast to the other. Emigrants to the goldfields of California, sooner than trust to the long and dangerous overland route or to the interminable journey round Cape Horn, found their way across the narrowest part of the continent, either by the Isthmus of Panama or by the San Juan river, flowing into the Caribbean Sea between the Central American states of Nicaragua and Costa Rica. And here again they met the British lion standing in the path.

A conflict was nearly provoked by a people not inappropriately named the Mosquitos. These natives occupied the stretch of coast reaching northward from the mouth of the San Juan river (that is, on the side of Nicaragua). Their chief ("who," said Lord Palmerston to the American ambassador, "is no more a king than you or I") had accepted British protection, originally because of his dealings with the British West India islands and our settlement of Belize. When his territory was invaded by the Nicaraguans a British naval force came to his assistance and compelled the aggressors to recognize Mosquito independence under British protection. This news, together with information that English agents were active in Guatemala and Costa Rica, excited American opinion. Palmerston responded to angry speeches in the Senate by instructing our minister at Washington to defend the action taken. The quarrel might have taken a sharper turn had not Polk been succeeded in the presidency by the more quietly disposed Zachary Taylor. Bancroft, the historian, was sent to London to ascertain the intentions of her Majesty's Government. Britain, he was assured, had no idea of extending her possessions in Central America. At this stage the matter was referred by the Foreign Secretary to Bulwer in Washington.

A more ambitious man might have perceived here an opportunity for settling all outstanding differences between Britain and the United States by an American Treaty of Utrecht. Instead, Bulwer wrote:

> Our great object . . . as it has appeared to me is to displace the discussion from the claims of Mosquito and Nicaragua, on which it is unlikely that the two Governments of Great Britain and the United States should agree, and bring it to the consideration of the canal on which it is almost certain their views will be identical.

That was, indeed, the crux of the dispute. The people

of the United States would assuredly never go to war in order to subject the Mosquito Indians to the rule of Nicaragua, however much they might resent European interference; but the practicability of a canal which should follow the course of the San Juan and thence be carried into the Pacific had long occupied many minds, promising as it did a short and easy route to the goldfields of California. It was the fear that such a waterway might be constructed by the British, or be dominated by a British fort at its mouth in the Mosquito territory, which armed the speakers in the Senate. Bulwer set to work. Within a month the draft of a treaty was agreed upon. In the first and eighth articles the contracting parties bound themselves not to obtain or to maintain for themselves any exclusive control over such a canal or to occupy or colonize or exercise dominion over any part of Central America. If either party were to entertain a scheme for constructing a canal it was to notify the other.

It was to be hoped, said Bulwer, that this treaty would put an end to the constant rivalry of the two Powers' agents in the distracted republics. Even as he wrote, however, a blockade of the ports of little Salvador was effected by a British warship and the island of Tigre seized in an attempt to collect interest due to British bondholders. Nevertheless, on April 19, 1850, the treaty was signed by Bulwer and the American Secretary of State, John Clayton. The eighth article was altered so as to extend the protection of the parties to any other canal across the isthmus that might be agreed on. The potential canal was practically placed under the protection of the two Powers.

When Palmerston read the treaty he perceived a danger in leaving out all minor matters of possible dispute. He instructed our minister to announce that the treaty was not to be understood as applying to the British colony of Honduras or Belize or its dependencies. The Americans sniffed suspiciously at this reasonable reservation. Concerned mainly for the canal, Clayton saved the treaty by persuading Bulwer to state his reservation in these terms as applying to "British Honduras, as distinct from the republic of Honduras, [and] . . . the small islands in the neighbourhood of that settlement which may be known as its dependencies."

It is still doubtful whether this reservation or its acceptance by the United States Government forms an integral part of the Clayton-Bulwer Treaty, which was ratified on July 4, 1850, and proclaimed by the President on the following day. The point is of little importance now. Britain long ago withdrew her protection from the Mosquitos, whose territory now forms indisputably a part of Nicaragua. That republic was, till lately at all events, garrisoned by United States marines; and ships pass from one ocean to another, not along the course of the San Juan river, but along a waterway strongly held by America.

But in 1851 both the English-speaking nations gratefully recognized Bulwer as a peacemaker. Perhaps because he corresponded so closely to their conception of a British aristocrat, he became a great favourite in the fashionable circles of Washington. From that capital he was transferred in January 1852 to the strangely different atmosphere of Florence. There was a lull in the Italian storm. Otherwise he might possibly have been tempted or instructed to interfere as actively on behalf of the Liberal cause in Tuscany as he had done in Spain. Of his subsequent mission to the Danubian principalities and of his conflict with the formidable Stratford something has already been said. Unlike his senior, he became less aggressive with the years. For seven years—from May 1858 to August 1865—he ably discharged his duties as ambassador to the Porte, without resorting to the over-imperious methods of his stern predecessor. He died in May 1872, unexpectedly at Naples, on his way back from a visit to Egypt, five years earlier than Lord Stratford, the title of Baron Dalling, which had been conferred on him in 1871, dying with him.

Bulwer was not a great diplomatist. Like Bentinck, he might have earned greater fame as the semi-despotic administrator of one of our Eastern dominions. No man could have commanded greater respect than he for the English name and the English character. It would be well if the accents in which he responded to the Spaniards' threats were more often heard proceeding from a British embassy.

INDEX

ABDU-L-MEJID, SULTAN, 231, 233, 241, 243, 246, 268
Aberdeen, George Hamilton Gordon, fourth Earl of, mission of, to Vienna, 171, 173; policy of, towards Grecian insurgents, 217, 218, 221; policy of, towards Turkey and Russia, 231, 233, 235, 239, 247, 258; mentioned, 272, 273; and the Spanish Marriages, 281 *et seq.*
À Court, William, afterwards first Baron Heytesbury, 180, 229
Acton, General Sir John, 118 *et seq.*, 141
Adair, Sir Robert, 144, 183, 185
Adams, John Quincy, 194 *et seq.*
Adrianople, Treaty of, 225
Ahmad Vefyk Effendi, 236-237
Albert, Prince Consort, 244, 258
Alexander I, Tsar, 133, 184, 187, 191, 193, 200, 202, 204, 206
Alexander II, Tsar, 265
Alison, Charles, 233, 238-239, 248
Alquier, Charles, 117, 123, 124, 133, 136
Alvensleben, Philip Charles, Count von, 59
Amherst, William Pitt, second Baron, 147
Amiens, Peace of, 116
Aristarkhi Bey, 253
Armed Neutrality, the, 32 *et seq.*
Ascoli, Duke of, 151, 156
Aumale, Henri, Duc d', 281
Aupick, General Jacques, 242
Austerlitz, battle of, 138

BALL, SIR ALEXANDER, 119, 131
Baraguay d'Hilliers, General, 261
Barras, Paul-François, Vicomte de, French Director, 82, 85
Barrington, William Wildman, second Viscount, 92

Barthélemy, François, Marquis de, 77, 78, 80
Bathurst, Benjamin, British agent, 184
Batt, Mr, 22
Beauharnais, Eugène de, viceroy, 169, 173
Bellegarde, Henri, Field-Marshal Comte de, 173, 176
Belmonte, Prince, 156, 159
Benedetti, Count Vincent, 261
Bentinck, Lord William Henry Cavendish, birth and early career of, 147; appointed envoy to Sicily and instructions, 147-148; returns to London, 149; returns to Sicily, 150; quarrels with Queen Maria Carolina, 150; demands of, 153; secures release of exiled barons, 156; relations of, with Sicilian court, *passim*; insists on expulsion of Maria Carolina, 158; first negotiations of, with Murat, 165, 166-170; defeated by Suchet in Spain, 170; relations of, with Murat, 172-180; proclaims Genoese republic, 179; admonished by Castlereagh, 179; recalled, 180; Governor-General of India, 181; death of, 181
Bentinck, Lady Mary, 162, 181
Bernstorff, Andreas Peter, Count, Danish statesman, 100 *et seq.*
Bligh, Mr, 229
Bonaparte, Joseph, 140, 146
Bonaparte, Napoleon, Emperor of the French, victories of, in Italy, 71; and Naples and Sicily, 116-178 *passim*; and Ottoman Empire, 184-190 *passim*; and Switzerland, 191-193 *passim*
Bosset, French commissary, 167
Bourqueney, François-Adolphe, Comte de, 233
Boyle, Rear-Admiral, 148

311

Bresson, Charles, Comte, 282, 288, 290
Brunswick, Charles, Duke of, 53, 54, 70
Bucharest, Peace of, 190
Bulwer, Sir Henry Lytton, later Lord Dalling, family and education of, 271; *attaché* at The Hague, 272; Secretary of Legation at Brussels, 273; secretary of the embassy at Istanbul, 273-274; minister *ad interim* in Paris, 275; transactions of, with Thiers, 275-278; ambassador to Madrid, 282; and the Spanish Marriages, 283-291; dismissal by Spanish Government, 302; vindicated in Parliament, 305; concludes Clayton - Bulwer Treaty, 308; quarrel of, with Lord Stratford, 266; mission of, to Istanbul, 309; death of, 309
Buol, Count, Austrian statesman, 250, 255, 259
Byron, George Gordon, Lord, 184

CABARRUS, COMTE FRANÇOIS DE, 83
Caccamo, Fra, 158, 164
Cadiz, Francisco de Asis, Duke of, 284 *et seq.*
Camden, John Pratt, first Marquis of, 131, 143
Canning, George, Under-Secretary, 74; and the negotiations at Lille, 76, 81, 84; Foreign Secretary, 183; policy of, towards Greece, 200-213; death of, 213
Canning, Stratford, afterwards Lord Stratford de Redcliffe, birth of, 182; education of, 183; mission of, to Scandinavia, 183; first mission of, to Turkey, 183; mediates between Turkey and Russia (1812), 187-189; recalled, 189; mission of, to Switzerland, 191; at Congress of Vienna, 192; affection for Countess Waldstein, 192; mission of, to Washington, 194; quarrel of, with Adams, 194-197; recalled, 198; mission of, to Russia, 201-204; ambassador to Turkey, 205-216; leaves Istanbul, 216; delegate to Conference of Poros, 218-219; signs convention, 220; censured by Lord Aberdeen, 221; returns to Turkey, 225; in Parliament, 227-228; appointment of, to Petersburg objected to by Nicholas I, 229; goes to Madrid, 230; again at Istanbul, 231; defrays cost of excavations at Nineveh, 236; tyrannical methods of, 236; mission of, to Bern and Athens, 239; encourages Porte to resist Russian demands, 240-242; created viscount, 244; and the dispute over the Holy Places, 246 *et seq.*; dines with Napoleon III, 248; withholds Allies' note from the Porte, 255; and outbreak of Crimean War, 257, 259; insubordinate attitude of, 258; counsels moderation, 259; during Crimean War, 260-265; and Florence Nightingale, 262; and Colonel Fenwick Williams, 264; and the Danubian principalities, 266; resigns embassy, 268; created K.G., 269; death of, 269
Canning, Elizabeth (*née* Alexander), afterwards Lady Stratford de Redcliffe, courtship of, by Stratford Canning, 198; marriage of, 204; mentioned, 205, 211, 215, 221, 237, 255, 262, 263
Canning, Harriet (*née* Raikes), 194
Cape of Good Hope, 75, 77, 81, 86
Cariati, Prince, 178
Carmarthen, Francis Osborne, Marquess of, afterwards Duke of Leeds, policy of, towards the United Provinces, 37-59 *passim*; policy of, towards Denmark, 103-110 *passim*
Caroline of Brunswick, Queen of England, 70
Caroline Matilda, Queen of Denmark, 100
Cassaro, Prince, 151, 158, 161
Castelcicala, Prince, 128
Castlereagh, Robert Stewart, Viscount, afterwards second Marquis of Londonderry, Sicilian policy

INDEX

of, 159 et seq.; attitude of, towards Murat, 171–180; disapproves of Bentinck's pro-Italian policy, 179; American policy of, 197; attitude of, towards Greeks, 199; death of, 198
Catherine II, Tsaritza, attitude of, towards Britain, 24–35; creates the Armed Neutrality, 32; and court of Denmark, 103; at war with Turkey, 105; death of, reported, 75
Cerulli, Giuseppe, 167
Ceylon, 77
Charles X, King of France, 212, 219
Charles III, King of Spain, 19
Charles IV, King of Spain, 114
Charles of Austria, Archduke, 137, 184
Christian VII, King of Denmark, 100 et seq.
Church, Sir Richard, General, 219, 240
Circello, Marquis di, 143, 148 et seq., 161
Clarendon, George Villiers, Earl of Clarendon, policy of, towards Turkey and Russia, 247–264 passim; policy of, towards Danubian principalities, 267, 268; and Spanish Marriages, 289
Clayton, John, 308
Clayton-Bulwer Treaty, 308–309
Codrington, Admiral Sir Edward, 213–214, 215, 217
Coffin, Lieutenant-Colonel, 166 et seq.
Columbia, river, 195
Cornwallis, Charles Cornwallis, first Marquis, 68
Cortes, Donoso, 285
Cowper, Lady, 229
Craig, General Sir James, 128 et seq., 141
Cristina, Queen Mother of Spain, 279–298 passim
Croker, John Wilson, 87 n.
Curzon, Robert, afterwards Lord Zouche, 238

DALRYMPLE, SIR JOHN, afterwards sixth Earl of Stair, 48
Damas, Count Roger de, 127, 136
Daun, Countess, 91

De la Cour, French ambassador, 251–256
Delacroix de Contaut, Charles, negotiations of, with Malmesbury, 73–76, 81
Disraeli, Benjamin, afterwards Earl of Beaconsfield, 305
Donkin, General Sir Rufane Shaw, 152
Drummond-Hay, Sir John, 237
Duncan, Admiral Viscount, 86
Duncan, Captain, 165
Dundas, Admiral Sir James, 249

EDEN, MORTON, afterwards first Baron Henley, 65, 75, 95, 99
Eden, William, afterwards first Lord Auckland, 4, 15, 21
Elgin, Thomas Bruce, seventh Earl of, 64
Elliot, Captain Charles, 306
Elliot, Sir Gilbert, afterwards first Earl of Minto, 24, 33–34, 89, 92
Elliot, Hugh, birth and family of, 89; minister at Munich, 90–91; at Berlin, 92; obtains possession of American delegates' dispatches, 93; minister to Copenhagen, 95; divorces first wife, 95–99; duel with Baron von Knyphausen, 97; supports Crown Prince of Denmark, 100–103; active mediation of, between Northern Powers, 105–111; secret mission of, 113–114; minister to Dresden, 114; second marriage of, 114; minister to Naples, 116 et seq.; holds aloof from Russian projects at Naples, 130; accompanies Sicilian court to Palermo, 141; disagreement of, with Sir James Craig, 141–142; recalled, 144; Governor of Leeward Islands, 145; Governor of Madras, 145; death of, 145
Elliot, Margaret (née Jones), 114, 145
Ellis, George, 72, 77, 80
Espartero, Baldomero, Duke of Victory, 280, 282, 296
Eugènie, Empress, 248
Ewart, Joseph, 43, 51, 59, 60, 106

FAGAN, ROBERT, British consul, 149, 152, 158, 160, 163
Ferdinand IV, King of the Two Sicilies, relations of, with Hugh Elliot, 116–142 *passim*; in Sicily, 146; relations of, with Lord William Bentinck, 148–180 *passim*
Fernanda, Infanta of Spain, 283
Fitzherbert, Alleyne, afterwards Lord St Helens, 36, 111
Florida Blanca, Francisco Monino, Comte de, 112
Fox, Charles James, 15, 34, 92; opposed to allied expedition to Naples, 143; recalls Hugh Elliot, 144
Fox, Major-General Henry, 144, 148
Francis II, Emperor, 65, 75, 166, 201
Francis, Hereditary Prince of the Two Sicilies, 151, 155 *et seq.*
Francis Joseph, Emperor, 250
Frederick II, King of Prussia, 16, 23, 92 *et seq.*, 99
Frederick, Crown Prince of Denmark, afterwards Frederick VI, 100 *et seq.*
Frederick William II, King of Prussia, 23, 47, 51, 52, 58 *et seq.*, 65, 66, 67, 110
Fremantle, Vice-Admiral Sir Thomas, 162

GALLO, MARQUIS DI, 118, 124, 127, 133 *et seq.*, 173, 178
Genoa, republic of, 179
George III, King of Great Britain, 63, 99, 111, 113
George IV, King of Great Britain, 111, 150, 163, 217
Germanos, Archbishop, 199
Ghika, Alexander, 267
Godoy, Manuel de, Duke of Alcudia, afterwards Prince of the Peace, 83
Goldemar, General, 152
Gorchakov, Prince, 258
Gordon, Sir Robert, 224, 225
Görz von Schlitz, Count, 34, 35, 47
Gouvion-Saint-Cyr, General Laurent, 121, 124, 127
Gower, Earl, 113
Grantham, Thomas Robinson, second Baron, 20, 35, 95

Granville, Granville Leveson-Gower, first Earl, 72, 77, 275, 278
Gray, Sir James, 17
Grenville, William Grenville, Baron, at Foreign Office, 62–85 *passim*, 143
Greville, Charles, 229, 305
Grey, Charles Grey, second Earl, 229
Grimaldi, Marqués de, 17, 18, 20
Guilleminot, General, 214 *et seq.*
Guizot, François Pierre-Guillaume, French statesman, 279 *et seq.*
Guldberg, Count, 101
Gülhanè, Charter of, 232
Gustavus III, King of Sweden, 105 *et seq.*
Gustavus IV, King of Sweden, 183
Gyslaer, Mynheer van, 46

HALL, SIR ROBERT, 172
Hamilton, Captain, 205
Hamilton, Sir William, 56, 63, 115
Hamilton, Emma, Lady, 25, 56, 63, 115, 117, 120, 129, 141, 166
Hammer, von, historian of Turkey, 193
Harris, James, senior, 13, 14
Harris, James, afterwards first Earl of Malmesbury, birth and origin of, 13; early years of, 14–17; Secretary of Legation at Madrid, 17; minister to Berlin, 21; minister to Russia, 24; marriage of, 24; protests against Armed Neutrality, 32; minister to The Hague, 37; supports Orange party, 40–55; negotiates treaty with Holland, 55–58; negotiates treaty with Prussia, 58–61; raised to the peerage, 61; special mission of, to Berlin, 63; mission of, to army headquarters on the Rhine, 68; escorts Princess Caroline from Brunswick to London, 70; conducts abortive peace negotiations at Paris, 72–76; conducts negotiations at Lille, 77–86; closing years and death of, 87
Harris, Harriet, afterwards first Countess of Malmesbury, 24–25, 34, 35, 48, 70, 89, 96
Hat-i-Humayun, the, 265

INDEX

Haugwitz, Count Christian von, 66, 67, 69
Hawkesbury, Robert Jenkinson, Baron, afterwards second Earl of Liverpool, 116, 198
Henry, Prince, of Prussia, 94
Herzberg, Ewald, Count, 58, 60
Hesse-Cassel, Karl, Prince of, 104, 105, 107
Holland, Elizabeth, Lady, 64
Holy Places, dispute over, 246 et seq.

IBRAHIM PASHA, 203, 204, 213, 219, 226, 227, 228
Ingraham, Captain, U.S.N., 244
Isabel II, Queen of Spain, 279 et seq.
Isturitz, Francisco Xavier de, 283, 285, 289, 303
Italinski, Andrew Yarvievich, Russian envoy, 188

JACOBI, spy, 152
Jarnac, Count de, 289
Jones, Robert, 169, 170
Joseph II, Emperor, 43
Jourdan, Jean-Baptiste, Comte, 69
Juliana, Queen of Denmark, 100 et seq.

KALCKREUTH, FRIEDRICH ADOLF, COUNT VON, 68
Kapodistrias, Count Ioannes, 191, 192, 218, 219, 225
Kaunitz, Count, 127
Keith, Lord, 98
Kinckel, Baron, 44, 51, 64
Knyphausen, Baron von, 96 et seq.
Kossuth, Lajos, 241
Koszta, Martin, 244
Krauth, Charlotte, afterwards Mrs Hugh Elliot, 95 et seq.

LA HARPE, FRÉDÉRIC CÉSAR, 191, 193
Lacy, Russian General, 129, 130–131
Lansdowne, Henry Petty-Fitzmaurice, third Marquis of, 302
Latour Maubourg, Marquis de, 186, 187
Lauzun, Armand de Gontaut-Biron, Duc de, 22
Layard, Henry, 235, 236, 238, 248

Lebanon, the, 231
Lee, Arthur, 92 et seq.
Leipzig, battle of, 172
Leopold of Saxe-Coburg, afterwards King of the Belgians, 225, 273, 280
Leopold, Prince of Saxe-Coburg, 282, 285, 287
Letourneur, French diplomatist, 77 et seq.
Leveson-Gower, Lord Granville—see Granville, first Earl
Lieven, Dorothea, Princess, 229–230
Liston, Robert, 91, 96, 111, 189
Liverpool, Robert Jenkinson, second Earl of (Baron Hawkesbury), 116, 198
London, Convention of, 194
London, Treaty of (1827), 218
Louis-Philippe, Duc d'Orléans, afterwards King of the French, 146, 163; and the Spanish Marriages, 278–293; deposed, 297
Lucchesini, Girolamo, Marquis, 64, 65
Luzzi, 133, 135, 137
Lyons, Sir Edmund, 239–240

MACFARLANE, GENERAL, 164
Mahmud, Sultan, 184, 199, 226, 231
Mahon, Philip Henry, Lord, afterwards fourth Earl Stanhope, 164
Maida, battle of, 143
Maillebois, Marquis de, 42
Maison, Nicolas-Joseph, Count, 219
Malmesbury, James Harris, first Earl of—see Harris, James
Malmesbury, James Harris, third Earl of, 245
Manhès, General, 172
Maret, Hugues-Bernard, afterwards Duc de Bassano, 77 et seq.
Maria (da Gloria) II, Queen of Portugal, 230
Maria Carolina, Queen of the Two Sicilies, 117–166 passim
Marie-Amélie, Duchess of Orléans, afterwards Queen of the French, 146
Marie-Louise, Empress of the French, 146, 151, 158
Masséna, Marshal André, 137
Masserano, Prince, 18

315

Maurokordatos, Alexander, 206, 272
Mehemet Ali, 203, 226, 227, 275, 277
Melvil, Commodore, 56
Melville, of Boston, 82–83, 85
Menshikov, Prince, 247, 250 et seq.
Metternich, Prince, 171, 200, 201
Micheroux, Cavaliere, 123
Miguel, Dom, de facto King of Portugal, 230
Miles, W. A., 112
Mill, James, 181
Miltitz, Baron, 207, 210
Mirabeau, Honoré - Gabriel de Riquetti, Comte de, 39, 48, 55, 112, 114
Mohammed Ali, 263
Möllendorf, Field-Marshal Richard, 68, 69
Monroe, James, President, U.S.A., 194
Montgomery, George Augustus Herbert, eighth Earl of, 170
Montmorin, Armand, Count de, 51, 52
Montpensier, Antoine, Duc de, 283, 284
Moore, Dr John, 22
Morpeth, George, Viscount, 72, 77
Mosquitos, the, 307
Mulgrave, Henry Phipps, first Earl of, 128, 131
Muñoz, Agustin, Duke of Rianzares, 280, 284, 285, 287
Murat, Joachim, King of Naples, 146, 152, 154, 155, 158, 165 et seq.
Murat, Caroline, Queen of Naples, 172, 175

NAPIER, ADMIRAL SIR CHARLES, 278
Napoleon III, Emperor of the French, 246, 266
Narvaez, General (afterwards Marshal), Duke of Valencia, 282, 283, 295 et seq.
Navarino, battle of, 214
Neale, Admiral Sir Harry, 205
Negapatam, 36, 56, 57, 58
Neipperg, Albrecht Adam, Count von, 175
Neipperg, Countess, 91

Nejib, Ottoman Foreign Secretary (Reis Effendi), 226
Nelson, Horatio, Viscount, 115, 116, 119 et seq., 149
Nesselrode, Charles Robert, Count von, 202, 203, 210, 229–230, 254
Nicholas I, Tsar of Russia, policy of, towards Grecian insurgents, 207–225 passim; sends help to Turkey, 227; personal objection of, to Stratford Canning, 228–230; attitude of, towards Hungarian refugees, 241–243; policy of, towards Turkey, culminating in the Crimean War, 246–260 passim; death of, 262, 265
Nicolas, 169

OLOZAGA, SALUSTIANO, 282
Omar Pasha, 259
Orange, Prince of—see William V
Orange, Princess of—see Wilhelmina
Ordal, battle of, 170
Orléans, Duke of—see Louis Philippe, King of the French
Orléans, Marie-Amélie, Duchess of, afterwards Queen of the French, 146
Otho of Bavaria, King of the Hellenes, 225, 239
Ottenfels, Austrian internuncio, 216
Otway, 301

PALMERSTON, HENRY JOHN TEMPLE, VISCOUNT, restrains Stratford Canning, 241; supports Turkey, 242–243; supports movement for Belgian independence, 273; threatens France, 277; policy of, towards Spain, 288–305 passim; policy of, towards United States, 306–308; mentioned, 225, 227, 228, 239, 258, 265, 268
Palombo, Giuseppe, 167
Panin, Nikita, Russian statesman, 24–30 passim
Parish, Henry, 205
Patiomkin, Russian statesman, 28, 30, 33, 35
Paul, Tsar of Russia, 75
Paulus, Pieter, 43, 44, 54
Peel, Sir Robert, 228, 231, 235

INDEX

Pein, 80 *et seq.*
Perregaux, French banker, 72, 83
Persigny, Jean de Fialin, Comte (afterwards Duc) de, 248
Pertev Bey, Reis Effendi, 212–213, 215
Pisani, Frederick, 233, 248
Pitt, William, policy of, towards France, 69–86 *passim*, 112–114; death of, 143; mentioned, 37
Pius VII, Pope, 178
Planta, Joseph, 196
Pléville de Peley, Admiral, 77 *et seq.*
Polignac, Auguste Jules, Prince de, 222
Ponsonby, John, Viscount, 274
Poros, Protocol of, 220, 225

Radziwill, Michael, 242
Raglan, Fitzroy James Henry Somerset, first Baron, 261
Railways, Stratford Canning's opinion of, 249
Reshid Pasha, 232, 240, 244, 253 *et seq.*, 273
Rewbell, Jean-François, French Director, 78
Rheineck, Baron, 220
Ribeaupierre, Aleksandre, Russian diplomatist, 211, 220
Rifa't Pasha, 234, 251
Riza Pasha, 232
Robins, Lieutenant, 242
Rose, Colonel Hugh, afterwards Baron Strathnairn, 249, 250
Ross, Charles, 72, 77
Rossi, Emmanuele, 170
Rush, Richard, 194
Russell, Lord John, 247, 254, 305
Russell, Odo, afterwards first Baron Ampthill, 238
Ryssel, General van, 50

Saida Effendi, Reis Effendi, 208 *et seq.*
Saint-Clair, Marquis de, 120, 122, 152, 158
Salm, Rhinegrave of, 45, 49, 51, 53
Sangro, Duke of, 164
Sartorius, 300
Saxe-Teschen, Albrecht, Duke of, 66

Sayre, Stephen, American delegate, 92
Schack - Rathelou, Joachim Otto, Danish statesman, 101
Schinina, Cavaliere, 172
Senegal, 78
Serbia, 235
Serra Capriola, Duke of, 119, 188
Serrano y Dominguez, General, afterwards Marshal and Ducque de la Torre, 295, 296
Seville, Enrique, Duke of, 284, 289, 290
Seymour, Sir Hamilton, 247
Sinope, disaster of, 259
Smith, Robert ("Bobus"), 81
Smith, Sir Sidney, 143
Sonderbund, the, 239
Sotomayor, Duke of, 298 *et seq.*
Stanhope, Lady Hester, 186
Stanislas, Poniatowski, King of Poland, 16, 23, 34
Stanley, Edward, Lord, afterwards fourteenth Earl of Derby, 245, 268, 302
Stanley of Alderley, first Baron, 238
Stein, 59, 60
Stephanaki Bey, 226
Stormont, David Murray, Viscount, afterwards second Earl of Mansfield, 32, 33
Strangford, Percy Smythe, sixth Viscount, 207
Strangford, Percy Smythe, eighth Viscount, 238
Struensee, Johann, Count von, 100
Stuart, General Sir John, 143
Suchet, Louis - Gabriel, Duke of Albufera, 170
Suffolk, Henry Howard, twelfth Earl of, 22, 92, 93

Talleyrand-Périgord, Charles-Maurice, sometime Bishop of Autun, 72, 81, 85, 87, 133
Tatishev, Dmitri Pavlovitch, 130, 132, 135
Thiers, Adolphe, 275 *et seq.*
Thouvenel, Édouard - Antoine, 266, 267
Thugut, Baron Johann Franz, 77

Thulemeyer, Friedrich Wilhelm, 47, 51
Townley, Captain, 243
Trapani, Count of, 281, 283
Treilhard, Comte J.-B., 84
Trincomalee, 56, 57, 58, 75
Trinidad, 77, 78

ULM, capitulation of, 137
Unkiar Iskelesi, Treaty of, 227

VALENTIA, GEORGE ANNESLEY, NINTH VISCOUNT, afterwards second Earl of Mountnorris, 149
Van der Spiegel, Laurens Pieter, 44, 54, 57, 60, 63
Vérac, de, 40, 45, 48, 50, 52
Vergennes, Charles, Comte de, 37, 40, 45, 51
Victoria, Queen, 233, 234, 258, 281, 303
Voronzov, Semen, Russian ambassador, 109, 113, 119, 131, 132
Voss, Fräulein, 49, 52

WAGRAM, battle of, 184
Waldstein, Isabella, Countess, 192

Wellesley, Henry, afterwards first Earl Cowley, 238
Wellesley, Richard Colley Wellesley, Marquis, 77, 80, 147, 186
Wellington, Arthur Wellesley, Duke of, 170, 207, 209, 210, 217, 225
Werelst, Mme de, 95
Westmorland, John Fane, eleventh Earl of, 255
Wickham, William, 80
Wilhelmina, Princess of Orange, 39–59 *passim*, 87
William I, King of the Netherlands, 272
William V, Prince of Orange, 36–60 *passim*, 87
Williams, Sir Charles Hanbury, 16
Williams, Colonel Fenwick, 264
Wilson, Sir Robert, 177

YARMOUTH, FRANCIS SEYMOUR CONWAY, EARL OF, afterwards second Marquis of Hertford, 63
York, Frederick Augustus, Duke of, 62, 64, 67
Ypsilanti, Alexander, 199

ZOGRAPHOS, 206

CPSIA information can be obtained
at www.ICGtesting.com
Printed in the USA
BVHW041254180322
631870BV00008B/89